the
experience
of
architecture

the experience of architecture

henry plummer

Thames & Hudson

contents

Frank Lloyd Wright, Wingspread (1937), Wisconsin,
spiral stair climbing the chimney to a rooftop observation space

places of possibility

the risk and necessity of undetermined space

One of the most crucial if overlooked aspects of architecture is the capacity of buildings to either support or diminish the spontaneous powers of human beings to act in space. These 'acts' take place whenever we have a chance to decide *how* we are going to occupy, move through or directly affect the place we are in. They originate in simple endeavours such as opening a door or closing a window, climbing a stair or crossing a bridge, changing level along a footpath or emerging in an urban square to find multiple routes and attractions ahead from which to choose. Regrettably, these countless undertakings have become so dull and uneventful that we barely notice them anymore.

There are times, however, when architecture elevates these customs to gratifying and exalting events, to true *actions* in the original sense of the word. Masses and cavities, floors and stairs, doors and windows draw us into a more consciously improvised kind of activity. In doing so, they call into play the underutilized gifts of our human agility and imagination, our motor impulses and sensory faculties, our powers to foresee and deliberate. We are invited to respond creatively to architecture, rather than react passively to its directives, transforming habits into deeds and promoting us from 'patients' to 'agents'. At these moments the act itself creates elation in the doing, intensifying our sense of existence.

This distinction is not merely philosophical, for spatial actions underlie some of our most cherished experiences. The verification of our own vital powers occurs, for instance, when climbing an unpredictable stair, bringing unaccustomed muscles into play and turning us into nimble, even acrobatic, forces. Or consider what happens when walking along a path that splits into alternate journeys: we are presented with more than one possible future and our capacity to venture in space is restored. We become causal forces, as well, when opening a door or swinging a shutter whose motion and effect is uncertain yet pleasing, suffusing their task with the freedom of play. Another modest example is found in a building endowed with secret depths we are able to discover, by simply opening a drawer or closet or climbing up to an attic or down to a cellar, peering into tiny architectural details to find something hidden within or probing through an episodic succession of rooms. In all these undertakings we are converted into protagonists in space: empowered to launch our own initiatives; cause effects; be doers of deeds in which we can shape our own immediate destiny.

At first glance, these unpretentious operations in buildings may seem so mundane they are of little consequence. But they are deeply significant insofar as they contribute to the sustenance of our being, rather than threaten us with non-being. They verify, essentially, that we are 'persons', not 'its'. The daily exercise of free will in settings where there is more than just one possible outcome – when negotiating a path or throwing open a window – is a fundamental way that people are able to express their own essential powers and secure a sense of their own dignity and responsibility, reaffirming they have some influence over their own experience and fate. Everyone, from infants to the elderly, needs to know they are capable of being *in control of themselves*, and not always under the control of others.

Unfortunately, this kind of room to manoeuvre in sites of continual opportunity is disappearing from the modern world. Though once abundant in the natural landscape and in buildings, spaces open to human action are threatened by two opposing trends – utilitarianism and spectatorism – the former making buildings overly reductive and constraining, and the latter making them overly entertaining and theatrical. On the one hand our materialist culture is turning architecture into a commodity based on economy and easy production, which in turn standardizes our behaviour in space. On the other, our culture of amusement is converting buildings into seductive and highly marketable fabrications that captivate us with their novelty, but also reduce us to the passive audience of a prearranged visual spectacle. We forget that architecture is not merely an object to express personal or cultural values or satisfy a craving for fame. It is also the setting for what French philosopher

Gaston Bachelard in *The Poetics of Space* called the 'passionate liaison of our bodies' with the world.[1] When this liaison occurs, architecture is no longer something we ogle from a distance or exploit for practical need, but the catalyst for our very existence as living forces acting in concert with the world.

On the basis of everyday activities in space is built our immediate awareness of knowing we are intensely alive, sensing each time we are able to *do something* that *makes a difference*. Environments that nurture our creative use of these spatial powers allow us to both project and realize our bodily existence, instead of reducing us to just another item among the objects surrounding us. While the field of architecture has been rather oblivious to this reality, thinkers in neighbouring disciplines such as philosophy, poetry and psychology have reminded us repeatedly that everyday actions are how we restore and construct a sense of wellbeing, and it is only during this exercise of freedom that we are most truly ourselves.

Laying the groundwork for understanding what is at stake in our ability to choose among possible courses of action are the writings of those concerned with the loss of this power in contemporary culture, as well as the necessity and means of its recovery. Among them are poets such as William Carlos Williams and Charles Olson, philosophers Hannah Arendt, Michel Foucault and Daniel Dennett, the environmentalist and microbiologist René Dubos, and psychiatrists including Bruno Bettelheim, Erik Erikson, R.D. Laing and Erich Fromm. According to evolutionary biologists, our essential attributes as a species would have never evolved in the first place if the world of our ancestors was as monotonous and numbing as the architecture surrounding us now. Diverse stimuli and challenges were likely a crucial determinant of our biological endowment, for they kept *Homo sapiens* adaptable. A wide range of opportunities and risks are no less essential today, for they allow us, through our decisions, to give complete expression to our human potentialities.

The spontaneous powers that architecture is able to inspire in people – prompting them to become what Laing calls the 'origin of actions' in space – is the subject of this book.[2] While this topic is inherently slippery and almost indefinable, there can be no doubt about its significance. We need to better understand how buildings can nourish or shrivel the existence of people as vital forces able to choose their own courses of action, so that we might regain the skill to knowingly shape a more responsive, sustainable world. Fortunately, there is a long history of achievement in this regard to draw upon, in settings from the archaic to contemporary, both urban and rural, in historic monuments and anonymous folk buildings and villages.

Enriching this tradition over the past century are a number of courageous architects who have given a prominent role to human agency in their buildings. Among these pioneers of the twentieth century are Frank Lloyd Wright and Le Corbusier, as well as contemporary architects from Tadao Ando to Peter Zumthor. But the majority of work in this humanist endeavour is by individuals who have remained, perhaps by necessity, marginal to the field: Pierre Chareau (the intricate meshing of mobile screens at the Maison de Verre in Paris); Aldo van Eyck (the many-sided rooms and passageways of Hubertus House in Amsterdam) and Herman Hertzberger (the polyvalent spaces, windows, floors and pathways of Centraal

Beheer in Apeldoorn); Carlo Scarpa (the acrobatic staircases and kinetically surprising doors of the Fondazione Querini Stampalia in Venice and Castelvecchio Museum in Verona) and Giancarlo de Carlo (the participatory footpaths and corridors of the Urbino dormitories); Riken Yamamoto (the reconception of traditional screens and topographic freedom in the multilevel pedestrian streets of Inter-Junction City in Yokohama) and Maurice Smith (the multifarious stairs and spatial fields of the Blackman houses in Massachusetts).

PROVING THAT ONE IS NOT A PIANO KEY

A fundamental question we can raise about architecture is whether it determines human behaviour or returns this power to people so they can govern their own spatial deeds. Buildings can deny us the chance to decide our own courses of action or, at the opposite extreme, can furnish a wealth of desirable opportunities that we are able to appraise and then take responsibility for. They can restrict the choice of available experience or restore our capacity to deliberate over many agreeable possibilities. At stake is nothing less than the faculty of human volition, whether or not the occupants of buildings are given the leeway to exercise their powers of decision and shape their immediate destiny.

The impact of architecture on human freedom is especially evident when liberty is denied, regardless of whether or not that denial is deliberate. One of the sharpest critiques of society's impingement on individual freedom is found in Fyodor Dostoyevsky's *Notes from Underground*, which elaborates on the inhumanity of buildings that interfere with personal will. Dostoyevsky suggests that the very core of human nature lies in capriciousness and unpredictability, and man's refusal to be categorized or limited by the decisions of others. No matter how comfortable, prosperous or contented a civilization might be, it will reduce a person's sense of vitality if it fails to satisfy their inherent desire to assert and confirm their own individuality in the face of society. 'And who knows', he reflects, 'maybe the entire goal here on earth towards which mankind is striving consists of nothing more than this continuity of process of attainment alone ... in life itself and not actually in the goal proper, which, it goes without saying, cannot be anything except two times two makes four, that is, a formula, and after all, two times two makes four is already not life, gentlemen, but the beginning of death.'[3]

Dostoyevsky points to architecture as a cultural tool of enforcing the erosion of human will, irrespective of whether its forms are convenient or charming. When doomed to live in a thoroughly efficient mechanical world, characterized as an 'ant hill', or an impersonal shelter that is little more than a glorified 'chicken coop', or even within the technical perfection and outward beauty of a gleaming 'crystal palace', a person's spiritual needs, particularly the need to overcome inertia and exercise autonomy, turn all the more desperate.[4] The only way one can prove to oneself that he is not a 'piano key', an object controlled and played by somebody else, is to make use of one's own 'unfettered' and 'simply independent choice', which is free of any goal and may even be contrary to one's material interests. These caustic observations touch upon a great truth, reminding us that our most fundamental *human* need is the ability to carry out actions of our choosing and retain some control over our fate. People are born with an impulse to transcend passivity and generate their own operations in space. This striving to become an agent, rather than being reduced to a patient, is in many ways what separates *Homo sapiens* from all other creatures on earth. By contrast, inert matter merely lies around, machines follow programmes and animals remain largely conditioned by instincts. Only humanity comes alive as a spontaneous creative force, able to assess a range of options and freely select a course of action, including one at odds with our comfort or animal impulses, and even in the midst of that course to alter or reverse its direction.

When a world of conformity has already made the environmental decisions for us, all we are able or expected to do is comply with and reinforce them. In this situation Dostoyevsky, along with most existentialist thinkers of the past 150 years, from Friedrich Nietzsche to Jean-Paul Sartre, call for a radical reawakening in which the most urgent thing to do is simply to choose choice. 'The essence of choice is not in the end, but in choosing', Luther Halsey Gulick reminds us in *A Philosophy of Play*. 'In the doing is the result. Happiness is not in the attainment, but in the attaining. "Life is in the quest" … It is the doing that makes the deed worthy of record, not the material outcome.'[5]

SPACE THAT DISSOCIATES POWER FROM THE BODY

Another perspective, again rather gloomy, which helps us to grasp the reciprocity of architecture and power is provided by Michel Foucault. In his chilling book *Discipline and Punish*, Foucault examines the insidious but generally hidden or disguised impacts of space that deprive people of self-control, suggesting that the growing regimentation of people and their acquiescence to cultural norms are dictated not so much by the direct commands of other people, but by the coercive force of physical environments that our culture has refined and propagated.

Against a backdrop of architectural techniques perfected to enhance the surveillance of inmates in nineteenth-century penal institutions, Foucault turns his attention to the way these systematic corrections of behaviour now permeate a range of everyday institutions and buildings. Reflecting the growth of our 'disciplinary' society as a whole, these mechanisms serve to invisibly economize human conduct nearly every minute of the day. At the heart of his argument is a direct correlation between spatial volumes and human power, particularly built forms that break down and eliminate our capacity as agents by constraining and streamlining our behaviour and reshaping it over time.

As in the training of soldiers, where individuals are moulded into virtual machines by a repetition of habits that become automatic, civilians can be rendered equally compliant by space that 'dissociates power from the body', Foucault writes, 'reversing the course of the energy, the power that might result from it, and turns it into a relation of strict subjection'.[6] Among the most common environments operating as 'formulas of domination' are repetitious and dreary spaces, which silently govern human activity. Any distraction from efficient use is eliminated. Human conduct is normalized by accustoming people to 'executing well and quickly the same operations'.[7] The only stimuli left are those that arouse a single obligatory reaction or that offer nothing but unappealing and uniform alternatives – either of which is effectively a command, for it has turned its 'choices' into forced or redundant moves.

Especially distressing about all these coercive architectural forms is the degree to which they have become pervasive and universally accepted, owing to their benefits for a mass culture. Architecture that has been reified into an instrument that quietly drills people, conning them out of wasteful activity, has the orderly and economic virtue of improving their utility and efficiency. As power is drained from the will in order to render the body more productive, increasingly docile and better conditioned for a stable consumer society, people are gradually trained into leading a complacent existence, one that is not unrelated to automata and, Dostoyevsky would say, to *animaux domestiques*.

While it might be easy to relegate Foucault's critique to the most reductive and barren kinds of commercial or institutional buildings, and consider it moot in the context of the dazzling imagery and amusing kitsch of contemporary architecture, the latter trends are in many ways more alarming, for they distract us from awareness about the loss of something essential – human causation – which is rapidly vanishing from the physical environment. We can still feel the erosion of freedom in highly restrictive spaces, but this humiliation is obscured when standing before a display of exotic building forms so visually striking they stupefy their audience.

The architectural spectacle, which seems at first to offer relief from an otherwise brutally practical world, is no less domineering than the disciplinary space, for it reduces our experience to the passive enjoyment of somebody else's creativity. I am referring specifically to buildings conceived to excite the eye while denying any real possibilities of action, diminishing our bodily freedom. Provided are many choices of sensation, but not choices of action. The importance of this distinction is made clear by Charles Olson in his essay 'Human Universe', in which he writes: 'Spectatorism crowds out participation as the condition of culture … If man is once more to possess intent in his life, and to take up the responsibility implicit in his life, he has to comprehend his own process as intact, from outside, by way of his skin, in, and by his own powers of conversion, out again. For there is this other part of the motion which we call life to be examined anew', Olson concludes, 'man's action, that tremendous discharge of forces.'[8]

It takes only a glance at the changing silhouettes of most major cities, and the role of sensationalism in today's architectural schools and press, to recognize the societal stress being given to aestheticized and photogenic end products, in which the potential creativity of people has been stolen by the architect. These glamorous objects constitute a large portion of our accepted architectural history and are magnets of architectural tourism vital to economic growth. Helping to hasten and strengthen this reversal of power in our consumerist culture is a cult of personality and glorification of virtuosic design.

Sadly, we are barely aware of what we have lost, because we are so well trained in a Foucaultean sense and because we are so complicit in the docile joys of entertainment. Reinforcing this ominous pleasure in human submission, and dissociation of power from the human body, is a growing and by now universal obsession with computers and smart phones, not to mention television and films, based upon sensational effects, all of which are making us into extensions of imagery that has been programmed by others, to which we can only react in predictable patterns. 'The serious threat to our democracy is not the existence of foreign totalitarian states', notes philosopher John Dewey in *Freedom and Culture*. 'It is the existence within our own personal attitudes and within our own institutions of conditions similar to those which have given a victory to external authority, discipline, uniformity and dependence', so that the real 'battlefield' for freedom is 'within ourselves and our institutions'.[9]

BIOLOGICAL ENDOWMENT

The innate human desire and capacity to weigh and decide one's own courses of action, and to do this wisely in the light of personal interests and limitations, is rooted in our collective evolution. People in the distant past who fell into habitual patterns of perception and movement, unable to adjust to shifting opportunities and threats, were likely to meet an early demise. This process must have encouraged the natural selection and refined the genetic constitution of humans who could intelligently deliberate risks and options, and then innovate by responding creatively to unexpected stimuli.

Our very consciousness as human beings likely evolved from a continual urge to explore and tinker with the world, contributing to the critical development of our cognitive, emotional and motor skills. The groundwork of human imagination lies in repeatedly investigating a range of possible futures, envisioning, initiating and taking responsibility for one's endeavours. 'Our ancestors, like us, took pleasure in various modes of undirected self-exploration, stimulating oneself over and over again and seeing what happened', comments Daniel Dennett in *Consciousness Explained*. 'Because of the plasticity of the brain, coupled with [our] innate restlessness and curiosity ... it is not surprising that we hit upon strategies of self-stimulation or self-manipulation that led to the inculcation of habits and dispositions that radically altered the internal communicative structure of our brains.' He concludes: 'These discoveries became part of the culture – memes – that were then made available to all.'[10]

Our basic faculties derive from the way our species transformed itself through a slow genetic alteration as our forebears responded with ingenuity to a wide range of environmental forces. The response to these forces by our ancestors helped shape what humans are, just as the environments of contemporary cultures act as selective forces that will continue to adapt people – at what may prove a serious cost – to an increasingly technically sophisticated but also lifeless and disembodied world. For now, we retain many attributes inherited from the evolutionary past, including our basic anatomical and physiological characteristics, as well as a primeval impulse to create and confirm ourselves in action.

The human body itself would have never developed on a ground as desolate as the modern world, a terrain so safe and comfortable, but correspondingly flat, mundane and uneventful, that it is crippling in its deprivations. A monotonous topography robs us of any chance to exercise our limber biological endowment, to perform minor miracles of agility as we move through space, innovating through our responses to challenging floors underfoot. Our powers for nimble motion are founded on aeons of daring manoeuvres by our ancestors in the high-canopy rain forests, and then the open woodlands and grassy savannahs of

East Africa where *Australopithecus* roamed, followed by the treks of prehistoric cave dwellers over glaciated landscapes in the Ice Age, all uneven terrains filled with hazards. 'If man had originally inhabited a world as blankly uniform as a "high-rise" housing development, as featureless as a parking lot, as destitute of life as an automated factory', notes Lewis Mumford in *The Myth of the Machine*, 'it is doubtful that he would have had a sufficiently varied experience to retain images, mould language or acquire ideas.'[11] While this is aimed at the austere and degrading environments of which Foucault also speaks, the squandering of our basic human traits could be applied as well to the visually stunning and disabling effects of today's more ostentatious architecture.

Our astonishing ability to scrutinize the world, interpret and improvise among various choices in the terrain, examine and uncover puzzling aspects of spaces around us, is born from millions upon millions of archaic deeds that assisted natural selection at the time the biological identity of *Homo sapiens* was being formed. Each challenge was slightly different from the next, calling for an inventive response to unexpected problems in the landscape. We are beneficiaries in our genetic codes of the efforts of our ancestors to survey and roam on a changeable landscape whose every point may have been filled with terror and threat, but also sustenance and joy. The marvel that we know as the human condition originated in part from living in a dynamic relationship with a world that was varied enough for people to innovate moment to moment, giving full play to their genetic potential to evolve as adaptors instead of specialists. By slipping back now and then to the untamed conditions of a primal world, we keep in touch with our sources by continually emerging from them.

Much the same point is made by René Dubos when writing about the evolutionary origins of human nature. 'The ability to choose among … possible courses of action may be the most important of all human attributes,' he writes in *So Human an Animal*. 'While every human being is unprecedented, unique and unrepeatable, by virtue of his genetic constitution and past experiences, his environment determines at any given moment which of his physical and mental potentialities are realized in his life … Since the physical and social environment plays such a large role in the exercise of freedom, environments should be designed to provide conditions for enlarging as much as possible the range of choices.'[12]

FREEDOM AND FREE WILL

The higher a species on a scale of mental and physical faculties, the more flexible its patterns of action – a scale of development that culminates in *Homo sapiens*. Evidently our predecessors were only able to emerge from the animal kingdom by repeatedly exercising their independence to govern themselves and transcend coercive instincts. Unlike animals, which react predictably and impulsively to situations, people are able to carefully consider a course of action. 'Human existence begins when the way to act is no longer fixed by hereditarily given mechanisms,' notes Erich Fromm in *Escape from Freedom*. 'In other words, *human existence and freedom are from the beginning inseparable* … In the animal there is an uninterrupted chain of reactions starting with a stimulus, like hunger, and ending with a more or less strictly determined course of action … In man that chain is interrupted … he must choose between different courses of action. Instead of a predetermined instinctive action, man has to weigh possible courses of action in his mind; he starts to think.'[13]

Freedom is also a fundamental way we engage the world outside ourselves. While liberty in the physical environment is only one avenue for achieving a sense of causation and self-esteem, it remains the most essential, for it can be exercised immediately and spontaneously, providing a stream of direct evidence about our individual powers and supporting the growth of an active, critical, responsible self. When we are able to act upon and with the physical world, we overcome not only the modern malaise of feeling alone and isolated, but also the impotence of feeling inept and small, as if we were nothing but a particle of dust at the mercy of external forces.

When this validation of human significance is repeatedly denied, our ability to act is paralyzed, posing a real threat to our freedom. We are told by psychiatrists that we are then only able to satisfy our need for belonging by abandoning the search for autonomy and finding new submissive ties with the world. Fromm traces a whole litany of modern ills to a growing frustration over unrealized freedom: as opportunities to exercise independence wane, we need these opportunities more and more, owing to what he describes as a process of growing 'individuation'. We have lost our earlier unity with the world: phylogenetically, as a species that has emerged from an animal state; culturally, as a society striving beyond a tribal existence; and individually, as we grow out of childhood dependence. We have lost all of these primary bonds and securities, to which we can never return, while the world simultaneously eliminates our chances to realize existence as autonomous beings.

Among our various 'escapes from freedom', Fromm remarks, is a willing submission to the power of authorities or culture at large and a desire to dominate others and the objects around us in order to bear the helplessness felt in an uncontrollable environment. Equally omnipresent is the growth of human destructiveness, which provides another means for overcoming a sense of powerlessness in the world by, quite literally, destroying it – or oneself. But the most pervasive solution to a feeling of ineffectiveness is simply to accept one's condition: to become a complacent spectator, conforming to the life of a powerless recipient of stimulation. But a steep price is paid for this existential numbing, for it demands the loss of one's feelings of self, and discarding the self by reducing oneself to a thing.

Manifestations of all these debilitating effects, and their illusions of individuality, are by now so prevalent that we scarcely recognize them anymore. In addition to our more obvious submissions to mass behaviour, a quieter kind of subservience appears in the manipulated and passive state of a consumer society: an intellectual compliance with advertising; a materialistic obsession with commodities; and a fixation on entertainment. I don't mean to overstate the capacity of architecture to solve these plights, but only to argue that it plays a role in their aggravation or alleviation.

The only way to overcome these problems, according to psychiatrists from Laing to Erikson, is to continually reaffirm *that we are* and have faith in *who we are* through the possibilities and responsibilities of individual action. The human self is only as strong as it is able to realize itself through its own initiatives and capacity to be operative and effective.

In a similar vein, Fromm observes, 'if the individual realizes his self by spontaneous activity and thus relates himself to the world, he ceases to be an isolated atom; he and the world become part of one structuralized whole; he has his rightful place, and thereby his doubt concerning himself and the meaning of life disappears. This doubt sprang from his separateness ... where he can live, neither compulsively nor automatically but spontaneously, the doubt disappears. He is aware of himself as an active and creative individual,' Fromm concludes, 'and recognizes that *there is only one meaning of life: the act of living itself*.'[14]

THE DIGNITY AND JOY OF HUMAN AGENCY

While buildings constitute only one realm in which we are able to exercise action, they serve a fundamental role in allowing us, throughout our lives, to participate in the world around us without eliminating our individuality. What matters above all in this dialectic is that the possibilities offered to us are sufficiently appealing that their selection can be undertaken as a personal act, one that is fully appropriated by each person as an agent able to take charge of and sway one's own fate, and through this moment of spontaneity experience genuine vitality and joy.

Among those who have helped deepen our understanding of action and throw light on its spatial implications is Jean-Paul Sartre. In *Being and Nothingness*, Sartre moves beyond the tired conflict between determinists and the proponents of free will by identifying action as the essence of freedom, arguing that 'it is the act that decides its ends and motives, and the act is the expression of freedom'.[15] Moreover, it is through the unfixed nature of an act – which may be partly shaped but is never determined by conditions or motives – that freedom is experienced. One who truly exists must 'learn his freedom through his acts', and by the same token can lose that freedom when unable or unwilling to act, so that freedom is always in a precarious state that must be continually renewed. Freedom is not something we inherit or possess, but comes into being *only* at the moment it is acted upon and experienced. 'Thus my freedom', he says, 'is perpetually in question.'[16]

Related ideas are put forth by Hannah Arendt, whose writings focus on the nature of power. In *The Human Condition*, she contends that agency is a unique and irreducible feature of humanity, for 'to act, in its most general sense, means to take an initiative, to begin ... to set something into motion.'[17] She goes on to identify action as the way people begin themselves, rather than begin things, and through these actions 'show who they are, reveal actively their unique personal identities and thus make their appearance in the human world'.[18] To act in this sense is to bring about a two-fold creation: the innovation of a deed, as well as the innovation of oneself, a disclosure of *who one is* and of what one is capable. Created more generally but fundamentally is a sensation and evidence *that one is*, that one exists as something more than protoplasm or machinery.

The human necessity of agency, despite its inherent challenge and anxiety, lies in the fact that it is only in action that existence attains concreteness and fullness. Through actions people become aware of their capacity to project their individual selves. 'For in every action', as Dante purported in *De Monarchia*, 'what is primarily intended by the doer, whether he acts from natural necessity or out of free will, is the disclosure of his own image. So it comes about that every doer, in so far as he does, takes delight in doing; since everything that is desires its own being, and since in action the being of the doer is somehow intensified, delight necessary follows ... Thus, nothing acts unless (by acting) it makes patent its latent self.'[19]

Certainly the conventional routines we follow throughout the day, and cultural demands for norms of behaviour, are vital for maintaining societal harmony and reducing our personal anxiety at feeling uncertain and alone in the world, but these are essentially periods of passive, if productive, behaviour. Without the wisdom of these crucial patterns of compliance we could not function individually nor could we live and work together, and they offer a wide assortment of daily benefits: conserving our energy; involving us in a give and take with others; bringing us stimulation and pleasure. These well-tried and universal conformities allow us to survive collectively and avoid anarchy, as well as feel more comfortable, untroubled and gratified. But while we cannot live without resort to this state, neither can we be content to live only in this state.

It is during breaks from submission to routine that we are able to confirm our capacity to be the originators and performers of acts, no matter how simple or trivial these acts might appear to others. Indeed, their outer appearance is irrelevant, for deeds cannot be externally observed, but only internally experienced as people project and realize themselves. Through these recurring endeavours we express ourselves, but also make ourselves. It is due to this dynamism of being human that philosopher Gabriel Marcel describes man as *Homo viator*, rather than *Homo sapiens*.[20] Each moment of decision for man the wayfarer stirs unease, as well as elation, for what is chosen through this process are facets of oneself and it is out of these decisions that the self emerges and grows. Much the same thought of life as a journey towards self-actualization was expressed by theologian Paul Tillich in his well-known statement: 'Man becomes really human only at the time of decision.'

ACTION IN ARCHITECTURAL SPACE

While the interwoven experience of choice and decision has been generally approached from a philosophical, psychological, social or political perspective, it holds equally profound implications for the physical environment. If agency is central to being human, then it must be equally indispensable to architecture, for the buildings in which we live are our primary sources of spontaneous action. Unlike the rugged landscapes of our ancestors, the venues for spatial endeavour today are by and large the sidewalks and streets, corridors and rooms of our homes and neighbourhoods, whose potential is shaped by architects and developers.

It is generally accepted that buildings express an attitude towards life, giving visible form to the values of their makers and culture at large, but less acknowledged is the way in which buildings express an attitude towards the people destined to occupy them. By their generosity or stinginess of opportunity for spatial action, buildings exert a dynamics of power that can inspire or deflate, an effect that continues hour after hour, year after year. 'We shape our buildings,' stated Winston Churchill with unerring frankness to the House of Commons in 1943, 'and afterwards our buildings shape us.'

The source of this 'microphysics of power', to use Foucault's term, lies in the fact that we are not able to act spatially in a vacuum, but only in concert with the opportunities afforded by a physical environment.[21] In a sense, the world acts upon us just as surely as we act on it. The masses and voids that make up our environment can sustain or frustrate our simplest urges to feel alive while engaging the world. Almost every moment of life occurs in a site whose form affects our chances to act in space – whether standing, leaning, walking, climbing, congregating, retreating, cooking, dining, reading, writing, working, playing, bathing, resting, sitting or reclining, alone or with others – according to the opportunities embedded within or deprived from its volumes.

The aim of this book is to study how our most elemental spatial actions are influenced by architectural form. I want to examine how specific built volumes and details, taken from a wide array of settings, can foster or deplete our powers of decision, placing most emphasis on the former since it is a precious, if largely eroded, resource in the present world, but also within an emerging architectural age. If our buildings are to make any pretense at being more than a commercial or aesthetic enterprise, architects will need to give greater concern to moulding space so that *other people* can verify their own existence as human beings.

What I propose is a reconsideration of architecture from the vantage point of spontaneous action. These exploits include manoeuvres over the shape of the ground, manipulations of kinetic built parts, interpretations of manifold volumes, discoveries of unknown spatial depths and the encompassing freedom of a field of action: these topics form the five chapters of the book. Each explores a different kind of human deed that, no matter how humble, produces a miracle – for something new comes into being, in oneself and new in the world. Each entails a prospect whose outcome is uncertain, but when this initiative is decided upon, set into motion and accomplished by the doer, it can result in a marvellous feat where a trace survives, as Arendt wrote, of 'the shining brightness we once called glory'.[22]

The broader purpose is to arrive at a better understanding of how people interact with space and to urge the rediscovery of architecture as a domain of human deliberation, a totality of possibilities that people can freely, but with tremendous vitality, engage with and explore. In this regard I want to question the conventional views of architecture as a useful or aesthetic object, and argue that it should also be considered a vessel of power whose opportunities, when present, completely elude being used or seen.

In the presence of a building that invites deliberation, we find a subtle array of potential interactions that only exist in a latent state upon or between the forms themselves, and should not be confused with the physical contours we are able to see and touch. We can imagine, foresee, test and remember these scenarios, but can never directly seize them with the eye or mind. Nor can we put them to use, for they are essentially useless. Whether a building is beautiful or homely, practical or wasteful is largely irrelevant from the standpoint of agency, since the precious thing offered by an empowering form is what it allows *us* to create in space. It is not the concrete volume itself that is important, but the imperceptible web of actions lying dormant around yet stimulated by that shape. The forms we are able to see and grasp are what we are able to act upon, rather than the action itself.

Space that is lavishly open to human volition requires exceptional generosity on the part of its architect. This kind of benevolence is blatantly missing from buildings reduced to highly efficient and stereotyped patterns, but is also missing from many of our most visually dazzling and celebrated buildings, since often the more excitingly original a product becomes, the less creativity is left for others. This presents a dilemma for any talented but conscientious architect, as the endowment of action for other people demands not only a willing altruism, but also a degree of humility, even anonymity, each posing a genuine threat to profit and fame in a consumer society.

To achieve truly actionable spaces, architects may need to radically modify the way in which they envision and conceive the buildings they design. Instead of striving for absolute forms whose experience is fully decided beforehand, architects may need to create looser and more undetermined forms whose experience is left open to and provides the resources for spontaneous decisions by future occupants – a weaving of infinite and almost 'accidental' opportunities and scenarios embedded within but able to spring from, at any moment, the armature of concrete form. In a sense, these structures remain unfinished, in contrast to more polished objects, for they await others to bring them, virtually and momentarily, to future completion.

The result of such a design process would not only be a material object, but also an immaterial node of intersecting vectors whose predominant characteristic is *energy*, the kind of untapped energy an architect is able to bestow but never control or regulate. Beyond the form from which it emanates, the end would not be a form at all, but an invisible flow of possible actions that can be improvised in different ways, at different times, by the changing inclinations of people. The end, as Olson notes, 'is never more than this instant, than you in this instant, than you, figuring it out, and acting, so. If there is any absolute, it is never more than this one, you, this instant, in action.'[23]

Frank Lloyd Wright, Fallingwater (1935), Pennsylvania,
stair and platform over mountain stream

1

floors of agility

The ground of the built environment is our primary source
of opportunities to bring the body alive as a creative force in
motion, exercising faculties of balance and agility inherited from
the distant past. When omnipresent and despite its necessity,
a predictably uniform ground of flat floors and repetitive steps
subjects us to monotonous, mechanical movement, dissociating
power from the body. More challenging and playful terrains –
variable staircases, shifting slopes, unexpected level changes –
give us a chance to interact and improvise with the floor, reviving
our bodily powers in space. The act of motion becomes, in part,
an end in itself, confirming that we are vital forces even as we go
about our daily routines.

22   Paul Klee, *Tightrope Walker*, 1923 (Kunstmuseum Bern)

The floor is not only the ground of our world, but also the springboard of our motion. Our simplest acts in the physical environment are performed on this surface while manoeuvring over its terrain. Although these prospects disappear on a flat, predictable ground, they multiply on one that is stepped or furrowed, tilted or curved, especially when these disruptions are marked by surprising and alluring features, inviting us to move creatively, rather than automatically, in response to the contours underfoot.

When negotiating uneven ground, a person's mobility is never reduced to gross forward motion, but entails an assortment of springy vibrations that control and surround the overall flow. Torso and limbs tense and bend with ever-shifting and often precise adjustments to emerging terrain. A miraculous anatomy within the legs is called into play to stretch and compress as it bounds forward to land securely on the next momentary perch, before launching again into the air. Soles and toes wrap around textures with a primate-like effort to grip and exploit each new surface, subtly attuning the gait and flow of the vaulting body. These tiny creative discharges are concentrated where nerve endings abound, being a little more sluggish in the torso and sensitive in the extremities. Our peripatetic gestures are not simple vectors but clouds of motor and sensory impulses enwrapping horizontal progress, numerous erratic adjustments of each footfall that bestow a personal aura on motion. These eccentric pressures and releases are not appendages to movement but a penumbra of barely noticed forces that infuse walking with autonomous power.

In the interplay of flesh and ground, a varied and uncertain surface ensures that our movements are always fresh, transforming muscular effort into innovative actions. But equally important to this enterprise is the distinct and rugged character of the surface we cross. These qualities determine whether a floor is exhilarating or dull, and worthy of our pursuit. A topography that is unique and unmistakable, with clear and differentiated challenges that are instantly recognizable (even if never seen before), adds a special intensity and extra kinesthetic depth to motion. The grasping and releasing of lush terrain, revelling in our bodily skills at the height of play with the ground below, brings about a primal freedom known only to man. The experience carries us back to our origins, to the earliest gropings of infancy and further back to the beginnings of the human adventure.

Human faculties shaped aeons ago in a gravitational matrix of earth and trees require a periodic return to unsure terrain, where stimulating yet risky contours disrupt habitual and often mechanical motions. Everyone from the newborn to the aged needs unprotected places with challenges suited to their own capabilities, where they can test the limits of their limbs, senses and brains, so that each of these powers becomes an extension of the will. This kind of self-creative research, with its solitary trials and errors, its sudden surprises and strenuous encounters, is a simple yet fundamental act of facing the unknown and building self-reliance.

Most importantly, every surge over an uncertain floor calls the body itself back to life, as an impassioned tangle of flesh and bone, a figure struggling to burst from its frame in a wave of being, restoring our very existence. We make ourselves more vital and real by learning that the body through which we exist in the world is, for that moment, vital and real. The body is substantially *alive* and *there* in its strains and efforts, as it responds and adjusts to distinct yet ever-new conditions. Brought to awareness is a visceral and muscular presence, but also creative faculties roused to cope with an unpredictable ground. Whether one's body is graceful or awkward, it is pulsing with power.

Brought forth, as well, in these limber manoeuvres are the underlying motives of the self, an often hidden force at work that is beneath awareness yet flickers with impulses. In spontaneous acts of strolling over a challenging terrain, the 'I' wells up and appears, expressing itself through marvellous deeds and taking charge of its own destiny. This simple experience brings about an exquisite mutation of being, revealing something of one's innermost persona – exposing hidden aspirations and fears, capacities and limitations, but also something of who one potentially is, helping reshape and strengthen one's identity.

THE DOCILE EFFECT OF FLAT GROUND

Just as the terrain of the world can empower the body, it also can drain that power away, for its contours are urgently needed to supply opportunities on which we can act. The constructed ground over which we commonly walk – the floors in our homes, the continuous ribbons of sidewalks, the broad pavements of streets and plazas – depletes our power if it fails to respond to our presence and stimulate our faculties, presenting merely a uniform surface stripped of human deeds to perform.

On a floor that is perfectly flat and level there is no chance to interact with its surface, nor bring into play an extraordinary agility inherited from aeons of human evolution. Each contact with the standardized surface is the same, from every dull slap of the feet to every tedious stretch of the legs. Each dreary footfall weans us from a give and take with the ground, diminishing our responsibility and in a very real sense subduing and breaking our animal spirits, killing the spontaneity within us. The levelled floor gradually drills the human body into a kind of robotic motion. Nobody trips or falls on the unbroken plane, nor is anyone slowed when gliding over its vacant texture. But neither does anyone feel alive as a creative force in motion, since the horizontal plane has pacified the body and robbed it of power. By the same token, this floor presents an ideal terrain for machines and for people willing to move like machines, since it is totally divested of any interruption to easy and *a priori* motion, rewarding only the foot tamed by habit. There is no floor better suited to the routine behaviour of mass culture.

I am not suggesting the elimination of level floors, which provide benefits of practicality, accessibility and safety. Rather, I wish to propose that their omnipresence marks a new kind of danger for human existence. To live out one's life on a harmless and predictable ground would seem, at first glance, to assist the preservation of life. But, paradoxically, life as we know it is an evolving structure that resists monotonous conservation and demands instead a perpetual renewal by forgoing the comfort of a steady state. A sterile ground puts our agile faculties to sleep and conveys that we are impotent and automatic creatures, diminishing our sense of being animate. To put it more bluntly, the habitual ground that conserves life by eliminating risk is in reality a mechanism that, when universal, depletes and perverts the human spirit.

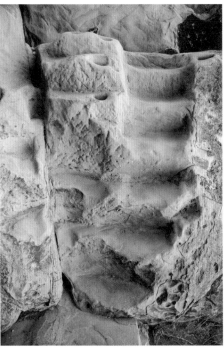

VERNACULAR STAIRS AND FOOTPATHS

Illuminating the idea that inventive motion transcends the benefits of physical exercise, and constitutes a fundamental responsibility of architecture, is Bernard Rudofsky in *Streets for People*. The primary human value of walking, he suggests, is that it grants us the freedom to stroll without any narrow aim or purpose. Among our exploits on foot, he notes, 'the act of descending a staircase ... represents the highest form of peripatetics', and for people who are strolling together, 'discoursing on this stylized slope demands a high discipline of give and take, and more than a touch of stagecraft'.[24] Rudofsky finds the apotheosis of creative walking in the urban staircases of Italy – notably Rome, from the divergent inclines to Michelangelo's Campidoglio and the twelfth-century church of Santa Maria in Aracoeli, to the monumental flights of Alessandro Specchi's demolished Porto di Ripetta and the iconic Scala de Spagna.

Our most resourceful climbs, of course, occur in the natural landscape, where geology and erosion have produced infinitely varied slopes, hills and mountains, tangled with roots or littered with rocks. Where wild terrains have been conserved, they remain as challenging as those on which our species emerged, continuing to summon extraordinary faculties of agility, balance and endurance, crucial to human evolution. While this kind of ground has largely disappeared from the everyday world, it remains a presence and perpetual attraction – as Rudofsky brought to widespread attention in the exhibition 'Architecture without Architects', held in 1964 at the Museum of Modern Art, New York – in vernacular hilltowns, whose rugged terrain is barely transformed and percolates up through the floor of the settlement.

Downward flight (left) and detail (right) of
rock-carved steps, Acoma Pueblo, New Mexico

Oia, Santorini, Greece, cliffside stairs; winding stair and
earthen ledges; sensuous rooftop stair, ever-changing
increments and footing of steps (clockwise from top left)

The twelfth-century village of Sky City at Acoma Pueblo (p. 25), for instance, set atop a sandstone mesa west of Albuquerque, New Mexico, can still be reached by its original means of access, a meandering climb through cracks and folds of vertiginous cliff. The invigorating yet treacherous route winds through slender crevices and over boulders, its journey eased slightly by roughly carved treads that merge into the natural slopes and ledges of bedrock. Phases of easy but changing terrain intermingle with an adventure close to rock climbing, where handgrips are as important as footholds and every muscle is brought into play. This experience doesn't entirely vanish atop the mesa, for even here paths rise and fall over outcrops of rock, turning every walk into a moment-to-moment challenge.

Analogous if less strenuous footpaths are etched into thousands of Mediterranean hilltowns, from the Iberian Peninsula to Greece, Morocco to Tunisia. In these largely neglected building cultures we still find surviving traces of a fundamental human heritage. Dramatic landforms press into and mould the shape of the floor, leaving the earth only slightly tamed and partially paved to enhance its access to human movement. Among the most dexterous but exciting footways are those carved into the volcanic cliffs of villages dotting the Greek island of Santorini. Precarious inclines wind unpredictably along and up and down the steep terrain, clinging above one another as they connect and cross over the roofs of the cubic houses. The stairways of the small town of Oia (opposite), carved into the island's northwest promontory, are among the most daring. Each flight perpetually widens and narrows, curves and bends in unexpected tacks, developing rhythmic passages that transform their beats with every footfall. Some phases clamber over massive boulders left in place, and others scale walls free of rails. Uneven repetitions of tread and riser invite the climber to closely interact with an incline that is simultaneously alarming and compelling, magnifying the deeds of ascent.

Oia's stairs are certainly hazardous, but they are also among the most vivifying climbs ever shaped by human hands, reminding us that we have to risk staying alive in order to actually *feel* alive. The value of such risks should not be confused with gambling, however, for climbing entails free choice, not compulsion. The climber actively shapes his own chances, rather than submits docilely to fate, and is always able to slow down or pause, manoeuvre more carefully or veer onto an alternate route. He takes his life in his own hands, accepting the peril of injury as the admission price for action in space. Only in places such as these, where we are vulnerable and life is uncertain, do we fully encounter the freedom of action needed to truly venture in space, discovering hidden frailties and fears that we have the chance to overcome.

In *The Prodigious Builders*, Rudofsky contrasts the unruly flights of Santorini's stairs with the monotonous and disabling stairs of modern life. 'The dancing rhythms of the steps, with their startling pauses', he writes, 'are rarely registered by the plantar nerves of those who all their life have been conditioned to walk like mechanical toys and thus lost the sprightliness that nature bestows on man and beast alike ... The varying height, width and depths of the steps are the despair of the city dweller. To scale but a short flight, he needs the crutches of railings and banisters. In fact, they are written into our building regulations.'[25]

Less earthy and primitive yet abundant with their own adventurous textures and inclines are the stairscapes of Italian hilltowns such as Sorano and Perugia, Urbino (above) and Ostuni (opposite). Magnificent flights plunge and cascade through slots carved from a dense urban mass, each inciting a distinct gait that may unexpectedly slow or quicken, constrict or broaden, bending at times into soft curves or sharp angles or splitting into multiple streams with contrasting direction and character, some steeply rising to the dwellings above.

An ever-shifting pace of steps eliminates all routine motion and each newly emerging rhythm keeps the climber awake and involved. Each part of the leg, complementing the balancing forces of a twisting torso and swinging arms, is synchronized in a complex yet highly creative act in space, turning locomotion into a precious moment of being. The result is a kind of rapture in which the combination of 'adventure, fun, wonder, risk and ordeal', to apply the words of Diane Ackerman in *Deep Play*, elicits 'a cyclone of intense alertness, a marginally frightening state in which I exist entirely in the tense present and feel quintessentially alive'.[26]

Even when appearing flat, the hilltown floor, like the earth, is generally sloped to some degree, its periphery further disturbed by folding terrain at building thresholds. Similarly, the memorable presence of an Italian piazza can derive as much from a distinguished gradient underfoot as from the shape of enclosing walls: consider the steep, fan-shaped bowl of the Piazza del Campo in Siena (p. 30), the southerly slant of the Piazza Grande in Arezzo or the inclined stone carpet of Montepulciano's own Piazza Grande, all breaking into multiple tilts around the edge. While strolling over a floor that 'slants down just a little, so little that it is not noticeable to the eye', as Bachelard notes in *Air and Dreams*, 'you will find wings growing,

Intersection of five stairs in Ostuni (above)
and curving staircase in Urbino (opposite)

Fan-shaped and sloped pavement, Piazza del Campo, Siena

little wings on your feet, your heel will have just enough light, delicate … energy to let you fly. With a very simple movement, your heel will change the descent into an ascent, the walk into a soaring.'[27]

Beneath the overall shape of its surface, the pavement of a hilltown prompts a further creative role in its tactile challenge to human feet. Even through the soles of our shoes we can feel the floor's uneven texture. The assemblage of rounded or pitted elements invites our feet to curl around each raised surface and step lightly over the cracks between. Unlike a smooth concrete sidewalk, to which most of us are now fully accustomed, a mosaic-like surface of brick or stone offers a pavement in relief to which we must constantly pay attention (above), but that rewards our involvement with a tonic for the foot. Though the uncertainty of vernacular textures and inclines may not have resulted from conscious design, and may simply be an unsquandered geologic gift enhanced by spontaneous craft and robust materials, it nevertheless demonstrates how the ground of our world might, in places, nurture more inventive movement.

GRAVITATIONAL CURRENTS

Among the world's great staired villages, one of the smallest yet most diverse is the enchanting white maze of Sperlonga, perched above the Tyrrhenian coast between Rome and Naples. Cutting through the dense settlement are numerous intersecting stairways, their twisted routes following the slope but also squeezing through narrow chasms overlooked by windows and stoops, dropping through cliffs of brilliant white walls, compressing and dark where tunnelled under buildings and frequently meeting at shared landings, only to suddenly split apart and race on at wildly contrasting angles.

Giving an unforgettable character to each phase of stair is the unique incline and course of its steps, inviting an equally unique kinesthetic experience. One supple winding flight contains alternating counter-curves in opposite directions. Another forms a plunging cascade, gaily covered with laundry and bouquets of flowers and lined at either side with small ledges for doorsteps, whose startling pauses and syncopations slow down and disrupt movement (above). Nearby is a rough chasm that rips diagonally across the hillside in a series of abrupt angles, giving the climb a staccato beat. Just around the corner is an intersection of multiple stairs, whose tangle of lines spreads into faster and slower increments, while quivering back and forth in minor directional shifts (opposite). In each footpath it is not so much the steps themselves that challenge and reward human action, but their uniquely shaped vectors and evolving surprises that keep the climber engaged.

Evidently something beyond the physical realm, and exceeding vision, has been introduced to and now pervades the inclines of this village. Unlike the inactive floors of conventional architecture, Sperlonga's floors are permeated with heightened forces and

tensions of gravity. Appearing not to the eye but to the body in motion are active gravitational currents within the air along each cascade, streams of forces into which we bodily enter and take part while travelling through them.

To borrow an analogy from quantum theory, wherever the ground is broken open and made incomplete it is, in a sense, no longer inert and static. The ground is transformed from a neutral object into a magnetic region, like an atom whose outer 'valence shell' has been 'destabilized' and 'ionized' by an input of energy that enlivens the element and gives it the power to move, change and interact with others. Correspondingly every juncture and cascade of ground along an indeterminate slope is suffused with its own unique gravitational currents, a voltage that may be invisible but is nonetheless so tangible we can anticipate its presence and carry its experience in the memory of our muscles. We feel currents seize hold of the body, as if entering a moving river, and sense the way it resists or transports us as we climb through its force field. We sense an accelerating tug as we plummet through air to levels below and a backward drag as we spring to higher levels above.

Zig-zag staircase (above) and episodic
stairs (opposite), Sperlonga, Italy

Wharton Esherick Studio (begun 1926), Pennsylvania, red-oak
spiral stair, with intersecting stair to the kitchen and dining room

The enriched gravity at Sperlonga thickens our movements like some sort of germinating ingredient in space. Where currents pick us up we can wade into them, propelling ourselves through surges and waves, occasionally a torrent or trickle. By swimming through the shifting resistance and tensions of gravity, we are able to inscribe our own glorious powers in space. Not only do we feel a play of forces on our body, sharpening senses and wakening faculties, but we are also invited to become living forces ourselves as we drive through the viscous currents. A related point is made by Erik Erikson in *Childhood and Society*: 'Take *gravity*: to juggle, to jump or to climb adds unused dimensions to the awareness of our body. Play here gives a sense of divine leeway, of excess space.'[28]

The unique yet ever-changing calculus in each flight of steps exerts infinitely varied forces upon us, calling forth an evolving, almost balletic response to engage its shifting currents and still move about as we please. Each bounding launch sets into motion a throng of velocities that transforms rapidly through space and time, and which can only be resolved by an equally complicated spatiotemporal counterforce of limbs and torso traced into air and at each landing, a spry motion performed off-balance on footholds that are unpredictably wide or narrow, rough or slippery. Our motions are at once more primitive, as well as more nimble, the fruits of exercise and evolution. Our moves at times feel weightless, gesturing lightly in the air, but are also more fleshy, with a sagging mass to discover and carry. We take on a more voluptuous existence, returning us to our bodies in two ways: causing us to dwell more deeply within the skin, while transcending the skin's limits as if liberated from its frame. We become, for a time, moving centres of expressive force, rather than puppets of forces controlled by others. With every self-delighting gesture in these gravitational fields, each of us sketches into the air '*I am*': I am a 'person', rather than 'it'.

ACROBATIC STAIRCASES

It would, of course, be impractical, not to mention hazardous, to form extensive fields of gravity in our buildings and cities, especially for cultures obsessed with economies of effort and time, but also rightly concerned with architectural access for all – including those of us with physical challenges.[29] At times we need to move quickly, without distraction, and there are obvious merits of security and comfort in flat floors, and of movements that free us from having to constantly pay attention to our feet. The few architects who seem to have wanted to accommodate these polar demands have shown great ingenuity in combining flat floors with small concentrations of daring movement, so that people may move about with ease yet occasionally return to their bodies in manoeuvres that can reach high-wire intensity.

A small but astonishing instance is the rough-hewn staircase of red oak built by sculptor and furniture-maker Wharton Esherick to link three levels of his home in Malvern, Pennsylvania (opposite). No two treads repeat precisely in this spiral structure, whose cantilevered blocks of wood twist about an equally twisting vertical post, echoing the torsion experienced in the climber's own torso. Mid-flight, the stair splits into two different routes, one angling left to the kitchen and dining area, the other coiling up to a sleeping loft over the studio. Halfway along the rise to the kitchen is a ledge for the telephone and space to write,

an event that complicates climbing with a revolving and balancing act of the torso amid careful footwork. Smoothly undulant wooden railings, and in one case a mastodon bone, follow the ascent without any uniform line or thickness, prompting while freeing the climber to improvise handholds along the way. A person must be fully alert and agile to climb this stair, but is rewarded with a tremendous elation and degree of involvement. When asked if anyone had ever been hurt on his stair, Esherick replied: 'No, it's too dangerous.'[30]

A similar interest in compact yet invigorating climbs capable of disrupting habits can be followed in the architecture of Carlo Scarpa, whose floors of horizontal planes often shift level with unexpected increments. The new floors of the renovated Fondazione Querini Stampalia, in Venice, are set slightly above and not fully covering the old floors (above), leaving them often surrounded by continuous channels and shallow rims that control flooding during the *acqua alta*, but also provoke an up-and-down motion as if stepping into a boat, a resonant experience in this water city. The canalside arrival by gondola (opposite) entails an especially elaborate sequence, whether ambling down to or up from the water. For those departing, the thick treads of Istrian stone begin at a curb above the floor and then twist and turn in a loose concatenation of squares, with each slab given a bevelled corner to vary

Carlo Scarpa, Fondazione Querini Stampalia (1963), Venice,
canalside stair (above) and steps up and over rim of new floor (opposite)

the assembly and complicate the flow, descending along a continuous but unforeseeable sequence, before splitting into divergent routes that lead to two metal gates onto the canal – an adventure that heightens when the water rises to surround the steps. Much of this discursive language continues into the small garden behind the gallery, its upper terrace of water and grass reached by steps that veer sideways with treads that are not always where one expects them.

Even the brief but daring climbs between a lower pavement and upper grass terraces at the Brion Cemetery in San Vito d'Altivole, Italy, involve topographic peril and delight. Stutter steps (opposite) offer each leg a different tread, and at times slide obliquely to challenge feet with unfamiliar diagonal components in the vertical motion. The high point in this dual kinesthesia, described by Scarpa as 'climbing in space', is the marble staircase at the heart of the Olivetti Showroom in the Piazza San Marco, Venice. The line of ascent strays subtly off to the right in an angular drift, while guiding the climber to a corner office on the mezzanine. One's legs are induced to shift to the right while lifting clear of each tread, a dual motion that brings lateral forces and muscles to bear, making the act more three-dimensional. The broad hovering sheet of marble at the stair's base, essentially a bottom tread widened to form a threshold and landing, gestures in two directions – aiming down the room's axis to the doorway onto the piazza, and leading off to a secondary entrance – so that the stair incorporates four different, if barely noticeable, inflections that vitalize motion in space.

All these experiments in human agility at critical junctures, 'celebrating the marriage of flesh and air', as Wallace Stevens says in his poem 'Life is Motion', culminate at Scarpa's Castelvecchio Museum in Verona.[31] Gallery floors are loosened from walls by shallow channels around the perimeter, giving a mild levitation to each raised surface. At the same time, the displacements cause rifts where rooms meet each other or adjoining corridors, so as to subtly waken and ennoble each arrival or departure. These edges of possibility turn especially adventurous in the outdoor niche at the northwest corner of the courtyard, where a nexus of circulation routes at multiple levels also serves as the meeting ground of the contrasting historic eras of the castle (p. 40). The lowermost routes link the garden and gallery wing to the Torre del Mastio and Reggia galleries beyond, but do this indirectly along a sequence of stepped digressions that twist and slide the body in space. The route winds about itself as it slips over an excavated moat, before zig-zagging under the old city wall in a series of bridges with changing overlooks onto archaeological excavations.

Similar but more airborne motions occur in the diagonal bridge above, from which branch multiple stairs to link gallery levels, and lead to a battlement walk along the river and up to a passage atop the city wall. The one still point in this complex gravitational field is the fourteenth-century equestrian statue of Cangrande I della Scala (p. 41). But even here a stair winds down and around the epicentre of this huge figure, providing an intimate view from beneath while extending out on a cantilever of steel and concrete. This projection bobs ever so slightly up and down under the influence of a person's weight, so as to punctuate a site rich in chances for exercising bodily faculties, while giving the sedate museum experience an undercurrent of risk and adventure.

Carlo Scarpa, Brion Cemetery (1977), Italy,
stutter steps with tombs beyond

Carlo Scarpa, Castelvecchio Museum (1973), Verona,
overview of discursive routes around and below the statue
of Cangrande I della Scala (below) and puzzle-like sequence
of pavements and bridges underneath bridge wall (opposite)

THE SPRIGHTLY JAPANESE FLOOR

Scarpa's penchant for slight displacements of floor, linked by brief yet refreshing climbs, is distantly rooted in his admiration for traditional Japanese architecture and gardens. The many slight shifts in Japanese floors derive, in part, from the pragmatic need to escape damp earth in a wet climate, but also from a cultural urge to differentiate territorial zones: a lowermost level of stones or pounded earth (*doma*); an elevated timber floor (*engawa*) for the intermediate levels of corridor and veranda; and an uppermost floor of *tatami* mats for sitting, dining and sleeping (above). Important consequences of this stratification are the modest yet psychologically momentous leaps that recur throughout the day in moving from one of these worlds to another, marking but also charging each boundary with tiny gravitational currents.

Further complicating agility at each new level of a house or temple is a ritualized changing of footwear, aimed to reduce the transfer of dirt inside and to make each level slightly cleaner and purer than the one below (opposite). Outdoor shoes are left where the earth or street meets the inner wood floor, and slippers are removed at the edge of the *tatami* mats, which means that each climb is infused with the balancing act of removing or slipping on various shoes, as well as twirling around to leave each pair ready for easy departure, or in some cases placing outdoor shoes on a shelf or flat stone reserved for this purpose. All these intricate twists and bends, and rotations in the midst of ascent, transform otherwise simple motions into feats of equipoise, where many different forces converge to be creatively balanced and counterbalanced.

Sutejiro Kitamura, Kitamura House (1944), Kyoto, stepping stones
and bench at main entrance (above) and veranda and *shoin* (opposite)

Stepping stones to the teahouse at Kitamura House (top);
sawatari-ishi ('steps across the marsh') at the Heian Shrine
(1895), Kyoto (above)

Human equilibrium is stimulated differently in the Japanese garden, especially in each unique series of stepping stones (*tobi-ishi*), whose ever-changing intervals invite a light, graceful movement. The stakes of a misstep are exaggerated by setting off the elevated stones from a soft, delicate earth not to be touched by human feet. These fragile settings range from carpets of moss and beds of raked gravel to the waters of a stream or pond, the latter taken to acrobatic heights when approaching the Kitamura teahouse (opposite), springing along the erratic series of cylindrical piles at the Heian Shrine or stepping out to a stream to wash one's hands as a prelude to tea at the Katsura Imperial Villa.

The essence of Japanese stepping stones lies in the way their journey enlivens walking while shunning routine or inattentive motion. The size, shape and texture of each stone are distinct and unrepeated, ensuring that each deviates slightly from those before and after, and thereby calls forth a newly improvised footfall. Further expanding uncertainty is an evolving arrangement and course of stones. They are generally not fixed along a straight line or sequenced with equal intervals, but placed to sporadically shift direction with unexpected gaps between. The progression may be vaguely continuous, then abruptly angle off to one side, take unexpected diversions or twists and intersect other series of stones that swerve off in contrasting courses, all of which help to slow down motion and tap extra levels of skill in the feet, magnifying deeds in space.

The most precarious motion occurs as garden stones rise when approaching a veranda. The ascent turns especially thrilling at Katsura in two garden paths that climb up to the elevated verandas of the Middle and Old Shoins (above). Flatter stones give way to ever-higher boulders and their routes begin to stagger almost haphazardly, causing the walker to bob up and down along the ascent, suggesting 'the desultory flight of a butterfly'.[32]

Katsura Imperial Villa (17th century), Kyoto,
rising stepping stones to the Large Veranda
and Moon-viewing Platform at Old Shoin

Human exploits on other stone series at Katsura are amplified by crossing eventful garden textures, whose passing allure of moss and roots diverts the eye and widens the margin of error in movement, as seen in the stepping stones to the Shokatei (above). The route established by square-cut granite blocks skirting the Onrin-do traverses bands of smaller, closely fitted stones (opposite), and in one instance a pebbled rain gutter. In all these cases one has the impression of a long and momentous journey, where motion is enriched with pauses and twists, turning this way or that, bending down to see a detail with greater clarity, balancing on one stone or another – and for visitors today to do this while also aiming a camera.

The indeterminate garden walk has parallels with the game of Go, which originated in China more than 2,500 years ago and spread to Japan in the seventh century AD. In the game, players set black and white stones on a board to mark out key strategic positions, to be subsequently filled in according to circumstances, while in the garden walk the first stepping stones placed by the gardener function as initial markers, their vague choreography then completed by positioning other stones between. The rough plan of action in Go, a technique called *fuseki*, as Kiyoyuki Nichihara points out, is essentially the same as the initial stone placements in *yakumono* ('things with a purpose') garden design, their preliminary moves deployed as 'focal points for action based on an idea of what the future situation will be'.[33]

Another peak of agility occurs when arriving at a teahouse, enhancing awareness that one is about to enter a world set apart from everyday life. While perched atop rising stones, visitors slip off their shoes and bend to squeeze through a small door, the *nijiriguchi* ('crawling-in space'), an act meant to induce humility but also requiring dexterity, making people conscious of their bodily contortions and, hopefully, grace. This passage rite is

preceded by an even more astonishing feat along the garden path to the Fushin-an teahouse (p. 48, top) at Omoto-senke, Kyoto, eliciting an elaborate manoeuvre through a sliding door, a *nakakuguri* ('middle crawl-through gate'), in a freestanding wall. After scrambling up the rocks on one side, a person must then stretch in mid-air through a square opening, without aid of a floor at either side, and, while straddling this opening, balance his weight while withdrawing the rear foot and recovering his balance on another stone on the far side.

Even a simple bridge in the Japanese garden has acrobatic undertones. At their most delightfully primitive these crossings are reduced to a single stone slab set over a 'river' of moss or pebbles, or actual water. The Shirakawa bridge at Katsura (p. 48, bottom), for instance, is a granite monolith only slightly chiselled when taken from the quarry, its upper surface then further roughened to stimulate the foot while enhancing traction. The water-crossing slab to the *amanohashidate* ('bridge to heaven'), also at Katsura, has a slight upward curvature, prompting a mild kinesthesia of ascent and descent, a curving trajectory taken to

Katsura Imperial Villa, square granite stepping stones
passing the Onrin-do (above) and stepping stones over
roots and moss to the Shokatei (opposite)

Katsura Imperial Villa, Shirakawa bridge (above);
Fushin-an teahouse, Omote-senke, Kyoto, *nakakuguri* (top)

Murin-an villa, Kyoto, zig-zag timber bridge (above);
Katsura Imperial Villa, arched earthen bridge (top)

far greater heights in the steep, earth-covered bridges that begin and end with near-vertical steps (p. 49, top) – a gravitational adventure derived from China.

A special place in the Japanese repertoire of light-footed motion belongs to the zig-zag bridge, as in the recurring offsets of paired boards at the garden of Murin-an Villa (p. 49, bottom) in Kyoto or the scissor-like sequence of boards at Kōraku-en Garden in Okayama. These narrow gangways set over water overlap as they shift to the side, and continue to deviate back and forth in a series of fresh angles in space. For a brief spell one walks in a line along one tack, only to then simultaneously twist and step diagonally while countering centrifugal forces and transitioning to a new vector in space. Brief periods of linear motion while dangling above water alternate with lateral moves and a realignment of the torso, heightening the experience of perpetually losing and regaining balance in a graceful interplay of muscle, tendon and joint.

VERTIGINOUS EDGES

The intensity of freedom on an open bridge exemplified in the Japanese garden illustrates another kinesthetic feat that would be deflated by parapets or railings. When nearing either hazardous edge, a fear of falling pushes up into the conscious mind. The roots of this terror include the sensation of being unprotected and of easily toppling off the side, plunging to uncertain perils below – feelings that make one tremble, even if only in the innermost part of the psyche. A faint vertigo further threatens balance, bringing added attention to each footfall, while tapping into reserves of willpower to assess and overcome the threat. It is precisely the repeated and successful experience of this kind of challenging operation, while triumphing over fear and risk, which underlies, as Erikson writes in his essay 'Play and Actuality', the 'restoration and creation of a *leeway of mastery*'.[34] It is no wonder, he continues, 'that man's play takes place on the border of dangerous alternatives and is always beset both with burdening conflicts and with liberating choices'.[35]

A more elusive if nonetheless deeply felt power that is also roused on the unrestrained bridge is a virtual experience of levitation, originating in what Bachelard calls the 'aerial psyche'.[36] We do not merely walk across but *soar over* the bridge and what lies beneath, enacting a primal urge of mankind: the ineffable happiness of flight. We take pleasure in briefly leaving the earth and escaping its terrestrial bonds, to loft over the world below, seeming to hover momentarily in air. We overcome the hold of gravity when adventuring in the heights, a height that can be felt but not measured, lingering awhile in this state immune from the laws of nature, before gliding back to terra firma.

A related component in traditional Japanese architecture that exploits these tensions and triumphs over danger is the open veranda, its wooden floor devoid of rails and hovering precariously over a lush and pristine garden (opposite). People can sit or stroll, congregate or meditate along these edges of possibility brought into communion with nature. There is no barrier to disturb the view, but neither is there any safeguard to prevent tumbling off the side. A slight misstep or loss of balance could easily result in slipping off the wooden platform. While the actual height above ground is slight, the perceptual and psychological height is enormous, for the exquisite landscape below is meant not to use but to behold and inspire, a place closed to touch but open to dreams. Peril intensifies this reverie, strengthening the awareness of having been brought right up to the boundary of two different worlds.

The open edge of a bridge or veranda also implies an open future. There is an electrifying sense of being back in control of one's destiny, for we know that we *could* easily leap off if we wish, that we have been granted the power to do so and might even do so by accident if we become distracted, lose our footing or get too near the brink. There are few analogies in the West to this simple kind of human responsibility, but among them is the small platform dangling over a mountain stream at Frank Lloyd Wright's Fallingwater (p. 20) in Mill Run, Pennsylvania, and the floating terraces of Mies van der Rohe's Farnsworth House in Plano, Illinois (overleaf). The planes of white travertine held in white steel frames at Farnsworth hover like two magic carpets above the grassy, sometimes river-flooded earth. Pervading each is a zone of peril, as well as a euphoria that can't be seen but is acutely felt, where menace is brightened with possibility – a kind of tightrope from which one might fall but can equally prevail over hazards and fear in a barely noticed but splendid deed.

Joju-in Temple, Kiyomizu-dera, Kyoto,
open veranda and *tsukubai* (water basin)

Although open edges have largely disappeared from urban public spaces, a splendid exception to this distrust of freedom is Venice, where stone *fondamente* keep the city floor in close touch with canal and lagoon, giving every stroll an undeniable risk and elation. Cutting into the waterside pavements are stairs descending to meet gondolas and gangplanks to water taxis. Replacing the floor during seasonal floods are long trails of wooden planks, compressing pedestrian traffic into precarious footbridges. When poised along any of these precipices, our vertigo becomes both a knife-edge of anxiety and a symbol of our right to exist as truly human beings. Our fate is put entirely back in our own hands and, for a time, we are deliriously incarnate forces in the world, rather than machineries of atoms or pliant meat.

Mies van der Rohe, Farnsworth House
(1950), Illinois, floating travertine decks

SKY CITIES AND RESIDENTIAL EYRIES

Magnifying the freedom of vertigo and human ventures into air, while protecting all but the suicidal, are small mountaintop cities in Europe, crowded at times up to the very edge of a cliff: Bonifacio at the tip of Corsica; Saorge and La Roquette-sur-Siagne in the Alpes-Maritimes and Rocamadour and St-Cirq-Lapopie along the Lot in France; the Andalusian villages of Montefrio and Alhama de Granada in Spain; Marvão and Monsaraz in Portugal; and the Italian hilltowns of Vernazza (p. 54, top left) and Civita di Bagnoregio. These lofty villages are piled above and seem to hang over river valleys or rocky coastline, originally for defense but now giving daily life an exalted sense of being on high or, as Bachelard

Vernazza, Italy; Thera, Santorini, Greece; cascading roof
terraces and houses, Foinikia, Santorini; staired descent
to cliffside house, Thera (clockwise from top left)

described it in *Air and Dreams*, the grandeur of living in an 'aerial state', in a world endowed with 'aerial dynamism'.[37]

To illustrate aerial dwelling at its most primitive yet most invigorating, we must return to Santorini, whose black and red volcanic bluffs are dotted with hundreds of small white houses perched in the contours. The towns of Oia and Thera (opposite, top right and bottom left), along with the hamlet of Foinikia (opposite, bottom right) lying between them and Thirasia set on a facing clifftop across the caldera, are built up from tier upon tier of footpaths, stairways, rooftops and courtyards, each overlooking dozens of others like steep amphitheatres pressed up to the precipice. Space falls away from one to the next, and further down to the distant sea, so that one is continually flirting with danger. Accentuating the precarious footholds, dangled hundreds of metres above the sea, are visible signs of seismic activity in the cracked walls and rubble that has cascaded down the cliffs.

Introducing a spiritual dimension to the aerial life are sanctuaries perched on mountains, intent on dwelling closer to heaven and far from the secular ground below. At the monasteries of Mont-St-Michel in Normandy and Mount Athos in Greece, or the small chapel of St-Michel d'Aiguilhe (below) atop a volcanic cone in Le Puy-en-Velay, France,

St-Michel d'Aiguilhe Chapel (969), France

people are able to commune with the sky from ecstatic yet terrifying heights. 'There dwell the gods, there a few privileged mortals make their way by rites of ascent,' wrote religious historian Mircea Eliade. 'He who ascends by mounting the steps of a sanctuary or the ritual ladder that leads to the sky ceases to be a man; in one way or another, he shares in the divine condition.'[38] But even apart from these aspirations, and while one may know it is impossible to fly, there persists an awareness of living among the clouds and birds and sharing in their conquest of gravity.

The journey to reach such a lofty world is itself a feat, for it entails an arduous and perilous climb, and for the believer a passage rite whose difficult path makes possible a new mode of being, overcoming death to be reborn. The Greek monasteries of Metéora (meaning 'hanging in the air') are perched on towering sandstone pinnacles, whose forms seem faintly ominous and almost alive. The geologic masses, into whose cracks the buildings claw a tenuous foothold, evoke internal tensions and pressures, a kind of petrified muscle and bone vented with strange dark orifices, suggesting something that might any moment shudder and move. The isolated pillars rise so perpendicularly from the Peneiós plain that, for centuries, the dizzying ascent could only be made by wooden ladders of 30 m (100 ft) or more in length, or in nets drawn up by a rope and windlass. Recent stairs chiselled into the cliffs have not lost all their vertiginous power, being steep and narrow while tightly wound up naked rock and overhanging the abyss, retaining a trace of mystic ascension.

Among twentieth-century buildings where people can reach for the sky, especially pronounced is the aerial freedom felt in the San Francisco Bay Area houses by Joseph Esherick, suspended over steep and supposedly unbuildable sites. Exemplifying this danger and bliss are Cary House in Mill Valley, Bermak House in Oakland, McLeod House (opposite) in Belvedere and Oestreicher House (p. 58) in Sausalito, dwellings that fully embody Bachelard's 'poetics of wings'.[39] A sense of sharing the freedom of birds in air is reinforced by entry bridges and balconies cantilevered into the treetops. The tremor of nervous excitement and hazard does not disappear inside, where tall windows extend from ceiling to floor, some to capture entire tree trunks, others to frame a slice of landscape similar to a Chinese scroll painting, where the eye can scan an entire progression from mountain peak to valley floor.

Another high-wire act derives from Esherick's hollowing interior cavities to create overlooks within. Stairs climb high walls and lofts dangle above double-height rooms so that one might be gazing onto a floor or cascade of floors below, and then further down through windows to steeply descending trees and earth, compounding the aerial intensity of each point in space. The dweller is immersed in 'one of those impressions of happiness that nearly all imaginative men have experienced in their sleeping dreams', as Baudelaire admirably put it, where they 'felt freed from *the powers of gravity*, and, through memory, succeed in recapturing the extraordinary *voluptuousness* that pervades *high places*'.[40]

Avian freedom and vertiginous power are equally felt, if differently aroused, in the Douglas House in Harbor Springs, Michigan, by Richard Meier. The house consists of a narrow stack of floors and mezzanines wrapped with glass, jutting into the treetops with elevated balconies and lookouts, interlaced and bordered with bridges and staircases,

one stair dangled over the falling ground and a ladder descending the shear foundation, all perched high above Lake Michigan. Continuing this precipice into the units are interior windows and floors cut away from the walls to open glimpses to other levels. Visually amplifying the sense of adventure are pure white forms that keep drawing attention to nature outside, while bathed in constantly changing colours that meld the house into the sky.

A more urbanistic aerial world developed in the work of Paul Rudolph, turning most precarious in his own ateliers and homes. The rail-less stair of his house in New Haven, Connecticut, for instance, scales a wall on openly cantilevered treads, seeming to float free in the air and offering climbers little resource beyond their own balance and footwork. This experience was carried further in his 58th Street office in New York, where a number of mezzanines spun around and overlooked, with little restraint, the three-level void of the rooftop space. Rail-less stairs combined with catwalks and improvised paths over flat file cabinets upon which several desks were mounted, along with Rudolph's own desk overlooking the atrium, gave the entire design a dangerous yet electrifying character described by one writer following its demolition as 'Rudolph's dare-devil office'.[41]

The intoxicating blend of agile play amid risk became the central motif of Rudolph's own experimental penthouse at 23 Beekman Place, also in New York, a masterpiece of vertigo that capitalized on bird's-eye views of the city. Scores of unbounded floors, stairs and bridges, as well as Rudolph's cantilevered drafting table high above, overlook the living room, using

Joseph Esherick, McLeod House (1962), California

Joseph Esherick, Oestreicher House (1968), California

openly tiered mezzanines as the basic components of the house. Transparent plastic in surprising places further erases the already diminished sense of stability, while enhancing the sense of lightheaded feats, from Plexiglas floors and staircase treads to a sink and bathtub, also in Plexiglas, which serve as skylights to rooms below. Especially ingenious is the narrow steel staircase in a guest apartment, which winds around itself while climbing through space, its rail-free danger compounded by surface reflections that visually erode the structure's security, as well as its restriction and certainty.

THE GRACEFUL FLIGHT OF RAMPS

As the floor begins to tilt, all of our kinesthetic faculties are brought into play to remain balanced while counteracting gravitational forces with powers applied through our angled feet and swinging torso and limbs. This kind of creative navigation is a central experience of the ramps in Renaissance villas, or equestrian coils such as the Rundetårn ('round tower'; p. 60, top) in Copenhagen, whose inclines take off from the earth in a low trajectory, to then bend or curve around on themselves and keep altering the course mid-flight, complicating kinesthesia with centrifugal forces. The entire body comes alive as it strains to generate lift and propulsion, drawing arms and legs into action with a miraculous blend of energy and equilibrium, coordination and endurance. The climber is made intensely aware of the relation between his centre of gravity and the lifting and pushing pressure of legs, as well as the need to carefully keep shifting weight to balance and rebalance the body in motion.

This graceful kinesthesia became a primary source of aerial dynamics in the architecture of Le Corbusier. His inclines range from steep angles calling forth conscious effort to gently sloped floors that induce a subtle gliding sensation, and in the case of the chapel of Notre Dame du Haut in Ronchamp, France, inflect movement into a counterforce of incoming light.[42] Beyond disrupting habits and stimulating the body in flight, the inclines keep activating the muscular role in a *promenade architecturale*. This dual fascination with simple means to conquer gravity and soar into the air rivals Leonardo da Vinci's preoccupation with the complex forces at play on ramps and the construction of human flying machines, as compiled in his famous notebook *Sul volo degli uccelli* ('On the flight of birds'). But Le Corbusier had the advantage of reinforced concrete, allowing him to build ramps that lift off the ground and hover in space, empowering their climbers to share in that weightless suspension.

An early example of this unconfined joy is the slender incline that cuts and weaves through the Villa Savoye (p. 60, bottom), in Poissy, only to continue outside and keep slanting up to the sky. The human significance of this trajectory derives not from formal properties, but from the way it stimulates creative feats, combining gentle ascents with twists and turns, and changing speed or pausing to rest while assessing emergent opportunities. But the intoxicating freedom also stems from a muscular exercise no longer bound to the external pressures of work, efficiency or time, allowing people to leisurely glide between the two poles of human existence. A similar liberation develops along the outdoor ramp resting on piers at the Carpenter Center for the Visual Arts at Harvard University, in Cambridge, Massachusetts, whose S-shaped route angles off the sidewalk and into the

Le Corbusier, Villa Savoye (1931), France, staircase and ramps
(above); Rundetårn (17th century), Copenhagen, spiral ramp (top)

air, a sensation not unlike the initial uplift of an aeroplane. As the take-off curves towards the building entrance, new counterforces are brought into play as the body responds to centrifugal pressures, similar to banking around a curve, a complex of forces that reverses along the descent on the far side.

The avian powers instilled in concrete by Le Corbusier have been revived, and at times transcended, by Japanese architect Tadao Ando in his threading of inclines to, through and around buildings. This emancipation from gravity is fully exploited at the Otemae Art Center, in Nishinomiya, where the ramp, after veering and lifting off the sidewalk, angles up and through the building as in the Carpenter Center, but here continues an upward climb on the other side. The airborne flight lofts over a hillside, seemingly free of earthly cares, only to tightly turn and angle back up to the topmost floor, allowing the climber to feel momentarily free of work and academia, as well as the building's physical security and geometry.

The low-flying ramps of Ando's Himeji City Museum of Literature have the unusual virtue of defining outdoor and indoor circulation. Museumgoers approach up a gentle incline that travels over sheets of water flowing in the opposite direction, magnifying the impression of speed and complicating the climbing action with invitations to pause, twist and bend at the waist to better admire the sounds and sights of the cascade below. The ramp reappears inside, but now in the form of a downward spiral skirting a cylindrical wall faced with exhibits, so that the balancing act of descent is mixed with frequent pauses and turns to take in displays on either side, recalling Frank Lloyd Wright's Guggenheim Museum in New York.

CATWALKS: FROM THE EIFFEL TOWER TO ARNE JACOBSEN'S STAIRWAYS

The act of climbing while mastering vertigo reaches a peak in very high structures open to air and scaled by foot. Anyone who has climbed a tree as a child understands the source of this triumph. Even in towers protected by railings the core of this deed survives, and where the restraints are perceptually dissolved and easy to slip over, there remains a real sense of danger while freely moving about in the heights.

Epitomizing these endeavours is Gustave Eiffel's iconic tower (p. 62) for the 1889 World's Fair in Paris, where different kinds of soaring acts take place throughout its giant iron web, eliciting a tremendous tension of euphoria and fear, vitality and mortality. At the same time the structure lifts off the ground, it dissolves into air, with restraints reduced to exceptionally thin members and often carried down to the platform or staircase so that one is continually gazing down through the lattice to a series of lower and lower floors. While the lift undermines most of this exploit, the stairways offer a thrilling climb as they zig-zag through openwork girders and piers and pause at a succession of outlooks, weaving a labyrinthine flight through a multitude of levels and turns, all dangled over entrancing scenes with a bird's-eye view of the city below.

Related in spirit, and a masterpiece of vertiginous flight, is the episodic climb shaped by John Wellborn Root for the Rookery Building (p. 63) in Chicago. Springing off the mezzanine to cantilever over the atrium is an iron staircase that continues to change as it rises upward, its sense of vertigo and climbing on air made palpable by perforated risers and filigreed

banisters. The oriel stair tightens above to a vertical spiral, which eventually breaks through the atrium's glass roof and continues on through its own glass tube to connect all eleven storeys above, its corkscrew deeds reinforced by overlooks and glimpses of atrium below. This spinning motion, where a climber's body churns up while continually recalibrating its forces, twisting the torso at the same time that legs and feet negotiate ever-changing angles of steps, has its adventurous roots in Bramante's spiral staircase at the Vatican and the double-helix of the Château de Chambord in France, but is unsurpassed at the Rookery.

The art of perceptually erasing while physically ensuring the safety of a staircase is exemplified in the wiry flight to the doctor's study at the Maison de Verre (p. 64), designed by Pierre Chareau, along with Bernard Bijvoët and metalworker Louis Dalbet. Every surface is porous and wispy, and every member thinned to an unsubstantial black line, an effect heightened by porous treads and the give and creak of tenuous steel. A related, if more vertical and caged, experience occurs in the spiral stair climbing the chimney of Wright's Wingspread at Wind Point, Wisconsin. The cage offers handholds while twirling upwards through falling light, to eventually corkscrew through the roof and culminate the twisting motion in a panoramic sweep over the trees to Lake Michigan.

The conquest of gravity by floating on air was a hallmark of Danish architect Arne Jacobsen. The exquisitely slender staircase of Rødovre Town Hall is reduced to almost nothing as it leaps into and rises through a well of space. The attenuated steel frame holds thin stainless-steel treads, separated by open space, rather than risers, and edged with transparent sheets of glass and railings narrowed to ultra-thin lines, making the structure a feathery thing that appears to hover without any effort and granting a climber the same experience, enhanced by minimizing every obstruction to views below. The weight of the stair is taken by steel rods suspended from the ceiling and painted red to detach them visually

Gustave Eiffel, Eiffel Tower (1889), Paris,
staircase interlaced through pier

John Wellborn Root, Rookery Building (1886), Chicago, spiralling flights
of stair beneath (top) and over (above) the glass roof of the atrium

from the magically floating staircase (above). A final touch to this lightheaded experience is a tall glass wall facing the stair, into whose unbounded space the stair seems to vault and whose illumination filters through every part of the structure, making it further melt away.

Jacobsen's rousing mixture of thrill and terror forms the central feature of the monumental atrium in the Bank of Denmark in Copenhagen. The entire flight is hung out in space beyond the security of an end wall, and linked to each floor by a short bridge. Amplifying the giddy sensation are the stair's six-storey height and the exaggerated emptiness of the huge room, all drawing attention to the naked climb, while turning it into a miraculous ascent up a structure that seems able to levitate without any tangible support. Whereas at Rødovre daylight is exploited to dissolve away safety and amplify human deeds, here it is achieved by shadows and their magnification of faint yet constantly fluid reflections picked up on the glassy edges.

Arne Jacobsen, Rødovre Town Hall (1956), Copenhagen, staircase (above);
Pierre Chareau with Bernard Bijvoët, Maison de Verre (1931), Paris,
auxiliary stair to doctor's study (opposite)

Le Corbusier, La Tourette (1960), Éveux, pivoting bronze door,
containing within it a smaller door for individuals

2

mechanisms of transformation

The kinetic elements of buildings (doors, windows, shutters and gates) that we are able to directly control and finely adjust with our fingers and hands, and sometimes our entire body, can give us the power to immediately alter the space around us in meaningful and desirable ways. But just as important as these results is our participation in making them happen. When we are drawn into a muscular and dexterous interplay with architectural mechanisms, and when their motions are playful and the effects magical, rather than predictable and dull, the operation reveals something beyond its practical merits – evidence that we are human beings able to exert real influence on the world, who are capable of the unexpected and have the power to cause effects, rather than merely be affected.

The universal attraction of pleasing objects that can be set into motion or reshaped in wondrous ways appears in the first small actions of infants. These elemental toys take different forms and appeal to varying aspects of each child's emerging body and imagination, but invariably at their heart is a desire to produce effects in the world by transforming the state of an object in a direct and personal way. Each manipulation, no matter how modest, confirms to the child that he or she *can* act, *can* have a creative impact and *is the source* of these self-guided powers. In a broader sense, this 'small world of manageable toys', Erikson tells us, offers 'a harbour which the child establishes, to return to when he needs to overhaul his ego'.[43]

The doll's house, to take a familiar example, is not a spectacle on which to passively gaze, but an arena of action in which a child can exert a great deal of personal influence and feel emotionally involved and part of his or her world, as well as inclined to lavish care and affection on something so responsive. The components can be endlessly adjusted to suit undefined and make-believe events, testing the arrangements of miniature figures and furniture. A similar blend of malleability and enchantment underlies the appeal of toys as diverse as pull-along or push-along buses and cars, soft toys such as teddy bears, the small yet realistic figures of toy soldiers, arks abundant with paired animals, model trains directed by hand, puppet theatres and perhaps the most mutable of all, building kits with wood blocks, interlocking bricks or erector sets. There is no limit to the imaginary scenarios that can be formed with these protean things, nor to the range of ways a child is empowered to shape and reshape their appearance. This power derives from pliability, but stems no less from the tactile and visual appeal of the things themselves, giving them a capacity to evoke, in the inventive mind, many possible acts of marvellous change.

Malleable effects brought about by direct human influence do not lose significance at the end of childhood, but remain vital to adults of every age, for their essential motive, in the words of psychologist Karl Groos, is to find 'joy in being a cause', exploring the latent mutation of things plastic with change and revealing that we are producers of those effects.[44] If man 'experienced himself as entirely passive, a mere object', echoes Fromm in *The Anatomy of Human Destructiveness*, 'he would lack a sense of his own will, of his identity. To compensate for this, he must acquire a sense of being able to do something', Fromm continues, 'or to use the most adequate English word, to be "effective" ... To be able to effect something is the assertion that one is not impotent, but that one is an alive, functioning, human being. To be able to effect means to be active and not only *to be affected*, to be active and not only passive. It is, in the last analysis, *the proof that one is*. The principle can be formulated thus: *I am, because I effect*.'[45]

I would argue that the immediately mobile elements of architecture, those we are able to transform directly through the force of our hands and imagination, can carry a trace of toy-like play that transcends their otherwise useful functions and satisfies a fundamental human need to be a source of action. But these pliable elements, including doors and windows, can only engender true human action when they are not reduced, as they generally are today, to dull and characterless things whose motions are habitual, predictable and merely pragmatic, or when their mutations have been disembodied by diverting operational power to electrical current and on-off switches. Real powers of self-affirmation can only come from mobile elements whose operation retains a trace of mystery, whose effects are not fully decided or even evident beforehand, and, most importantly, whose kinetics are able to elicit fascination and wonder.

Metamorphic building parts that can be guided by the human body – ranging in size from cabinets to entire walls and ceilings, with components that may slide or swing, move up or down or rotate about pivots – allow people to personally impact and transmute their world. They are able to assess and envision possible motions in advance, and continue to do so while directing and testing, finely adjusting or readjusting, the course of movement. When the outcome is uncertain and puzzling, and the transformation stimulates not only our skin, but also carries into our fingers and hands and further into shoulders and back, underpinned by pressure in the feet and legs, we experience a deep inner power to act upon and reshape the environment. In doing so, we are given a chance to reanimate the world around us as well as our own existence, for each modulation recreates itself and us anew.

It is important to keep in mind that the creative range of transformative elements can extend beyond the things themselves, for they have the potential to alter or govern the atmosphere within a space, modifying its ambience of light or shade, temperature, sound or smell, not to mention its relation to surroundings and often the universe beyond. A splendid example is the skylit Picture Room of Sir John Soane's Museum in London. On three walls are large hinged panels containing paintings, each of which can swing open to display hidden pictures behind. These panels, Soane himself noted, enable the room to hold as many paintings as a gallery over four times as large, and for the pictures to be seen at varying angles and under differing light conditions.

The panels on the south side of the room are especially impactful, for they can be swung open 90°, one by one, to expose an array of watercolours of Soane's own work. In doing so, they transform not only themselves and the room they enclose, but also open a huge window onto a skylit recess beyond – crammed with additional pictures and sculpture, beyond which is the window to an outdoor court; at closer range is an overlook to the Monk's Parlour below – with the added effect of mixing side light into the raining light from above. Manipulating these huge shutters can elicit surprise while completely altering the lighting and acoustics of this rather small room, including its ties to the outer world.

INTERPLAY AND DISCOVERING THE SELF

The importance of equipping architecture with kinetically indeterminate parts, which people can ponder and set into motion, bears heavily on the value and necessity of play for people at every stage of life. It is no wonder that play forms the innermost core of the human condition, and has been a central theme of existential philosophy for, according to Sartre, it 'releases subjectivity'.[46] As a consequence of our inherent need for causal awareness, 'as soon as man apprehends himself as free and wishes to use his freedom ... then his activity is play', and in playing is 'bent on discovering himself as free in his very action'.[47] Indeed, it is only in

play, when released from goal-directed tasks and involuntary behaviour, that we are able to transcend our utility and know that *life itself* has intrinsic value. In this regard we should also remember the celebrated statement of poet and philosopher Friedrich Schiller: 'Man only plays when in the full meaning of the word he is a man, and he is only completely a man as he plays.'[48] Because we play and as long as we do so, we will always be more than inert objects, instinctual creatures or automated machines.

As with freedom and action, play is inherently dialectical and should be thought of more accurately as 'interplay' between people and the world around them. The operable panels of Soane's Picture Room, for instance, or the sweeping red gate and pivoting walls of the Morella Boarding School in Spain (above and opposite), by Enric Miralles and Carme Pinós, transcend any narrow goal since there is always some amazement and doubt in the effects, and their motions exalt and bring alive the entire body in its exercise of power. These mechanisms are practical and beneficial, but during their operation a person is loosened from these results and enjoys a self-confirming delight in regulating the speed and trajectory of the movement itself. They remind us of a basic truth that adults have often forgotten: playing does not consist of arbitrary, detached or idle activity, to which it is often erroneously linked, nor to an alienated kind of busyness, fantasy or relaxation. On the contrary, play marks the heights of human involvement in the world. We do not depart from the world in play, but suddenly enter and interact with it for the first time, every time, as creative participants.

'Play is a function of the living,' we are told by historian Johan Huizinga, for it is the very essence of 'voluntary activity'.[49] In *Homo Ludens: A Study of the Play Element in Culture*, Huizinga examines the cultural manifestations of play in everyday life, with most of his focus on the play occurring between people, and between people and society. But one might

Enric Miralles and Carme Pinós, Morella Boarding School (1994),
Spain, pivoting wall to the main hall (above) and pivoting steel
entry gate on wheels, shown open (opposite)

mechanisms of transformation   71

question whether his stress on a mode of play that is the opposite of seriousness – arising in the ploys and tactics of 'games of strength and skill, inventing games, guessing games, games of chance, exhibitions and performances of all kinds' – does not emanate from something more fundamental, the kind of play that emerges during and only exists through each person's interactions with the world. It is within this primordial ground of being and its continued renewal that architecture serves such a pivotal role, starving or nurturing our capacity to perform deeds and realize our existence in the here and how.

Increasing evidence comes from psychiatry that play is not only enjoyable, but is also the facilitator of a lifelong process of human wellbeing and self-restoration. In *Playing and Reality*, psychoanalyst and pediatrician Donald Winnicott argues that playing is essentially a search for the self, paralleling Hannah Arendt's concept of action as a disclosure of the self. 'It is in playing and only in playing that the individual child or adult is able to be creative', he writes. 'And it is only in being creative that the individual discovers the self.'[50] Each playful act exposes the presence and traits of our personage. Our predilections are revealed, our capacities tested and new potentialities in our latent personality are tapped and brought into being. We achieve the precious sensation of being fully incarnate, giving us proof we are causal beings, able to control and improvise effects in the world. At the same time we are shown what is distinct and unique about us, including our aspirations and limitations. It is the 'summation' of all these experiences, says Winnicott, and their 'reverberation' in the body and mind, that provides 'the basis for a sense of self'.[51]

Evidently the self-identity of each human being is not a static construction achieved by the end of youth, but a fluid configuration that evolves and remains susceptible to atrophy throughout life. To remain healthy, this living structure requires perpetual renewal and self-cure through play until the end of one's lifetime, for play, remarks Erikson, is 'an infinite resource of what is potential in man'.[52] Moreover 'in order to be truly adult', every person 'must on each level renew some of the playfulness of childhood and some of the sportiveness of the young,' and beyond this must 'remain playful in the centre of his concerns and concerned with opportunities to renew and increase the leeway and scope of his and his fellow man's activities'.[53] Winnicott carries the implications of play further by suggesting that play is actually *how* we communicate since it is the *essence of* dialectical activity. 'On the basis of playing is built the whole of man's experiential existence,' he concludes. Without play people are reduced to one-way communication, which 'belongs to psychopathology or to an extreme of immaturity'.[54]

Offering an evolutionary perspective on this matter, René Dubos noted that the success of *Homo sapiens* as a biological species stems from its ability to respond creatively to stimuli and challenges, a response that is manifested primarily in a human desire to explore the world around him. 'Such exploratory activities have much to do with what is generally called play', he wrote, 'but they constitute in reality an effective manner of establishing through experience a close relationship with the outer world. People in primitive tribes also explore their environment and thus acquire a deep knowledge of its resources, and its dangers. Even in the most civilized and technicized societies, play remains essential for the acquisition of knowledge, especially for self-discovery by the child and the adolescent. The drive to explore and to play probably contributes also to the continued growth of the adult. It may well be true that,' he concludes, 'when we are no longer young we are already dead'.[55]

While bodily play in our mass society has been demoted to a frivolous activity reserved for children, that portion of existence that is so far unusable in a consumer-based and cybernetic culture, it remains the activity most associated with creative living for all ages. The traditional playground limited to children, a tiny oasis in an otherwise flat and petrified world, is, despite its happy encounters, the most disturbing symptom of the debasement of human play in our society. If play is crucial to our existence as human beings, it should be more widely available and woven into the everyday world, forming sites where people of every age and physical skill are given the chance to renew their selfhood. In such places each of us would be able to recover some of the playfulness lost after childhood, and re-establish contact now and again with our developmental and evolutionary origins.

THE RED HERRINGS OF MACHINE ARCHITECTURE

A brief mention needs to be made of the deceptively playful devices, stripped of direct human control, being exploited today as kinetic spectacles by some architects. Admittedly, some of these monstrous machines are hypnotic to watch, but their operation has been programmed beforehand and is powered by electric, rather than human, energy. Personal action is shrivelled down to the flick of a switch, and the kinetic change is a fixed performance arranged in advance. Among the most impressive of these enormous automata are the contrived theatrics of Santiago Calatrava, which reduce the observer to a passive spectator who can only marvel from afar at the pre-engineered performance.

The most mind-expanding of the past century's machine architecture has remained unbuilt, above all Cedric Price's pioneering Fun Palace, which has since developed into an annual celebration of arts and science in East London. The steel structure of this remarkable invention forms the scaffold for a kit of prefabricated walls, ceilings, pivoting escalators and modular stairs to be moved about and assembled or disassembled by a travelling gantry and cranes, permitting improvised spaces to come and go, whose playful adaptations have the appeal of a great erector set but make us forget the slow and groaning technology needed to implement change. The underlying notion that architecture could be a flexible interactive structure, rather than a fixed unresponsive one, continued in his Potteries Thinkbelt project, which utilized railway cars on derelict tracks for a mobile university in Staffordshire.

Emerging from Price's exuberant vision was the imaginary 'Plug-in City' of Sir Peter Cook and Archigram, with its adaptable, interchangeable units. This was followed a decade later by Price's most famous offspring, the Centre Georges Pompidou in Paris, by Renzo Piano and Richard Rogers, whose bolted-on elements and partitions can be moved and repositioned according to varying activities. But in all these impermanent structures, it is well to remember that basically they are form-shifting industrial machines, employing superhuman technologies to put colossal things into motion with an equally superhuman display of mobile power, the latter so sluggish we can barely follow it. The mobile spectacle, whose effects are controlled by hidden mechanisms and designated operators, or more impersonally by remote switch, is stripped of any visible link to human initiative. But even if this link was visible, we should not forget that the hand or trigger is never our own.[56]

Unlike Price's joyful kinetics, whose inner workings are essentially transparent and fully displayed, subsequent generations of kinetic theatrics tend to conceal the power behind their own sensational mutations, or worse, envision absurd and histrionic machines that seem to be striving to not only mirror, but also celebrate the loss of self in a cybernetic society and dystopian world of science fiction. These mobile contraptions convey dark futuristic narratives, a nightmarish world of machines that are out of control and now control us. We should bear in mind here the cautionary words of philosopher Martin Heidegger: 'We will, as we say, "get" technology "spiritually in hand". We will master it. The will to master becomes all the more urgent the more technology threatens to slip from human control.'[57]

MODEST SLIDING SCREENS OF JAPAN

Architecture's most humanely responsive kinetics are not spectacular but inherently modest, being small and light enough for people to immediately guide and control them with their hands. These improvisational elements are generally placed at critical boundaries and thresholds of buildings, where they can exert great influence over a room and its relation to neighbouring space and the outdoors. The mutations make it possible for people to instantly connect or separate adjoining realms, finely tune the desired balance of refuge and outlook, or nuance the flow of light and sound, temperature and smell. The chance to regulate so many important qualities invests people with real power to take actions worth making, and to do this at once through the force of their own imaginations and bodies – and, more generally, retain some control over part of a world that is largely determined in advance.

For the richest culture of modulation we must turn to the traditional architecture of Japan, where an extraordinary repertoire of mobile parts evolved over centuries that permit nearly infinite modifications of mood and space. By layering rather simple panels, diverse in permeability and function, it became possible to subtly regulate daylight, privacy, contact with nature and protection from the weather. Fundamental to this mutability is a manageable size and weight of panels, allowing a single person to easily slide or rotate each of many related units, and often remove and place them out of the way in a storage cabinet. Equally crucial is the fine carpentry of tracks in the floor, into which panels fit perfectly and glide quietly, turning the simplest pull of a screen into a graceful and pleasing action.

The greatest concentration of movable panels occurs around the periphery in close layers of parallel sheets. To keep that boundary fully responsive to changing conditions, a number of varied filtrations are employed, resulting in multiple tracks for a single opening, with each track carrying one of many partitions, whose superimposition allows control over much of the perimeter. Sliding along the outermost tracks are solid wood shutters (*amado*), deployed to protect against storms and intruders, but also reduce heat loss in winter. In the morning these shutters are removed to open the interior to light and fresh air, transforming the building into a pavilion. During hot summers the boundary facing into a garden can be

subtly adjusted by unfurling rolls of *sudare*, knotted together from strips of bamboo and hung from the eaves as a porous curtain (above). These loosely assembled blinds intercept sunlight while remaining pervious to air and view, and have the further advantage of easily rolling up or down, at times drawn up out of view and others partially unfurled or stretched like a veil from ceiling to floor.

Translucent *shoji* screens form the innermost lining of the perimeter, gently diffusing the light they receive and reappearing inside to propagate the illumination from room to room. Giving their motion a sensuous as well as practical power is a construction of thin wooden frames, onto whose outer face are pasted sheets of coarse and long-fibred paper. Sliding *shoji* can instantly change a room's size and enclosure, but also its overall feeling and atmosphere, opening to make a room expand and merge with nature, or closing to bathe it in a soft white glow (p. 76). The more a room is enveloped by this peaceful illumination, the more it acquires a

Yoshijima House, Takayama, outer *sudare* and inner *shoji*,
including sliding screens in the transom above

Taizō-in Temple, Myoshin-ji, Kyoto, comparison of closed
and open *shoji*, with *sudare* partly unfurled beyond

'dream-like luminescence', according to Jun'ichirō Tanizaki, a 'feeling as though some misty film were blunting my vision. The light from the pale white paper,' he continues, 'creates a world of confusion where dark and light are indistinguishable.'[58]

Adding an extra dimension to these kinetic powers are the *yukimi* ('snow-viewing')-*shoji*, as surrounding the *shoin* of the Kitamura House, in Kyoto, by Sutejiro Kitamura. Beyond their sliding movements and ease of removal, the *yukimi-shoji* contain two layers that can be vertically adjusted, one paper and the other clear glass, allowing the former to slide up and open a horizon onto the garden without exposing the room to rain or cold.

Complementing the *shoji* within rooms are similarly sized and lightweight but opaque sliding screens (*fusuma*), whose frame is pasted on both sides with sheets of heavy paper (as seen in the Honmaru Palace; above). The result is a sliding wall that can block out light and cut down on sound. Working within their own network of rectilinear tracks and in combination with *shoji* and fixed walls, the *fusuma* permit endless permutations in the character and awareness of rooms, and the relations between rooms and with nature.

Sliding panels can be moved singly or in tandem to close off a space or fuse it with others, retain a slight refuge while opening up a discreet glimpse or wide vista, closing the building into separate cells or opening it up entirely to gardens. Unlike Western doors that open or close holes in the wall, Japanese partitions open or close the wall itself, and finely regulate the scope and direction of sightlines. Complementing these broad spatial powers are small sliding screens with specific and highly focused effects: the *marumado*, a circular window augmented sometimes with *shoji* screens; the *mairado*, a wooden partition to access the bath or toilet; and the *muso-mado*, whose sliding panel of alternating gaps and boards can ventilate the kitchen or bath.

Honmaru Palace, Nijō Castle, Kyoto, multiple spatial
interactions with sliding *fusuma* and *shoji*

One last device perfected in Japan must be mentioned: the *shitomido*, which is used to enwrap large ceremonial halls in Zen Buddhist temples (above) and such imperial villas as the Kyoto-gosho. These batteries of huge wooden panels are hinged at the top, allowing them to be swung out and up like a series of garage doors and fastened horizontally with metal clips to which they attach, so that the perimeter can be opened up fully or partially to the veranda and world beyond.

It is surprising that so few Japanese architects have attempted to translate these mobile powers inherited from the past into a language suited to current materials, technologies and tastes. One of the few exceptions is Shigeru Ban, most simply and theatrically in his Curtain Wall House in Tokyo, a cube whose open corner is protected by a huge curtain. The two-storey membrane of white fabric, which Ban acknowledges 'takes the place of *shoji* and *sudare* screens',[59] can be pulled closed for privacy or drawn back to open the house up to the city and aerate its interior in summer.

In a series of subsequent houses with transformative themes, from the 2/5 House in Hyogo to the Wall-less House in Nagano, Ban installed a range of mutations. Especially changeable is his Nine-Square Grid House in Hadano, its entire volume sandwiched between roof and floor planes, and two facing side walls, allowing the interior to be opened or closed according to seasonal and functional demands. Sliding partitions, stored in the hollow side walls, can be easily inserted and guided along a grid of tracks. Completing this fluctuating network are removable sliding-glass doors on the north and south sides, allowing the entire house to be subdivided into rooms or opened into a single pavilion, fused with nature – a sleek white abstraction of the traditional house.

Zuishin-in Temple, Kyoto, horizontally hinged *shitomido*, held in place by metal fixtures with long rods bent into hooks (*shitomizuri*)

SIMPLE BUT REWARDING VERNACULAR DEVICES

Paralleling, if never quite reaching, the subtlety, diversity and scope of their Japanese counterparts are a number of ingenious kinetic elements developed in the vernacular architecture of the West. Each is cleverly devised and suited to its purpose, while transcending productive use through its range of control and kinesthetic rewards. Something beyond work occurs when the simple opening of a door or window stimulates our creative faculties, with pleasing but uncertain effects that infuse labour with playful delight.

Magnifying the significance of these modest actions woven through air is the reality that a door or window is never merely a physical threshold, but also forms, as Bachelard has stressed, a 'psychological threshold' where complex fears and desires mingle. The dual hinged panels of a traditional Dutch door (below), combining the behaviours of a door, window and gate, to take a simple example, may have been invented to keep animals out and children in, while allowing the passage of light and air. But it also governs a primeval balance of security and adventure, feelings of shelter from external threat and of being in touch with

Double-hung Dutch door, Netherlands

the world. Control over this great rhythm of retreat and outlook, which resonates deep in the human psyche, allows the mutations to far exceed their more obvious physical and practical benefits. Furthermore, the operator's body is drawn into a highly resourceful and supple action as it manipulates dual latches and, in some cases, bolts that retract and slide back in place, or a door-wide bar to be lifted out and later returned.

Similarly, the opening of a well-crafted door from the past (above and opposite) is rarely a bland or bodiless manoeuvre. The operator becomes intimately involved with the door's own weight and inertia, the sensory meeting of knob or handle with the skin and joints of the hand, the momentum of its mass and the unpredictable muscular tension needed to finally slow the door and bring it to rest. Often giving the eye and mind an extra dimension of enterprise is an array of devices used for security – the handling of multiple locks and keys, gripping and then sliding or twisting heavy bolts, manipulating clamps or levers and, for the visitor, grasping and raising a metal knocker whose impact when released produces a loud, often distinctive acoustic event.

Analogously the operation of a doorbell need not be reduced to a small button with a preset sound, as demonstrated in the Bavarian town of Rothenburg (p. 82, left), where arrival is announced by manipulating a marvellous doorbell unique to that building, and in some cases choosing among multiple doorbells that ring at various levels inside. Smooth brass or wrought-iron handles cast into sensuous shapes appeal to human flesh, inviting fingers to wrap around them, fitting the hand – a wonder of human evolution, with some of the densest nerve endings on the body and the richest source of tactile feedback – about a plainly voluptuous object, and then pulling down on a thin metal cable attached to bells that ring above, inside or out. The muscular act of gripping and tugging, and precise degree to which one pulls or repeats the motion, sets off a slightly different intensity, rhythm and duration

Sainte-Chapelle (1248), Palais de la Cité, Paris,
vertical and horizontal bolts of the west doors

Fontfroide Abbey (founded 1093), France, gallery door
with iron knocker, sliding bolt and door knob

of chime. Compared to the sterile and programmed sound of an electric doorbell, triggered by the meagrest touch, Rothenburg's doorbells exalt the human deeds they foster, while rewarding them with sensory pleasure.

A related synesthesia occurs in the detonation of a Zen temple bell used to summon monks to prayer, as well as to simply mark time or signal important ceremonies (above, right). The intermingling of sensory acts begins with lifting a weighty mallet by hand, and then swinging it through an arc to strike a massive bronze bell, whose vibrations extend back into the fingers and arm. The lifting, swinging and striking produces a surprising and pleasing aural event, an extraordinarily low tone with deep resonance that carries over a great distance. The sound begins with the clear clean tone of an impact strike, followed by the prolonged reverberation of a low rumble, which then dissolves into a decaying resonance that can last up to a minute, a sound felt to be calming and highly conducive to meditation.

The deep satisfaction felt in a door responsive to human initiative can also derive from a window endowed with latent mutations that are unexpected and full of wonderment. Consider, for example, the colourful painted wooden shutters of old Dutch towns (opposite), especially those with combinatory or nested motions. Some streetside shutters are hinged to open up and down, rather than across, turning the shutter into an impromptu sunshade or shelf. More complex are the large banks of shutters in the tall leaded windows of seventeenth-century Dutch houses, which can be subtly adjusted to control the illumination of long, narrow rooms lit from one side. These finely tuned lighting effects were carefully studied by Steen Eiler Rasmussen, who described their typical form as a 'four-framed window with a shutter to each frame that could be opened or closed independently, so that the light

Wrought-iron doorbell, Rothenburg (left) and wooden mallet
and bronze bell, Juko-in Temple (1566), Daitoku-ji, Kyoto (right)

could be regulated at will ... the light could be dimmed down to a most mysterious gloom. Or all of it could be concentrated on one spot, leaving the rest of the room in semi-darkness. No one has employed these effects with greater skill than Rembrandt, as his paintings show. They also show the wealth of textural effects that could be produced by this special lighting method.'[60] Rasmussen goes on to discuss how similar shutter manipulations were used by Vermeer to produce the delicate moods of his paintings.

Related controls over light and air must have also been a concern in otherwise fortified castles, palaces and monasteries, for their deep windows were often given self-embedded shutters to permit control over conditions of the recess and room beyond (p. 84). Light, view, breeze and sound can be roughly governed by opening or closing the overall windows and shutters, and more finely regulated with smaller hinged flaps inside the panels, expanding the scope of action. Especially intricate shutter systems were invented by American Shakers in the nineteenth century, who were renowned for merging practicality with simple beauty. These include adjustable wooden transoms for ventilation, and so-called 'Indian shutters'

Horizontally hinged shutters, Delft, Netherlands

that slide horizontally over windows and eliminate winter drafts. On the ground floor of the huge granite dwelling house at Enfield, New Hampshire (opposite), a four-shutter system was built into each window to finely modulate light and outlook. Each of the dual-hinged shutters can be folded in half, allowing it to assume three different positions – fully closed, half open, or fully open – so that each window has, in effect, over eighty permutations. The degree of participation increases as people deliberate and test the latent positions and motions of shutters, finding pleasure in the way smaller hinged orbits pass inside the larger orbits of multifold panels. When opening all the shutters at once, something equally marvellous occurs, for they disappear, as if by sleight of hand, into the recesses of reveals.

Similar wonders await those opening Carlo Scarpa's paired shutters for ocular windows in the Olivetti Showroom (p. 86, bottom) in Venice. Attracting the hand with their colour and texture, the paired grids of teak and Brazilian rosewood slide in opposite directions to disappear in the wall, revealing two other layers of modulation beyond: transparent glass panes that can also slide out of the way, and beyond these a pair of hinged windows,

Château de Beynac, France, small dual
shutters within each pair of shutters

Great Stone Dwelling (1841), Enfield, New Hampshire,
permutations in the four-fold shutters

Carlo Scarpa, Olivetti Showroom (1958), Venice, sliding wood shutters and glass panes with hinged glass windows beyond (above); Brion Cemetery (1977), Italy, individual door inside pivoting funeral door to chapel (top)

whose operation adjusts relations to the piazza outside. The self-embedded shutter finds a counterpart in large doors containing smaller ones (sometimes called Judas gates). The overall panels can be opened for large vehicles, and the smaller panels near the ground for the more frequent passage of individuals, giving the door two different roles and operations, augmented by other acts. The carriage door, for example, can be opened to admit horse and carriage, or today more likely cars, or remain shut as people squeeze through its smaller opening. The same nested motions appear in large church doors, able to open fully for crowds or partially through a door sized for individual worshippers. A recent parallel is the Brion chapel, where a small door of ebony and glass is set within a large concrete door for funerals (opposite, top). Its structure of iron and white cement rotates on a square steel pivot hinge running from ceiling to floor, the larger plane taking a different arc than the flap it contains.

GENEALOGY OF MODERN KINETICISM

From the standpoint of its atrophy of manual control, architecture's dual threat of immobility and automation can be seen as a process of disembodiment, and in this sense a betrayal of man. Those few built parts retaining a role for human operation – standard hinged doors, double-hung windows, sliding curtains, Venetian blinds – are stripped of any real action that would confirm our power to be a cause and, more broadly, feel a sense of responsibility in the physical world. By failing to exceed their functional purpose, eradicating play from work, these mobile remnants virtually destroy the possibility of human deeds.

Fortunately this trend to fossilization and cybernetics has been resisted by architects concerned with preserving some human dignity in modest acts of kinesis. Among them is Wharton Esherick, who fitted the doors of his house and studio with hand-carved latches and handles of satiny rosewood (p. 88), no two of which are alike, with shapes and textures inviting fingers and skin to touch and engage their mechanisms. People doing so become the locus and source of action by entering into a toy-like play with the intermeshed parts, whose movements and repercussions are enthralling but never immediately apparent. In a similar vein, Esherick's light-pulls are tiny metal figures that startle and delay our grasp, and lamps are hung from long wooden arms that swing through space in wide orbits. The largest kinetic element is a trap door to the bedroom operated by rope and pulley, facilitated by a rising and falling counterweight. In each loving marriage of use and delight is an idea about the core of life that echoes the words of Robert Frost in his poem 'Two Tramps in Mud Time':

> ... Only where love and need are one,
> And the work is play for mortal stakes,
> Is the deed ever really done
> For Heaven and the future's sakes[61]

The most widely known effort of the twentieth century to overcome architectural fixity is the Schröder House in Utrecht, by Gerrit Rietveld. Transforming the entire upper floor are sliding partitions that can define or erase the boundaries between four spatial quadrants, converging at a central skylit staircase. Each easily handled partition is made from a lightweight sandwich of bituminized cork faced with sheets of beaverboard. Reminiscent of Japanese sliding screens but lacking their subtlety and sensuous pleasure, each group of panels is arranged in layers and slides within parallel tracks, made by recessed grooves in the floor and a steel T-section in the ceiling, so that each room can be opened to varying extents and directions. The partitions can all be opened at once to create a large collective space, or partially deployed to subdivide the floor into two to four rooms. The movable windows of a shared entry hall around the stair permit the core itself to be open or glazed.

An irresistible spirit of mutation extends into other components. Meeting at the iconic south corner are two mullionless windows, hinged to outwardly swing in opposite directions to perceptually erase the seam of enclosure. Furnishings were shaped to stimulate dexterity and intrigue, notably a cabinet in the living–dining area that resembles a Constructivist sculpture, its differently sized painted boxes fitting into a largely hidden framework. Boxes can slide out in varied ways with uncertain directions, turning its volume into a three-dimensional puzzle in which inspired play transcends practical merit. Serving more than a decorative role are Mondrian-esque colours applied to each mobile element, a Dutch tradition stretching back through centuries of vernacular building. Primary colours catch the

Wharton Esherick Studio (begun 1926),
Pennsylvania, rosewood door latch

eye and lure the hand, calling attention and bringing joy to what is transformable, with hints of how things might move.

While mutability was never a central concern of Frank Lloyd Wright – apart from Ocotillo, his 'little desert camp' in Arizona, rigged like a ship with 'white canvas wings' spread 'like sails' over wood frames, with hinged canvas flaps that 'may shut against dust or open part way to deflect the desert breezes into the interiors' – it became a prominent feature of many architectural details.[62] At Taliesin West are small features with unexpected motions emphasized by brightly painted colours. A skylit corridor skirting the cabaret theatre (above) also serves as an adjustable filter with long hinged shutters at either side, the outer swinging in and up beneath a skylight and the lower swinging down to open a window onto the theatre. The panels can be closed to isolate the theatre from daylight or distractions, or swung open and out of the way to infuse each space with light and air. This playful freedom reappears in other unpretentious elements, from the cantilevered entry gate to the small square shutters over the openings in Wright's living quarters, each extolled with Cherokee-red paint.

Glazing takes on a protean role at Fallingwater in Pennsylvania, beginning with the transparent hatch of the living room (p. 90), its promise of adventure strengthened by resemblance to a ship's hatch and all the freedom of space that implies. Still partly a door in its access to the stair leading down to the stream, but also a window to nature and source of ventilation, the hatch expands creative control through its operable sheets in two different planes: a pair of vertical panes swinging apart and three horizontal panes sliding in tracks. Equally adjustable and full of amazement are the corner windows of two west bedrooms, where six pairs of hinged panes can be swung open to the waterfall and startle the eye by

dissolving a corner. Alongside is a vertical casement that swings through a quarter circle cut from the desk, so that altogether thirteen panes can be brought into play in three different folds of the window (opposite).

In Paradise Valley, Arizona, six pairs of puzzle-like doors control the marriage of house and desert in the atrium of Wright's Price House. Each pair of doors meets along a vertical line obscured by surface reflections, while their outer edges are notched along a diagonal zig-zag to mesh with tapered piers of concrete block. Complicating the motion is a vertical pivot placed off-centre to allow each door to fold back against the pier and maximize communion with the landscape. The enchantment of this operation also derives from the way in which Wright hid the pivoting structure to create both doubt and fascination about a mutation that seems devoid of any obvious support or orbit. But it is also due to the facing of doors with a delightful collage of turquoise and gold, which, when in motion, sets off a dazzling sparkle – a mixture of bafflement and delight that is equally present in Le Corbusier's hand-painted pivoting door at Ronchamp (p. 92).

Frank Lloyd Wright, Fallingwater (1935), Pennsylvania,
casement windows and vertical window in bedroom (above)
and glass hatch in living room (opposite)

mechanisms of transformation 91

Paul Rudolph's foray into kinetics at the Walker Guest House controls two-thirds of the entire perimeter. Located on Sanibel Island, Florida, the elevated cubic dwelling is wrapped with horizontally hinged plywood shutters, two on each tripartite façade, and counterweighted by visually prominent steel balls, painted red and suspended from a rigging of steel cables and pulleys. Panels can be raised singly or collectively to vary the home's connection with weather and the sea, while also serving as sunshades and ventilating elements, or lowered and bolted to provide a shield from storms or prowlers when the family is away. These changes are not merely physical, for 'when the panels are closed, the pavilion is snug and cave-like', Rudolph notes, 'when open, the space psychologically changes and one is virtually in the landscape'.[63]

How lighthearted these motions appear by contrast with the gravitas of Le Corbusier's huge bronze door at La Tourette (p. 66), in Éveux, France. This tremendous dark plane of patinated metal, containing a smaller door for individuals, carries a trace of the countless hands that have pushed it open. To enter, one must first withdraw a large bolt from the floor and twist it in place, then press one's shoulder and torso into the mass to initiate its swing.

Le Corbusier, Notre Dame du Haut (1955),
Ronchamp, pivoting south door in action

The bronze structure is noticeably heavy and initially resistant to pressure, but astonishingly smooth once set into motion. When rotating through its 90° arc on a hidden pivot, the door rapidly gains momentum and calls for an unexpected counter-effort of muscular tension to slow it down and, while holding it steady, resetting the bolt in the floor, to find it has opened a wide passage into the church and thrown a shaft of light into the darkness.

A related desire to impart play to elemental things appears in the houses of Louis I. Kahn, where visually strong mobile elements have the tactile appeal of a wooden puzzle. Adjustability at the Esherick House in Philadelphia is centred on the largely glazed rear elevation, its south-facing windows framed by a thick lattice of cypress wood. Set into the deep reveals of some openings are shutters of the same wood, enabling wide control over light, sound and temperature, and views to the garden and park beyond. Eight pairs of shutters in the double-height living room are hinged and stacked, one above the other, to open or close in diverse permutations. When all of the inset shutters are open, the entire wall turns transparent; when closed, the exposure is cut in half. The quality and amount of daylight can be subtly managed, for the shutters combine with fixed central windows to produce different shapes, directions and flows of light. Manual control also appears in slender ventilation panels dividing the living-room bookcases, reminiscent of Le Corbusier's *pivotant aérateurs*, and, with some humour, in a large wooden drawer in the bathroom that slides from the wall to convert the bathtub into a sofa.

More condensed and intimate are the recessed window boxes of the Fisher House in Hatboro, Pennsylvania. The living-room window seat (p. 93) is especially commanding, set into a structure of folded glass and forming a kind of cockpit encompassed by beautifully crafted oak components, some of which move to finely adjust the ambience. The seat itself contains hidden cabinets, and at either side are shutters that can stay open in storms without allowing rain inside. Recessed windows with more vertical shutters appear in other rooms, their operable panels moving inside glazed wooden boxes. Each allows the control of qualities residents care about, such as natural light, summer breezes and the sounds of nature. They also entice human hands and fingers with seductive woodwork, and in this respect bear a close resemblance to Japanese puzzle boxes (*himitsu-bako*), whose sensuous wood elements can only be opened by a complicated series of manipulations, perhaps simply squeezing in the correct spot or twisting several small parts in the correct sequence to eventually open and reward the player.

MECHANICAL MARVELS OF THE MAISON DE VERRE

The intensely perplexing yet enchanting motions of Pierre Chareau's Maison de Verre give continual proof of the causal powers of human beings. Manually operated elements, from doors and windows to screens and cabinets, perform work at a practical level but also introduce a mischievous dimension of surprise and paradox that exceeds any immediate purpose. They possess what Hannah Arendt calls the 'character of startling unexpectedness', which 'is inherent in all beginnings and in all origins ... The fact that man is capable of action means that the unexpected can be expected from him, that he is able to perform what is infinitely improbable.'[64]

Even the more business-like tools of the house – from a sliding stepladder along the bookcase (opposite) to a retractable stair between Madame Dalsace's sitting room and bedroom (p. 96), along with a number of sliding panels, pivoting screens and frameless pivoting doors – have an intricacy of exposed moving parts and unforeseen beauty of motion, exalting their service while raising it to an entrancing event. About these inventions architectural critic Kenneth Frampton has written: 'The mechanization of the Maison de Verre was extensive and (such was the calibre of Dalbet's craftsmanship) economically conceived and precisely executed. In many of the details the strength of the material used is pushed to its limits. Typical of this is the mobile book wall ladder, which travels on a carriage made out of a single bent metal tube. The remote-controlled steel louvres to the salon and the opening lights of the main façades are thus by no means the only *éléments-mécanique type de la maison*. On the contrary,' he concludes, 'mobility permeates every detail of this house, from adjustable mirrors to pivoting closets.'[65]

The most bewitching mechanisms are devoted to the most sensitive boundaries. The ground-floor entry hall, originally shared by the doctor's office and a stair to the living space above, was a particularly delicate threshold that called for different degrees of modesty according to the time of day. The solution was a gauzy veil around the stair (p. 97), whose transparency could be adjusted to increase or decrease visual penetration. Access to the stair is provided by a quarter-cylinder of glass and perforated metal that rotates out of the way, but there is no immediately obvious method to open this unconventional door, which doesn't fit into a frame of jambs and lintel, but instead hangs loosely in space. The pivoting points are largely hidden and the precision-made hardware and tracks guiding motion are

Pierre Chareau with Bernard Bijvoët, Maison de Verre (1931),
Paris, sliding stepladder of the living-room bookcase

only vaguely suggested by black steel arms above and below, nor is there a handle to reach for. It is only by taking this sensuous veil in the hands and setting it into tentative motion that one is able to glean *how* and *where* it moves.

Alongside are slender, perforated 'butterfly' screens (pp. 98 and 99, top). Each pair of vertical screens, set behind and attached to the pivoting frame of a large sheet of glass, can mysteriously fold open or closed to regulate visual contact between the domestic and medical worlds. Left closed they muffle the view, but when opened up to 90° they produce greater but still not complete transparency, and at its extreme the entire structure of screens and glass can be swung open to completely merge the adjoining realms. Yet here again the operation is neither apparent nor fixed in advance, and involves the doer in an intimate process of drawing near to peer into joints, then exploring the parts and their possible motions, a process involving incredulity and elation. Adding an extra dimension of play is the sensual surprise of each mechanism's weight and texture, and smoothly gliding arc through space – a 'startling unexpectedness' that penetrates into one's fingers, arms, shoulders and torso.

A different array of kinetic marvels is built into the master bathroom on the top floor. A pair of freestanding storage units of bent duraluminium can pivot open or closed to access or conceal their contents, and in so doing alter the room's enclosure and link to corridors. The butterfly motion of each unit is twofold, combining rotation around a central pivot with the sliding of that pivot to fully insert the oblong volume into its shell. This scope of freedom exempt from any single function or obvious movement continues into other parts of the loosely defined room, from cabinets with overlapping doors rather than handles, whose drying racks pivot outward, to a dual screen consisting of both a pivoting towel rail and privacy panel of perforated metal that can subtly modify the visual ties of shower and bathtub.

Maison de Verre, retractable stair with details of cables and pulleys (above); overall view of veils around staircase, shown closed (opposite top); details of the pivoting and curved screen to the staircase (opposite bottom)

The gleeful and dumbfounding orbits of motion recurring throughout the Maison de Verre make us aware of a world of things conceived as vehicles by which an elusive and transient reality comes into being, mirroring the changeability of life itself (opposite, bottom, and pp. 100–1). It is not the finished object that is important, but its events of cinematic motion and their improvisatory effects. But these supple flights through space and time exist only in latent form, in the joints and mobile range of each mechanism, awaiting and requiring human acts to set them in motion and guide their course. A piece of architecture has moved inside the body, so to speak, allowing a person's acts to become the subject of their attention.

Maison de Verre, four stages of veiling and openness in the glass and metal screens (above); view up stair to family quarters when screen assembly is fully open (opposite top); pivoting screen wall of maid's bathroom (opposite bottom)

Maison de Verre, wheel and gear assembly for operating windows
(above); hand-cranked windows in the patients' waiting area (top);
wheel-operated ventilating louvres in the living room (opposite)

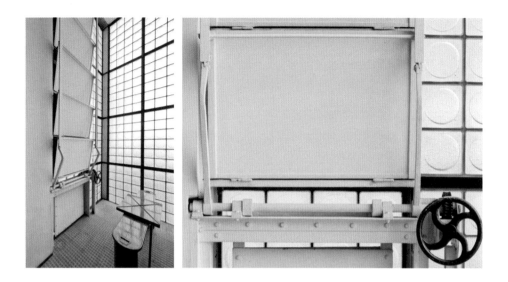

Paralleling Chareau's kinetic inventions were the innovations with mobile sculpture that emerged in the 1920s and '30s, but powered by electric current, rather than human hands. Just as Chareau was conjuring a realm of miraculous motions in which people are able to shape their own experience, Marcel Duchamp introduced the concept that viewers of art should abandon their passive role and become creative participants, if only mentally, in completing works devised to stimulate and sustain their involvement. Duchamp made his first attack on 'retinal art' with the mobile experiments of his *Rotating Glass Plates*, followed by the puzzling *Rotary Demi-sphere* and *Rotoreliefs*; at the same time, Naum Gabo produced his geometric *Kinetic Construction*. When activated, each of these works presents to the eye a virtual volume, a transient image traced in the viewer's imagination by its scope of vibration or speeding trajectory. Several years later, in his first *Light-Space Modulator*, László Moholy-Nagy developed the idea of sculpture as 'the relationships of energies', merging theatricality with art and conceiving form as an unfolding event.

While kinetic sculpture has largely remained a spectator art, it has expanded our understanding of form to include the poetics of motion, and begun to envision the shapes these energies could take in space. But it took someone with the child-like instincts of Alexander Calder to loosen motion from the artist's control and endow it with unpredictable forces. Calder began to employ mysteriously balanced and counterbalanced elements constructed from wood, wire and sheet metal that move collectively, as if by magic, in a slowly spinning and interactive temporal sequence that suggests an acrobatic playfulness. Unlike the programmed machines of his colleagues, Calder's hanging 'mobiles' are free of preconditioned change since they are solely aroused by air movement or human touch, heightening their spontaneity and freewheeling character. Because of this quasi-random motion, whose chain of cause and effect appears as a series of connected trajectories, wind-sculptor George Rickey later described this art as 'the morphology of movement', an ambition still unfulfilled in its implications for architecture.

THE POETIC MUTATIONS OF CARLO SCARPA

Another master of the art of motion, Carlo Scarpa, enlarged at length on the art and mystery of kinetic architecture, beginning with the exquisitely detailed shutter system of the Aula Magna at Ca' Foscari, overlooking Venice's Grand Canal. To periodically screen this meeting room and lecture hall from an adjoining corridor, the intervening glass wall was overlaid with a remarkable series of operable panels. Pivoting off timber posts on a complex assembly of iron and brass pivots, each pair of shutters can be folded together to open views into the room and canal beyond, or unfolded to form a discreet visual barrier (opposite).

It is the manner in which the shutters open and close, however, that is of paramount significance. The panels intrigue the eye initially with uncertainty about *how* they might move, and about *where* to place one's hand and exert force. Bevels mark the boundary and invite touch, but then one slowly becomes aware of the curious and complicated mechanism of the pivots and, when the shutters are fully retracted, an intriguing metal catch below into which the shutter slips and causes one part to rotate upward and click smoothly into place (below). Within this phenomenology of motion lies a pregnant tension, an evasive presence and revelation that are able each time to provoke wonderment and, in William Carlos Williams's words, 'startle us anew'.[66]

Carlo Scarpa, Aula Magna (1956), Ca' Foscari, Venice, closed (top) and
open (above) shutters; detail of pivoting assembly (opposite left); clasp
with a double rotation to receive and hold each shutter (opposite right)

Carlo Scarpa, Olivetti Showroom (1958), Venice, sliding and rotating gate guided by a brass-faced steel track (above left) and radiator cabinet with plaster-faced grilles and brass corner clasp (above right); IUAV (1977), Venice, suspended sliding gate, with black steel frame and stone slab on wheels (top)

Scarpa's fascination with protean beauty reappears in the mysteriously moving doors and gates of almost every building he designed (opposite, top). We are immediately drawn to these captivating things, but their material weight and flow through space are only disclosed at the very moment of bodily contact and force, in acts that are manifold, rather than singular, and develop with gratifying shocks. Beyond their invitingly sensuous form and texture, the devices are endowed with metamorphic change, enigmatic joints, perplexing degrees of sliding or rotational freedom and the equipoise of intermeshed motions.

A recurring apparatus in Scarpa's repertoire is the dark metal screen set parallel to, but offset and distinguished from, the glazed entry it protects (above). The perceptual independence of boundaries produces a collage of operable systems in successive layers, causing their opening or closure to set off a cinematic transparency. Sheets of interwoven black steel and smooth glass modify one another and render each more ambiguous, a visual tension between superimposed linings that turns fluid as the gate slides past. But an extra surprise has been inserted to complicate the action, for each part of the gate hangs from two different pivots that slide in adjoining but separate tracks (opposite, bottom left), their channels beginning parallel and separating when nearing the end wall, with the innermost track veering off through an undulant curve, allowing each sheet to swing 90° flush with the wall and out of the way.

Another mystery exploited by Scarpa is the interlocking of sumptuous doors that often, with a sense of wit and a surreal twist, hide utterly pragmatic building services. The radiator cabinet nestled within a column of the Olivetti Showroom (opposite, bottom right), for instance, is accessed by hinged grid panels held in place by an alluring but baffling

Carlo Scarpa, Castelvecchio Museum (1973), Verona,
woven black steel gate overlapping glass door

Carlo Scarpa, Fondazione Querini Stampalia (1963), Venice,
interlocking brass doors to electrical cabinet (above); closed
(opposite left) and open (opposite right) travertine door in the gallery

brass clamp. Equally enigmatic are the large hinged panels of the electrical cabinet at the Fondazione Querini Stampalia, whose L-shaped and polished brass doors interlock in a vague rectangle (opposite). The offset and shape of the joint between imply two different doors and motions, but there is no indication of how or where the panels might swing. At the same time the metal, patinated by human touch, with small circular cutouts at the corners that expand the breathing space between sheets, capture the eye and lure the hand, inciting us to test different pressures and motions – experiments that eventually disclose counter-movements in opposite directions.

A similar mixture of promise and paradox in the Fondazione Querini Stampalia is conveyed by the gallery's travertine door (above). Is this strange stone slab devoid of handles an immovable piece of the travertine wall, or a source of access to what lies behind? Spatial gaps have perceptually loosened the slab from its wall plane and offer hints of space beyond. But it is especially the Z-shaped cutout at the top that suggests mobility, and vaguely entices one's hand to push upon the stone sheet – exerting pressure here and there, feeling the rough mineral texture so different from a nondescript doorknob, but also finding an unexpected mass and resistance. Within the many reciprocal doors devised by Scarpa can be found a spur to trial and error that approximates solving a jigsaw puzzle. As in the latter's dovetailed pieces, the components imply related parts that suggest a capacity for manipulation, movement and fitting together, but never expose the act in advance so as to keep the future open for participants. To operate a door is not only to gain passage, but also to bring an unforgettable event into being that lay dormant a moment before.

Forming another small masterpiece that bears little resemblance to stereotypical hinged doors are the pivoting doors at the rear of the Brion chapel (above), leading to a cypress grove housing the priest's graveyard. Pivots are inset to give an unexpected orbit to each iron-framed leaf infilled with concrete. But of equal fascination is the volumetric mutation of doors, owing to their L-shape in plan, and the surprising way that they block window slits at either side when fully open. Adding to our curiosity is the hardware of motion: cylindrical Muntz metal collars and pivots above and below, rotating on ball bearings housed out of sight, and milled with a fluting that echoes the concrete profiles of the building. The act of opening is enhanced further by small bolts that slide in and out of hollow discs rising from a mysterious drain. We are invited to tinker with and, through our initiatives, discover something unknown, rather than merely using the door to perform a preordained task.

The peak of secret operations at Brion is saved for the corridor leading to a water pavilion (opposite, top), a place set aside for contemplation. Walking through the dark passage sets off puzzling echoes from under the floor, an acoustic mystery followed by a thick glass door obscured in shade to confound the visitor. This door is not hinged, nor does it move upward. After some clumsy experimentation, it is found to open by grasping the top edge and pushing it *down* with all of one's weight through a slot in the floor, making it disappear though bodily pressure. As soon as this pressure is released, the door rises back up, but now bathed in the water hidden below, producing through this dripping image an epiphanic moment, as if the door were being raised from the dead and reborn through an act of immersion. At the same time the door's movement is accompanied by unexplained creaking and scraping sounds that emanate from the far side of the wall, another mystery later revealed as counterweights suspended from cables that have been strung through an angular system of pulleys. The visual separation of door and counterweight prevents the act from ever being fully exhausted, while extending its influence through space and time.

Playful involvement brings to life other elements of the cemetery, extending into things as small as the handle of a marble anteroom font and hinged alabaster windows of the chapel to something as mundane as the jigsaw timber doors of a nearby service room, all of which

Carlo Scarpa, Brion Cemetery (1977), Italy, closed and open pivoting doors in the chapel (above); vertically sliding glass door and external counterweights (opposite top); rolling concrete funeral door, at right (opposite bottom)

are strangely heavy yet smoothly sensuous in operation. The mutual animation of doer and building depends in part on each action's unforeseen muscular engagement and pleasure, a surprise that turns especially strenuous in the steel-framed concrete gate for funeral services (p. 109, bottom), its bronze wheels and concealed ball bearings running along steel rails set into the concrete paving. One cannot anticipate being able to dislodge and move this massive object, but persistent effort sets the gate into motion, producing an almost superhuman feat analogous to the biblical story of opening Christ's tomb (Luke 24:2).

It cannot be overly stressed that the ultimate significance of Scarpa's kinesis, despite its evident beauty, is not to aestheticize but to empower the threshold. Mobile things are humanized by playful and enigmatic operations that increase our participation, as well as by seductions of skin and hand, imploring us to touch and grasp them, and to move in tandem with their own gestures in space, an erotic dance that is fresh and enthralling each time it occurs. In doing do, they glorify instead of stripping us of our deeds.

TOM KUNDIG'S 'GIZMOS' AND STEVEN HOLL'S 'HINGED SPACE'

In recent decades, new kinds of mechanisms have emerged that continue to translate human touch into kinetic marvels. Among these are the 'gizmos' created by Tom Kundig that largely define his Pacific Northwest architecture. The transformative appeal stems from a tough industrial character of moving parts and the way their kinetics are drawn out in space – through hand-operated wheels, cables and gears – along a highly visible series of interactive events. But their fascination also stems from unorthodox forms and procedures, so oversized and complicated in operation that they make an all-consuming ethos of play, touched with caricaturizing humour and bearing some resemblance to the sculpture of Swiss artist Jean Tinguely. 'For me, the machine is above all,' said Tinguely, 'an instrument that permits me to be poetic. If you respect the machine, if you enter into a game with the machine, then perhaps you can make a truly joyous machine – by joyous I mean free.'[67]

The devices animating Kundig's Studio House in Seattle, Washington, range from a towering front door that slices through its canopy as a combination door-window, to a kitchen island with concrete doors that roll upon bronze wheels guided by steel tracks in the floor. Larger still is the hand-cranked apparatus that activates a horizontally pivoting window-wall at the Chicken Point Cabin in Idaho. Using a precise balance of each half-wall and a set of mechanical gears, the 6-ton steel-and-glass window can be easily opened by one person. More ambitious are the beautifully rusted steel shutters that can be slid open simultaneously on all four sides of the Delta Shelter, in eastern Washington, by means of a large hand wheel, whose force is conveyed and magnified by drive shafts, spur gears and cables.

Though tied in spirit to the mobile delights of kinetic sculpture, Kundig reminds us that unlike sculpture's detached performance – 'mechanical ballets', as art critic Rosalind Krauss calls them – with preordained movements for physically docile spectators, a humanly based architectural performance can *only be enacted* by direct and intimate bodily engagement, as well as the playful testing of uncertain gadgetry and motions. The mechanics of Kundig's designs are at every moment guided by the strength and skill of each operator and can be

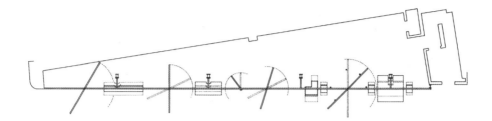

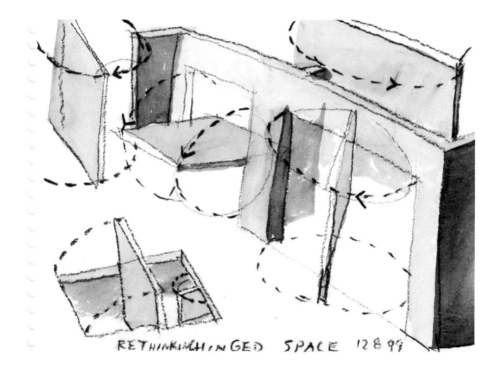

RETHINKINGHINGED SPACE 12899

stopped halfway, or even reversed if desired, instilling them with human powers absent from their artistic forebears. They exist to visibly convert one form of energy into another, and to transmit forces from one place to another, making light work out of something that would otherwise be impossible.

The long succession of translated movements and amplified forces in Kundig's inventions echoes in part the comical contraptions of cartoonist Rube Goldberg. While Kundig's gadgets lack the buffoonery of Goldberg's inventions, they share with the latter a painstaking elaboration, at times ostentation, of purely mechanical operations that are normally hidden or too small to see in our machines, turning them into celebrations of human will. More puzzle-like and spatially meshed are the mutations developed since the

Steven Holl, Storefront for Art and Architecture (1993), New York,
watercolour sketch of multiple pivots of concrete planes (above)
and plan showing pivoting concrete planes (top)

PARTICIPATING WALLS

Storefront 7/21/93 SH.

4.27.99 SH

Storefront for Art and Architecture, watercolour sketches of
interlocking puzzle-like pivoting planes (above) and early scheme
with corrugated planes turned into doorways and seats (top)

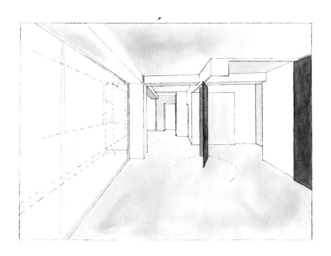

Steven Holl, Void Space/Hinged Space Apartments (1991), Fukuoka, Japan,
watercolour sketch showing three permutations of hinged space

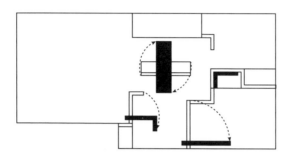

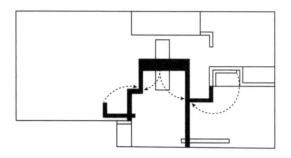

1980s by Steven Holl, who exploits a wide range of kinetic parts from small furnishings to huge interacting walls, often with a range of differently sized movements. Even the smallest ensembles are endowed with mysteries of motion, including cabinetry with a multitude of doors and drawers, some to be unexpectedly pulled out and others rotated through an arc. These operations, with obvious debts to Rietveld and Scarpa, gain added uncertainty from handgrips of differing form and location relative to motion, some being centred and others offset, some at the top and others the bottom of their compartments.

The mobile elements making up the urban wall of Holl's Storefront for Art and Architecture (pp. 111, 112) in New York appear cut out of the façade itself to create active and ever-changing relations between the gallery and sidewalk. A long series of pivoting concrete elements with contrasting shapes and motions makes up the boundary, turning something normally flat and static into a space-containing and space-shaping instrument. Flaps open inward and outward, with pivots either vertical or horizontal, so that some behave as doors or windows and others as tables or benches. These concrete folds, Holl notes, are 'arranged in a puzzle-like configuration'. When the panels are open, 'the façade dissolves and the interior space of the gallery expands out onto the sidewalk', he continues. 'The body is linked to the wall forms in the crude way that the shoulder is needed to push space out or pull it in' – though these acts, in actuality, are limited to gallery workers.[68]

Holl's ideas of 'hinged space' and 'participating walls' are especially responsive and diverse in his Void Space/Hinged Space Housing in Fukuoka, Japan, where the rooms

Void Space/Hinged Space Apartments, plan showing
arrangements of interlocking doors, walls and cabinets (above)
and watercolour sketch of multiple hinged cabinet (opposite)

of apartments 'interlock like a Chinese puzzle' (p. 113 and above).[69] At largest size are walls varied in shape that can pivot open, partly or completely, individually or in unison, to transform neighbouring spaces. Several L-shaped walls can be swung into corners or recesses, making them disappear, and other rotations allow walls to intersect and create new and unexpected rooms. At smallest size is a toy-like cabinet (below), reminiscent of Rietveld's, with doors both planar and L-shaped in plan that open out from three sides of the cube, permeating use with unusable play. The expansive range of manual control and continuity of energy through multiple scales with surprising effects, creates events far exceeding necessity. But it is this very extravagance that makes possible an arena of human interplay, transcending any narrow purpose or execution of work in architecture. It verifies that it is only in the searching for, rather than finding solutions, that we exist.

Giancarlo de Carlo, Collegio del Colle (1966), Urbino,
staircase landing widened into alcoves with seats

3

spaces of versatility

The common feature of spaces containing more than one possible action is versatility. Such a space is able to adapt immediately to different human desires and decisions, ensuring that considerable autonomy is left to each person to impose his or her will upon that volume, turning choices into acts of improvisation. The architectural source of this room to manoeuvre is multivalence, in which a number of appealing options fluctuate in the same volume – a space that is bordered with alcoves or bays, faceted by level changes or galleries, porous with colonnades or porticos. The uncertainty implied by multivalence is a positive feature, for it encourages different interpretations. As ambiguity loosens volumes from any pre-established control, people gain the leeway needed to navigate freely in space, gaining the power to take control of their immediate future.

In his famous painting for the Vatican, *The School of Athens* (above), Raphael depicts groups of figures arranged on an imaginary staircase. Some stand, others sit or sprawl on steps, while others lean against walls or settle arms into mouldings, one resting a book on a pedestal. Still others are spread out along the floor. Sitting on the lowermost step in the foreground is a figure traditionally identified as Michelangelo, propping his elbow on a marble block, supporting his head on his hand and seemingly in the midst of a drawing.

What is remarkable about this scene, in terms of human action, is the variety of ways its architecture encourages different kinds of interplay with the liberally shaped forms, textures, incidents and details. A special kind of liberty is portrayed that contains more than one desirable option and turns easily from one possibility to another. On Raphael's stair a person is free to select one of many latent interactions with some part of the overall space, a latitude that is echoed in a monastic cloister or arcaded court, or a colonnade such as at St Peter's in Rome, where one is able to wend and weave through countless gaps between columns, each slightly different in view and route, light and activity. In each instance, the zones permeate one another, producing an overlap of two or more zones within a larger volume, and it is precisely this versatility that allows a space to stimulate more than a single response and spark human initiative.

Also illustrating the underlying doubleness of versatile space is Thomas Jefferson's design for the University of Virginia, in Charlottesville (opposite). The axial control of the campus and bilateral repetition of units would seem at first to be the inverse of space open to alternate possibilities, but Jefferson sought a complex balance between order and liberty, in which there would be freedom within limits (ironically, the definition of human play). While the overall plan exerts a unifying force, the parts are loosened from the whole and

Raphael, *The School of Athens*, 1509 (Vatican, Rome)

remain diverse in experience, beginning with the slightly tiered terrain of the site. Each of five pavilions, along either terraced wing extending west from the library, presents a slightly different volume and portico, and the continuous colonnade enclosing The Lawn offers many options, from sheltering from the weather to leisurely strolling about the perimeter or taking a shortcut over the grass. The plinth of the library incites its own deliberation of routes to pursue, climbing over roofs or snaking through subterranean corridors. Here, we have the ultimate classical expression of a world that is equally authoritative and rebellious, cooperative and defiant.

Within the library is another clear demonstration of polycentric freedom in a collective whole, giving concrete form to the democratic impulses of a new nation. The cylindrical void and dome above pull the room together, while the perimeter becomes increasingly complicated with depth as the geometry loosens around paired columns framing a series of window bays (p. 120). The room allows people to gather in the centre or retreat to a quiet alcove, each a small room gleaming with light and with its own unique vista onto the campus. The alcoves themselves are not singular but plural, for they include an indistinct zone between and around columns, then an intermediary zone sheltered between facing bookcases, followed by the intimacy of a niche with deep window reveals. Movement, too, in this deceptively simple room provokes human decision, for one can cut through the domical centre or slip between columns, expanding the courses of action in a manifold space.

Thomas Jefferson, University of Virginia (1826),
colonnades and porticos

Long before any of these images of looseness are grasped in the mind, they are immediately felt in our muscles, those body parts acutely sensitive to freedom of motion and carrying, perhaps, a distant memory of our animal origins. We breathe more easily and our bodies instantly limber up where some leeway appears in the paths we traverse and the rooms in which we settle down, a margin of superfluous space whose residue has not been pressed into service and returns control to *us* over where and how *to be* in space. Only when not tightly packaged around a single, preordained use can space offer a range of undetermined actions that reflect our own changing needs. '[The philosopher David] Hume speaks of "a certain looseness" we want to exist in the world,' observes Daniel Dennett. 'This is the looseness that prevents the possible from shrinking tightly around the actual, the looseness presupposed by our use of the word "can".'[70]

By the same token, we instantly sense an absence of looseness and loss of control over events when entering a space that permits only one mode of moving or settling, making us feel constrained and unable to wander freely. There is no escaping the experience set before us, no matter how productive, pleasing or entertaining it might be. Such sites of human submission are an ever-present feature of the modern world: the uniform sidewalk; the monotonous plaza; the narrow corridor; paths devoid of sidings in which to retreat or pause; the room reduced to a single platonic geometry or the cell defined by a single function.

Less obvious but equally authoritarian in their denial and ultimate debasement of the human capacity to act in space are large empty volumes valued for extreme flexibility, which allow people to move about and rearrange furniture as they please. Analogous to flat ground that is open to many different versions of the same stereotypical movement, vacant flexibility is stripped of any real alternatives or contrasting qualities that people might desire and

Thomas Jefferson, University of Virginia (1826),
perimeter alcoves in the library

choose, for every 'choice' is virtually the same. Gone are any opportunities we might actually care about and that could empower us to act upon and with the environment. All that is left is a neutral and barren kind of container, its 'free plan' appearing to allow anything but inviting, sustaining and rewarding nothing.

More disingenuous is the space controlled within or without an architectural spectacle, whose flamboyant, ostentatious forms help one forget the loss of leeway in the spot where one stands. The formal display and decorative skin provide a kind of sugar-coated pill to make the indignities of docile space more palatable. As the pageantry intensifies, it seems to have a sedative effect on the human urge to search for, must less notice, the shrivelled and illusory choices in space. A related observation is made by the artist Robert Irwin: 'When performance goes up, the quality of the questions usually tends to go down.'[71]

AMBIGUITY

The construction of environments rich in options for human decision is not merely dependent on 'weak' versus 'strong' form, since vagueness alone does not provide the projects and deeds worthy of people's consideration (see p. 122). Alternate courses of action imply that set before us are the intensely appealing and real opportunities we long for. But they also imply not one option but many, so that we are able to see them fluctuate in a variable structure. As soon as space includes two or more interpretations, it becomes ambiguous. It moves back and forth between different possibilities. In terms of perception, its *gestalts* are multifarious, simultaneous, polyphonic and irresolute, rather than singular, separate, monotonous and absolute.

It is not surprising that the word 'ambiguity' has been stigmatized in our positivist culture, but it derives in its original sense from the Latin *ambiguus*, from *ambigere*, to be undecided, combining *ambi-* (both) and *-igere* (to drive, act or do), thus sharing linguistic roots with the word 'agency'. In terms of architecture, it is not an amorphous lack of clarity or physical presence that produces spatial ambiguity, but the existence of two or more latent values or renditions whose possibilities intermingle. It is only when these possibilities are desirable enough to stir us to action that architecture is truly responsive to our initiatives and becomes humanly relevant.

Ambiguous space implies a degree of uncertainty and doubt, making room for human deliberation, whereas this disappears in forms that are overwrought or narrowly defined. It also suggests, by its reduction of outward display and exhibitionism, a measure of restraint on the part of its maker. The sad news for architects who care about these matters is that in order to invest buildings with fluctuating chances for improvised action by other people, they must be willing to temper their own presence as a controlling force in the finished work. This does not imply tedious or undistinguished form, as architects from Bernini and Jefferson to Kahn and Scarpa have demonstrated, but it does require that a generous portion of the creative powers instilled in a building are bequeathed to others, rather than fully expressed and used up in the making. When a share of these powers are passed on as an embedded gift to people who will later experience the building, those occupants are elevated to actors able

Multiple ways to sit upon the Seine embankment, Paris; Piazza Grande, Montepulciano, alcoves with stone benches between columns; Michelangelo, Piazza del Campidoglio (1561), Rome, improvisational stairs and benches of the Senatore (top to bottom)

to invent and shape their own dramas, rather than reduced to spectators of someone else's dramatic form. While being provoked into action by appealing, even wondrous, possibilities, they are free to complete the scenario for themselves.

Taking this thought a step further is architect Peter Prangnell, who has argued that the freedom to act in ambiguous space is maximized when built forms are inherently modest. Where manifold things are characterized by understatement and anonymity, they become 'friendly objects', fully accessible to those coming into contact with them, since their forms can be more effectively taken over and absorbed into everyone's personal world. This power of easily shifting one's relation to an unpretentious form is immediately evident in the way, Prangnell wrote in an article for the *Harvard Educational Review*, 'children at play quickly change a table into a house; a house can become a ship'.

'It follows that the more explicit an object is in the sense that it has no ambiguity, the more difficult it is to use it imaginatively in any other way,' he continued. 'A plain wooden chest may be a seat, a stage, an island or a coffin. If the chest is decorated with pictures or painted signs, it can be easily recognized as a special chest but it will not lend itself so easily for use as a stage or an island. In the same way a bare attic may lend itself to more imaginative use than a completely decorated one. Obviously [it] will have … sloping ceilings, dormer windows, beams and stairs, which define particular volumes or places for our occupation. These features will immediately generate and connect with our desired actions and we can exploit … their latent potential to be released through our imaginations … If our buildings and cities are made as friendly objects, they will invite [our] participation. As friendly objects, they will have immediate purpose and withheld meaning. They will stimulate, through perception, our creative powers which are the basis of growth in all our activities.'[72]

DOUBLE-PERSPECTIVE IN 20TH-CENTURY POETRY AND PAINTING

In a compound space, where multiple zones of opportunity are contained in one overall volume, people are encouraged to see, but also imagine and contemplate, space through a kind of double-vision. The physical eye and the mind's eye see many in one, as well as one in many. Instead of being bound to a single rigid and predetermined perspective, people are enabled to grasp and assess space in multiple ways and from many perspectives, to move back and forth between many simultaneous facets and possible actions.

From the standpoint of human perception, simultaneity depends on conditions of transparency and interpenetration. These indicate, we are told by György Kepes in *Language of Vision*, 'more than an optical characteristic; they imply a broader spatial order. Transparency means a simultaneous perception of different spatial locations. Space not only recedes but fluctuates in a continuous activity.'[73] In other words, a viewer is offered two or more ways to see the same thing, and through this oscillation is drawn into and encouraged to take an active role in determining the visual experience. But we must keep in mind that unlike a painting observed from a distance, the compound architectural space invites more than retinal and mental action: it offers alternatives that people can also enter and act upon, continuing to revise and alter that act as new conditions or desires emerge.

The double-perspective aroused by a thing we can see and construe in differing ways, at different times, equips us to work on several different associative levels at once. While the reading of poetry is not the same as manoeuvring in buildings, the structure of poems can provide useful lessons for understanding versatility. Charles Olson put his finger on the taproot of participation by continually crossing out the word 'one' and replacing it with 'two', realizing that it is multiplicity, not singularity, which makes the world involving and energizing. 'One' is something to passively follow, while 'two' injects a vital moment of decision that draws the reader into action. This variability is a principal means by which Olson sought to turn his poems into instruments of creative reading, perpetually able to overcome the tendency for life to settle into habits.

Two other American poets, the contemporaries Wallace Stevens and William Carlos Williams, struggled to incorporate the reader in poems through a highly evocative linguistic structure that was rich in alternate ways of hearing and seeing the same words. Not coincidentally, they are the two poets of their generation most influenced by the new movements in painting based on concepts of simultaneity that were emerging in Europe at the time, from Cézanne's interlocking colour planes to the faceting and multiple views of Picasso and Braque. By contrast with poems that present a fixed perspective, Stevens and Williams were searching for a poetic structure that contains multiple perspectives and offers a somewhat broken and incomplete structure open to diverse manners of reading and interpreting phrases. Such a poem is no longer an expression but a dialectical medium that invites the reader to project *himself* into its world, and there actively engage and work out *for himself* each possible experience out of the latent options.

Williams was particularly close to the emancipatory images being pursued in the visual arts. 'Representing planes to denote volumes, Picasso gives so complete and so decisive an enumeration of the various elements which make up the object, that these do not take the shape of the object,' he wrote. 'This is largely due to the effort of the viewer, who is forced to see all the elements simultaneously just because of the way they have been arranged.'[74] He sought an equally open composition in his poems by incorporating words and phrases that invite the reader to fluctuate between interpretations that permeate and charge one another. Instead of producing clear and straightforward forms resistant to imaginative play and transfiguration, he created ones with multiple shadings and ambiguous structures that soften and disintegrate into a shiftier kind of reality. Unlike a pre-arranged thing that remains external to our existence, these nuanced things invite us to share in finishing and, to some extent, choosing their forms. Stevens conveyed a similar thought in imagining a poem in which the 'degree of perception at which what is real and what is imagined are one: a state of clairvoyant observation', so that 'reality is not what it is. It consists of the many realities which it can be made into'.[75]

As in a painting such as Picasso's *Portrait of Daniel-Henry Kahnweiler* (opposite) or a poem by Olson, Williams or Stevens, architecture gains simultaneity when its spaces are compound, rather than singular. This occurs in a building whose whole and parts avoid being overly fixed, fully defined and sharply divided, and instead are built up out of

incomplete qualities and zones that overlap with unclear boundaries to produce a shifting and shadier whole. Boundaries leak and connect, as well as partly divide. Components are to a certain extent transparent to one another, as well as discrete, and offer multiple facets of the some overall volume they occupy. This extraordinary doubleness, poised between reality and imagination, may extend into many facets, but its basic power depends first of all on escaping the command of a single, preordained future.

THE FREEDOM OF ELBOW ROOM
The liberating power of ambiguity bears upon the inherent human urge to be in control of and able to shape one's own immediate experience and destiny. Freedom is essentially a

Pablo Picasso, *Portrait of Daniel-Henry Kahnweiler*,
1910 (Art Institute, Chicago)

postulate of action but remains elusive, for it exists only as a possibility, rather than actuality. It cannot be grasped by mental thought or expressed in solid form, but only experienced in the present tense through its own exercise. Freedom may be dangerous to unity, but there is no human dignity without it, and so the risk of increasing and providing freedom must be constantly taken.

The exhilarating experience of freedom in architecture is broad enough to apply to almost every chapter in this book. An unpredictable flight of steps or variable window, for instance, contains the crucial latitude needed for us to decide how to exercise our bodily faculties or reshape some part of our world. We feel this kind of unconstrained power as long as the outcome is not inevitable. We may be surprised at our own cautionary fear or anxiety, but equally may bring to light unexpected interests and desires, as well as resources of dexterity and imagination. We may fall to the ground or fail to move a mobile object, but may also astonish ourselves with balletic moves or miraculous change. In either case, we are granted the leeway to decide events for ourselves and become R.D. Laing's 'origin of actions'.

But freedom finds its deepest roots and most complete exercise in compound space, where it is immediately sensed long before it is consciously grasped by eye or mind. Autonomy in space assures us that we are not 'manipulated objects', a feeling essential not only for people of all ages, notes Bruno Bettelheim, but also for those trying to recover from mental illness. The essential quality Bettelheim sought to instill in the Orthogenic School for autistic children in Chicago was a 'structureless structure', where patients could participate in all decisions that affected their lives, including the design of the school and their own rooms. 'Recovery from insanity is dependent on the patient's conviction that he or she is an autonomous human being,' he continues. 'Everybody is afraid of having his mind read or made up by others; everybody wants to have control over his own mind. The delusion that others can control his mind is common to the mental patient.'[76]

The architectural roots of autonomy, Bettelheim believed, are forms that avoid the institutional demands and patterns present in bland or redundant spaces, and instead are rich in attractive choices of variable action, including territories patients are able to spontaneously stake out and feel secure in. At every scale of the Orthogenic School, the patient is provided with two or more desirable possibilities in order 'to make it a real choice'.[77] And so the corridors were shaped into spaces for both movement and repose, combining invitations to saunter along them and rest in the sheltering alcoves. The basic aim was to construct options that would be gratifying to different people, and would satisfy the changing needs or desires of each person over time.

Related ideas have long been a staple of philosophical discourse. In *Elbow Room*, Daniel Dennett negotiates a way through perplexing questions about free will by juxtaposing two situations: those in which people have come under the control of something or someone else, and those in which people have acquired self-control. 'We want to be *in control*,' he writes, 'and to control both ourselves and our destinies.'[78] We lose control in situations marked by extreme order, which deny or restrict our choices, and regain self-control in environments with generous 'degrees of freedom'. The latter depend on a certain amount

Carlo Scarpa, Olivetti Showroom (1958), Venice, marble-slab staircase
(above); Katsura Imperial Villa, Kyoto, Shoka-tei teahouse (top)

of disorder to avoid confining or predictable patterns, and are full of the kind of operations we find rewarding. They are essentially marked by a generous amount of 'elbow room', which provides us with the room to manoeuvre. 'We want a margin for error; we want to keep our options open, so that our chances of maintaining control over our operations, come what may, are enhanced,' Dennett concludes. 'This implies that we would also like the world to be a certain way: full of variety, certainly, and with lots of sustenance and delight – but more important in this context: not so savagely demanding (given our needs and abilities) as to constrain our options to a bare minimum.'[79]

The architectural implications of Dennett's scenarios are immediately apparent if we compare the cellular structure of a standardized Western building with the interflowing compound space of a traditional Japanese house or villa. Instead of the former's uniform floors, tightly wrapped walls and flat ceilings, the latter presents floors that are broken into slightly higher and lower levels, and the combination of a few fixed walls with the changing enclosures of movable screens to produce interlocking and incomplete rooms, with ceilings that rise and fall to differentiate spaces below. Other facets appear in window alcoves with low wooden desks (*tsukeshoin*) and in the contemplative alcove of a *tokonoma*. Even a small teahouse, such as Shoka-tei at Katsura Imperial Villa (p. 127, top), is inherently double in its combined zones of refuge and outlook, contrasting adventurous areas with the intimacy of solid corners and complementing the focal point of a clay stove for heating water with ledges covered with *tatami* mats for sitting on while conversing or looking onto the garden.

An equally stark contrast can be drawn between a stereotypical modern stair, with its efficient channel and repetitive steps, and the indeterminate flight of steps designed by Carlo Scarpa for the Olivetti Showroom (p. 127, bottom). Both serve the practical function of climbing, but the former is so tightly formed around a single normative behaviour that it compels a person to climb in a stipulated manner. There is no invitation to pause, or climb in more than one way, a routine now so deeply ingrained it is drilled into our legs. Scarpa's stair begins from a different premise: to surprise and restore control to the climber and, despite its limited dimensions, offer a host of self-confirming acts. Steps of polished Aurisina marble widen in places to accommodate varying manoeuvres, cantilevering at one point into a shelf, and spreading and folding at the bottom into a bench where people can perch. Instead of confined to compulsory moves, the climber is free to climb in diverse ways and lean or sit in diverse postures.[80] This multivalence releases our imaginations and motor impulses to move at will within its framework of gratifying phenomena. The leeway provided does not exist as a physical thing, but a potential that people can only materialize for themselves.

The stair also illuminates the critical role played by architecture as a catalyst to spark our choices, precipitating human events. We cannot truly act in a vacuum, but only in tandem with environmental features that inspire and merit our decisions. Fromm describes this kind of incentive as 'one that *stimulates the person to be active*'. He notes that 'such an activating stimuli could be a novel, a poem, an idea, a landscape, music or a loved person. None of these stimuli produce a simple response; they invite you, as it were, to respond by actively and sympathetically relating yourself to them; by becoming actively *interested*, seeing and discovering ever-new aspects in your "object" (which ceases to be a mere "object"), by becoming more awake and more aware. You do not remain the passive object upon which the stimulus acts, to whose melody your body has to dance, as it were; instead you express your own faculties by being related to the world; you become active and productive.' In conclusion, Fromm states, 'because of the productive response to them, [activating stimuli] are always new, always changing; the stimulated person (the "stimulee") brings the stimuli to life and changes them by always discovering new aspects in them. Between the stimulus and the "stimulee" exists a mutual relationship, not the mechanical, one-way relations S>R.'[81]

COMPOSITE STAIRCASES

Whether stemming from gifts of terrain, accidental accretion or subconscious wisdom, common to the inclined footpaths of vernacular settlements is a relaxed and generous freedom of movement. Spatial channels widen and narrow along their length, folding the boundaries into nearly infinite corners and alcoves in which to spontaneously pause or rest. Beyond its overall slope, the hilltown path is often endowed with alternate textures from which to choose, juxtaposing stepped increments with a smooth ramp, for instance, or dividing the floor into ribbons of optional gradient.

A magnificent example is the Via Appia in Perugia, which flows down from the city centre in three winding streams of differing footholds (p. 130). '[Its] austerity ... is offset by its fine pavement, no one who walks this street can fail to note the texture of the stairs,' wrote Rudofsky in *Streets for People*. 'There is nothing monotonous in their execution; the height, length and width of the steps vary sufficiently to give each of three people walking abreast a different choice of surface – one of them may walk on conventional, rather shallow steps, the other may prefer the bordering narrow ramp, while a third ... may select one of the two inclines that flank the centre stairs. The latter is neither ramp nor steps but a blend of both, a pavement characteristic of Perugia's steep streets. Here, the steps are reduced to one-inch footholds that walk uphill – a joy for the goat-footed, a stumbling block or worse for the clumsy.'[82] Increasing the stair's deliberative range is an alternate route to the university on a far hillside. A derelict medieval aqueduct, intersecting the staircase along its descent, has been transformed into a footbridge that soars over the valley below, providing a more direct but exhilarating path to the same destination.

The hallmark of a number of celebrated staircases is an offering of divergent routes. In the tripartite stair devised by Michelangelo for the Laurentian Library in Florence, the climber is offered three differently tempting ways to the same journey's end.[83] The wide central flight is characterized by voluptuous steps that swell downwards, bordered at either side by indirect rectilinear routes that ascend without rails, before all three fuse to enter the reading room. In other monumental inclines, the options are reduced to mirror images that differ solely in direction and scenery, as in the magnificent if virtually identical double-staircases of Renaissance villas and Baroque palaces, culminating in the twin flights of Filippo Juvarra's Palazzo Madama in Turin, Italy, and Balthasar Neumann's Würzburg Residence in Germany.

View down Via Appia to Via Acquedotto, Perugia; overview of the intersection of
Via Appia and Via Acquedotto; alternate stairs at either side of Via Acquedotto;
Via Appia flowing beneath overpass (clockwise from top left)

Still symmetric but less controlled are the huge urban staircases of Alessandro Specchi's Porto di Ripetta and the Scala di Spagna (below). While presenting a manifold whole, each is endowed with many discretionary acts that people are able to choose and perform. Available roles built into the Porto di Ripetta can still be gleaned from eighteenth-century engravings: alternate speeds and routes of stairs, contrasting ledges for accessing water or unloading boats and varied ways to simply sit or sprawl on steps with differing sightlines onto the Tiber. The skewed cascade of the Scala di Spagna is even richer in its intersecting courses of action. Flights continually divide and converge along the incline with differently angled and shaped steps, their flow interrupted by periodic landings including two broad terraces that serve as belvederes from which to gaze onto the streetlife and fountain below. Further differentiating flights are narrow tiers of rectilinear travertine blocks with pedestals for lamps, offering ledges for sitting or reclining, perhaps leaning back with legs dangling off the side, and extemporaneous lodging points that recur in the bordering parapets and balustrades – all of which give the stair a simultaneity of diverse routes and points of repose.

The sumptuous staircase designed by Antoni Gaudí for Parc Güell in Barcelona (p. 132) keeps splitting into alternate journeys and is dotted with chances to pause and sit with varying postures and outlooks. Coated with radiant white tiles and flourishes of colour, the alluring double-stair begins as two angled routes that converge at an initial terrace, whereupon the strands diverge again but run parallel up to the next terrace, and the next, before separating one last time with divergent routes to the plaza above. While the parapet with rounded contours can also be sat on, the landings offer especially delightful throne-like benches, the first a convex seat with a tall, curving back, and the second haloed with colour and shaded from the sun by a concave recess.

Alessandro Specchi, Scala di Spagna (1725),
Rome, impromptu seating

ITALIAN PIAZZAS, BOTH GRAND AND INTIMATE

The most compelling composite space is the city square. It is not the size, however, nor the utility or beauty of this outdoor room that nurtures human action. Rather, it is a powerfully sculpted yet multiform and ambiguous shape, analogous to Jefferson's campus or Bernini's portico, which provides infinite chances for human decision about qualities we truly desire. The resources for vast numbers of people to be individually autonomous in the same overall space are especially evident in the urban cavities of historic Italian cities and towns.

The finest and most famous of these – the Piazza del Campidoglio (opposite, top) in Rome, the Piazza del Campo in Siena (opposite, bottom), the Piazza Grande in Montepulciano (p. 134, top), the small Piazza Pio II by Bernardo Rossellino in Pienza (p. 134, bottom), the Piazza della Cisterna in San Gimignano and the Piazza San Marco in Venice – possess voids that are vivid and memorable, as well as abundant with diverse features and contrary edges where freedom develops. These piazzas are unified and disparate, centred and decentred, authoritative and subversive. As a result, they can nurture the urban identity of huge crowds at civic events but also offer small groups and individuals the power to manoeuvre among many attractive possibilities, containing a wide margin for both error and improvisation. The 'intermingling of appearances' and 'scope for action' turn each cavity into 'an arena of free interplay', qualities Erikson considers essential to wellbeing and survival, for they offer a 'leeway of mastery' to hundreds, if not thousands, of people at once.[84]

In any of Italy's iconic piazzas, the strongly defined character of the container is immediately felt to loosen up along the floor and around the perimeter. Instead of rigid geometry, warping, creasing and bending occur at the foot of a remarkable enclosure. Walls relax as they alternately advance and recede, pressing into corners and niches

Antoni Gaudí, Parc Güell (1914), Barcelona, alcove
with concave bench on landing of the staircase

Piazza del Campo, Siena (above) and Michelangelo,
Piazza del Campidoglio (1561), Rome (top)

Piazza Grande, Montepulciano (top) and
Bernardo Rossellino, Piazza Pio II, Pienza (above)

around the edge, mingling various spatial choices. Other sites for action appear in the hollows of porticos and arcades in which to shelter, withdraw from the crowd or merely lean against a column. Where solid façades touch the ground they open to a variety of decisions by folding into public benches or entry stairs, whose steps and ledges offer extemporaneous seating, lining the void with numerous chances to manoeuvre and settle in the same overall volume.

Different modes of action develop around features pushing up through the ground, their small centres exerting attraction like islands in a flux of space (above). We can latch onto these stable anchors in diverse ways: sitting around the node of a wellhead; reclining against a lamppost; perching on a bollard or parapet. The multisensory delights of a great urban fountain, the central lure of many piazzas, should not obscure our appreciation of its other provisions for voluntary power. Surrounding the hypnotic play of water are myriad points of decision – ledges of varying form and dimension on which to stretch out or dangle limbs in cool water.

The floor of a great piazza supplies yet another source of manifold space. Slight displacements in slope or surface break up the floor into different angles or levels, producing many facets of one large surface. The same is true of the pavement itself. Huge carpets of stone or brick unite and distinguish the overall space, sometimes emphasizing a central zone, but this carpet then tends to shift texture or colour around the periphery to create an irregular fringe, an unruly edge more local and individual in character. In combining a comprehensive

Piazza della Cisterna, San Gimignano, improvised seating
around the octagonal travertine base of the cistern

whole with a profusion of smaller jostling domains, the Italian piazza constitutes one of architecture's greatest achievements of freedom for many, a place where people can feel communal unity while controlling their own experiences.

The same is true of the upper plaza at Parc Güell in Barcelona, where freedom develops around a uniquely configured edge (above). No two seats in the undulating parapet-bench around the circumference are exactly the same, for the alternating concavity and convexity ensures that each point is slightly different in angle of view and incident sun. Some positions thrust a person out to the central space, while others recede into quiet coves with unique vistas down to the gardens and out to the city. The sectional moulding of this sinuous bench in the shape of a seated human figure, coated with brilliant sherds of pottery, bring added attractions of comfort and colour to any location a person chooses.

WRIGHT'S 'SOVEREIGNTY OF THE INDIVIDUAL'

Leading the way at the outset of the twentieth century in associating architecture with freedom through a polymorphous shaping of rooms was Frank Lloyd Wright. The essence of Wright's composite language is most ingenious in his houses, and above all in the generous room to manoeuvre of the living rooms. Even at the heart of his modest Usonian houses, such as the Tracy House overlooking Puget Sound, near Seattle, Washington, is an overlap of many small zones within one large room. The diminutive living/dining room of the Pope-Leighey House (opposite), relocated to the grounds of Woodlawn plantation, in Arlington, Virginia, also exerts a collective unity shot through with smaller domains of a hearth, dining recess and intimate wood cove, combined with many small glimpses of nature and two panoramic windows. Equally significant, each domain is itself composite with its own unique balance

Antoni Gaudí, Parc Güell (1914), Barcelona,
sinuous bench around the grand plaza

of outlook and refuge, which can be altered by the slightest shift of location or orientation. In part it may be Wright's identification with what he considered the 'dream of freedom' and 'democratic spirit' of America that led him to pay as much attention to the 'sovereignty of the individual' as to the collective unity of buildings. Volumes were configured to place a 'premium upon Individuality as the highest possible development of the individual consistent with a harmonious life of the whole', and embodied his notion that 'the whole to be worthy as complete must consist of individual units, great and strong in themselves, not units yoked from outside in bondage but united by spirit from inside with the right to freely move'.[85]

It is important to recognize that Wright's 'individual units' are never neutral, redundant or mere formal alternatives, but are built up from choices of primal conditions about which people care passionately. He ensured that options are real incentives that invite and reward the deepest human urges: the hearth became an earthy site of primitive masonry and mesmerizing fire; the dining area possesses an ambience conducive to gathering over meals; and everywhere are sheltering alcoves complemented by glassy bays liberating in outdoor

Frank Lloyd Wright, Pope-Leighey House (1941), Virginia, overlapping zones in the living/dining room

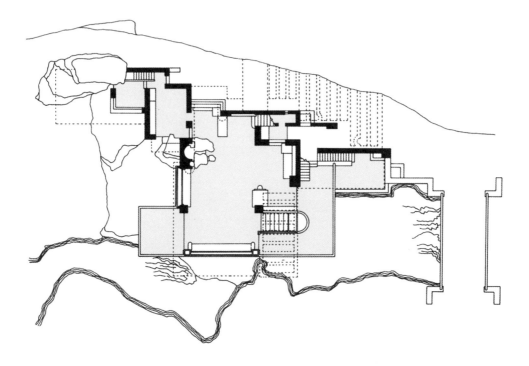

vistas. 'Buildings, at long last – like their occupants – may be themselves free', he wrote, when 'in every part of the building freedom is active'.[86] But Wright also understood that if left too vacuous, choices would not be free in any meaningful sense. The 'new liberation', as he called it, demanded opportunity and not just a loss of bondage.[87] It required a freedom *for* rather than merely *from* something. 'Escape is not freedom', he knowingly observed, for 'the only freedom we have a right to ask for is the freedom to seek.'[88]

Larger homes designed by Wright only expand this 'freedom to seek', extending the ethic to multiplex bedrooms, libraries, balconies and terraces. But the living room always remained the most fertile and rich with opportunity, endowed with acts that each family member could differently but intensely appropriate. The central core of Wingspread, near Racine, Wisconsin, for instance, is a pinwheel of quadrants set around the anchor of a huge fireplace. Each radial zone is differentiated while linked to its neighbours by low walls, level changes, ceiling heights and outward views, with the inward appeal of fire combined with the outward lure of a rooftop lookout. The ground floor at Fallingwater (above) in Pennsylvania is as multifarious as the land outside. Surrounding the volume of the living room are many locales with contrasting attractions that matter to us: a stone hearth resting on bedrock; an intimate dining alcove in one corner; transitional space for the entry with a bench set into a fold in the wall; a study enclosed by an 'L' of glass and overlooking the hatch to the stream; a seat nestled between columns and facing north back into the room; an equally bracketed

Frank Lloyd Wright, Fallingwater (1935), Pennsylvania, ground-floor plan

Frank Lloyd Wright, Taliesin West (begun 1938), Arizona, living room

seat nearby facing east to the outdoor stream, with cantilevered terraces at either side embraced by nature yet still part of the larger glazed room.

The extraordinary perimeter of Fallingwater, as well as the living rooms at Taliesin East in Spring Green, Wisconsin, and Taliesin West in Scottsdale, Arizona (p. 139), was conceived as a series of intermediate zones, turning the boundary into a deep, interpenetrative fringe of spaces that are inherently ambiguous. Instead of being reduced to a thin border, the boundary is expanded and staggered to create alternating inlets and peninsulas. Wright's pushing and pulling at this interface marries inside and out by extending each into the other while stitching together their polar conditions, and makes the boundary itself space-containing, inundating the edge with conflated qualities that people can ponder and act upon.

An analogy can be drawn between the improvisational nature of Wright's architecture and the experience of playing jazz, a musical form indigenous to America that was emerging in New Orleans, Kansas City and Chicago concurrent with Wright's prairie architecture. Jazz is based to an unparalleled degree on personal liberty set within limits, where each musician has the leeway to play off of and act on the melodies of the others. Unlike the strictly sequential beginning, middle and end of most music, jazz starts and stops without a predetermined narrative. Often considered the quintessence of democratic equality, jazz is essentially a performer's art, where the composer sets up a rough framework that individual musicians interpret with their own unrehearsed instrumental and vocal improvisations. Impulsive solo flights and 'breaks' momentarily take off on their own tangents, while challenging, stretching and complicating the unity of the whole – an improvisatory range that could as easily describe Wrightean space.

POLYVALENT FORMS OF HERMAN HERTZBERGER
Wright's liberation of space finds European parallels in the interiors of Le Corbusier and Alvar Aalto, as well as in the extraordinary feeling of participation created by Hans Scharoun for the Berlin Philharmonic. Surrounding the concert hall's central void is a complex wrapping of spatial sherds through which theatregoers can freely manoeuvre. This composite space begins in the lobby, where triangulated zones and level changes ensure there is always an undetermined margin around any normative course of action, enhancing deliberative powers as people linger between performances. The Cubist composition, developed both in plan and section, culminates in the auditorium itself. Facing the stage and surrounding its axis are differently angled domains for the audience, with each skewed and tilted plane having slightly different sightlines. Scharoun likened these fractured components to the terraces of vineyards, their irregularly cascading plots united yet always varied in space and orientation.

Displaying the same generosity of spirit but conceived with humility are the works of Herman Hertzberger (opposite), whose forms, especially those built between the 1960s and '80s, are intentionally poor in outward appearance but rich in desirable actions. Hertzberger has described this many-faceted wealth as 'polyvalence', calling attention to its heterogeneous meanings and interpretations. These 'inducements' provoke and inspire latent associations by people, stimulating choices that make a difference to their lives. By contrast

Herman Hertzberger, Centraal Beheer (1972), Netherlands,
axonometric of rooftop plaza over cafeteria (above) and
interior pedestrian street with alcoves and seats (top)

with authoritarian space, whose commands are exerted by excessive rigidity, repetition or expression, Hertzberger's paths and rooms are configured to liberate people by playing a wide range of secondary roles while remaining true to their primary function, melding spontaneous action with practical need and, in a more general sense, play with work.

The subtle infusion of voluntary options without making forms overly explicit reverses the now-common physics of power between buildings and people, redirecting control to the latter. In this regard, Hertzberger draws a correlation between architecture and a musical instrument. A piano or flute 'essentially contains as many possibilities of usage as uses to which it is put – an instrument must be played', he wrote. 'Within the limits of the instrument, it is up to the player to draw what he can from it, within the limits of his own ability. Thus instrument and player reveal to each other their respective abilities to complement and fulfill one another. Form as an instrument offers the scope for each person to do what he has most at heart, and above all to do it in his own way.'[89]

Analogous to the construction of a violin, Hertzberger sought to broaden and deepen the instrumental range of each built component, including its most easily stereotyped parts, often by simply folding an edge to insert a place for people to sit (above and opposite).

Foundations of walls crease into ledges, structural columns flower into tiny balconies with curved benches, concrete footings rise from the earth to provide shallow cylindrical seats, floor edges are slightly raised to offer footrests, metal balustrades are pleated into shallow benches and ledges and solid walls are indented with alcoves lined with warm woodwork and places to settle.

In his understated inclusion of play in unexpected places, Hertzberger knowingly drew from architectural history and the unnoticed details of many celebrated buildings, including the stone seats at the foot of columns in a portico and concave *miradores* of the upper roadway at Gaudí's Parc Güell, and the two facing window seats hollowed from a brick wall in the conference room of Sigurd Lewerentz's church of St Peter in Klippan, Sweden. Edging a path below the rampart of Scarpa's Castelvecchio Museum is a low wall that turns from a parapet into a high seat, then a low ledge and finally, within the wall itself, a footrest for a window seat overlooking the river. In a similar vein, the wood-framed glazing around the perimeter of Louis I. Kahn's Phillips Exeter Academy Library (all p. 144) expands into back-to-back window desks, whose surface is bent into an 'L' for diverse ways of working, complemented by a sliding shutter to control light, outlook and introspection.

Herman Hertzberger, Muziekcentrum Vredenburg (1978),
Utrecht, balustrade stretched into a seat (above) and balustrade
shelf and bench alcove along the staircase (opposite)

Antoni Gaudí, Parc Güell (1914), Barcelona; Sigurd Lewerentz, St Peter's Church (1966),
Klippan, Sweden; Louis I. Kahn, Phillips Exeter Academy Library (1972), New Hampshire;
Carlo Scarpa, Castelvecchio Museum (1973), Verona (clockwise from top left)

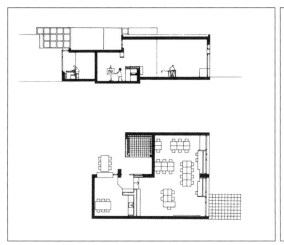

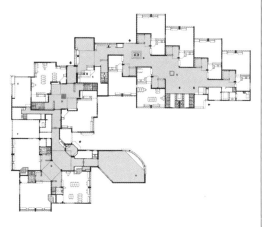

But unique to Hertzberger's nourishment of free will is the infusion of intensely plain materials with a tremendous scope of opportunity, shifting the focus of financial resources from appearance to action. An early masterpiece is the Montessori School in Delft (above), a humble construction of grey concrete and dark wood whose every part was conceived as a catalyst for the decisions of young children. The entry does not present a façade but an intermediary zone, full of possibilities – a sheltering recess near the door and a bay projecting into the landscape, its low parapet sized to the child and volunteering an ad-hoc bench or table while waiting for parents. This empathetic language of form, where deliberative wealth is fashioned out of inexpensive materials, extends into the dual levels of classrooms. Combined within an encompassing 'L', so as to stimulate interpretation at every scale, is a lower 'L' that is inwardly focused and intimate, and an upper 'L' that is outwardly gazing and adventurous. As at the entry, the threshold to each classroom is not a dividing line but an in-between place conducive to choice. Akin to the porch or stoop of a house, this domain is a slightly protected alcove where children can work between the control of the teacher and freedom of the hallway.

Most marvellous is the winding hallway linking classrooms. As opposed to the linear corridor common in schools, whose chillingly barren axis is easily supervised and hurries children efficiently from class to class, Hertzberger's corridor is a zig-zag volume that widens and narrows along its length. Children are able to both slowly meander and move more directly from one end of the school to the other, echoing the spontaneity of life itself. Along the way children can pause in a number of welcoming alcoves outside the stream of circulation, to work on their own or with others, or congregate at a spot in the floor where a cluster of seats can be removed and grouped about the pit they reveal. The transformation of a normally coercive corridor into a place of self-controlled movement and rest reminds us of Erikson's plea to 'take time', for 'in trifling, in dallying, we lazily thumb our noses at this, our slave-driver. Where every minute counts, playfulness vanishes.'[90]

Hertzberger continued to adapt the theme of polyvalence to buildings widely varied in type and size, from schools and apartments to office and institutional buildings, while

Herman Hertzberger, Montessori School (1966), Delft,
section and plan of a classroom (above left) and
plan of interior street (above right)

carefully attuning the choices in each to the limits and interests of each population. In doing so, the deeper significance of freedom of choice has remained a conscious pursuit. 'A thing exclusively made for one purpose', he wrote in the *Harvard Educational Review*, 'suppresses the individual because it tells him exactly how it is to be used. If the object provokes a person to determine in what way he wants to use it, it will strengthen his self-identity ... Therefore a form must be interpretable – in the sense that it must be conditioned to play a changing role.'[91]

MAURICE SMITH'S SPATIAL COLLAGES

In the Massachusetts houses of Maurice Smith, compound space is totally freed of dominant centres and closed cells. Among these few but exceptionally generous works are a residence in Groton (opposite) and an oceanside retreat in Manchester-by-the-Sea, both for the Blackman family, and his own experimental house in the town of Harvard. Each room in these deliberately unpretentious dwellings accommodates and is loosened around its explicit function, stimulating many ways of performing the same general action, as well as impromptu acts in the same space – a latitude Smith describes as 'slack' and 'spatial tolerance'.

The awareness at the Groton residence of being back in control of one's future begins on arrival, from the multiple attractions of wall and portico, to a winding path that keeps splitting and uniting along its journey to several doorways into the house. Incentives and routes open up with new margins of opportunity: columns appear within the flow to stimulate decisions and loosely guide turns; alcoves recede to accommodate pauses or liberalize motion; and at several points the route divides into plural streams with contrasting enclosure or view, allowing each person to chart his own course from more than one appealing way to reach the same destination.

'This is a place that prescribes nothing', wrote architect John Donat a few years after the house was built, 'an architecture that is intense without imposing itself on you, that has absolute clarity in spite of diversity and complexity, a place full of gentle ambiguities. You are channelled towards the way in firmly but gently – the way is indicated – but even under the structure of the entrance canopy ... you are not forced to pass under it but can slip by on the side ... No space seems deliberately *for* anything, each can be used as you please ... This is not just the pseudo-flexibility of anonymous emptiness (universal space!) but a place full of real options and opportunities that can be richly interpreted by whoever is living in it.'[92]

Echoing the work of Hertzberger, the main staircase illustrates a core human freedom – the chance to spontaneously move or rest. At its mid-flight turn, the landing extends into a loft with an opportune couch. A person can easily turn 180° to continue up or down the next flight, or just as easily pause to take in the sweeping panorama, or sit down on the couch, which hovers over the living room like a crow's nest. Each choice is enriched by differing views of the living room on one side and greenhouse on the other, extending beyond to adjoining corridors and rooms and further out to the landscape and sky. With a solid back at one end and open on its other two sides, the couch is also inherently compound – eliciting alternate ways to recline, from sitting up facing back to the stair to lying down and stretching one's legs while overlooking

Maurice Smith, Blackman House (1963),
Massachusetts, staircase landing and sofa above living
room (above) and beginning of entry portico (top)

the hearth. Quite apart from its explicit function, the staircase offers an open future in its choices of how to climb or rest, each alternative a real opportunity – not surprisingly, it became the owner's favourite place to read the morning newspaper. The scope of freedom afforded by this doubleness of motion/rest in a stair/seat calls to mind the staircase designed by H.H. Richardson for the Robert Treat Paine House in nearby Waltham (below), whose lower steps turn the corner to furnish a seat facing the entry, while the upward flight branches into a cozy alcove with an L-shaped bench, continually presenting the climber with more than one course of action.

Related double meanings at the Blackman House occur in the small but deftly detailed stairs to the lofts of each bedroom (opposite). These elevated sites to retreat, daydream, write or read expand the looseness and range of freedom within the bedroom, intensified by the dual appeal of a refuge that is also vantage point. The stairs themselves, whose steep, narrow and winding ascents call for modest feats of agility, offer more than a single role to perform, owing to the many small ledges and compartments beneath. Some areas are left open as shelves and others infilled with sliding drawers, so the stair is also a seat or table, bookcase or cabinet, an idea linked to the Japanese step chest (p. 150), whose drawers are tucked under a steep flight to the floor above. Underlying Smith's composite language is the art of collage, and it is not coincidental that small collages have afforded him a parallel medium to experiment with space. In its assemblage of overlapping fragments to make a whole, while exploiting the ambiguities of

H.H. Richardson, Robert Treat Paine House (1886),
Massachusetts, staircase with bench facing the door

things that are broken and half-seen, the collage invites its own evocative double-vision. One is able to imagine the whole from a part, and conjure up what lies beneath an overlay, recalling György Kepes's words about 'simultaneous perception' when a person employs both the physical eye and the mind's eye to see two or more things in the same location.

In the collages of Braque and, later, Kurt Schwitters, mysterious fragments interlock into larger forms to activate an inquisitive observer. Fractured elements taken out of their expected context exert a shock upon the eye and induce the viewer to participate in reconstructing the parts in their entirety. A diversity of elements – pasted strips of paper, newspaper clippings, playing cards and varying textures beyond those of paint itself – are arranged into a balanced and dynamic order. Of central importance is that this order can only come about through a creative leap of imagination, whereby the components begin to communicate with each another as well as the eye and mind observing them. In Smith's collages an analogous but more three-dimensional assemblage is developed out of strips, screws and bits of metal and glass, some on the surface and others elevated in air, and it is only a small jump from this structure to his buildings, where rooms are assembled from a tremendous array of jigsaw-like volumes and peppered with myriad corners and alcoves, all of which activate people through unexpected chance associations and interpretations.

The collage of architectural space is, of course, a more elusive and arguably more difficult art, for it requires a three- and four-dimensional overlap of conflated things, not merely of subjects for the eye, but also of actions for the body in space. This makes the buildings devised by Smith all the more impressive. Take the living room at Groton, for instance, its constellation of space no longer a 'room' in the conventional sense, for it is built up out of dozens of different virtual rooms whose components can never be singled out, sharply distinguished or fully grasped in a single glance. More important is its simultaneity of attractive actions, where a large group can gather as one in the overall volume, while smaller groups are equally comfortable

in alcoves or level changes that break up the unified space, and individuals can find their own ledges on which to perch or corners in which to retreat, allowing many people to be together and alone in many ways at once.

GIANCARLO DE CARLO'S PARTICIPATORY ARCHITECTURE
The additive forms of vernacular architecture, built up slowly over time by individual and collective wills, offered a model of humane accretion for architect Giancarlo de Carlo in his search for a 'participatory architecture'. His encouragement of people towards greater control over the buildings they inhabit, from the earliest stages of design to later occupation, is embodied in works ranging from the hillside dormitories for the University of Urbino and the diversely hollowed Magistero for its School of Education, to his multitiered Villaggio Matteotti for factory workers in Terni and colourful cubic housing on the island of Mazzorbo, near Venice.

Sumiya Pleasure House (1641), Kyoto, *kaidan-dansu* ('step chest')

De Carlo was deeply troubled over the waning of human influence in architecture, and the way in which oppressive and autocratic structures so often appropriated that power. 'The fundamental difference between an authoritarian architecture and an architecture of participation,' he remarked in an interview, 'is that the former begins with the premise that to solve a problem it is necessary to reduce its variables to a minimum, to make it constant and therefore controllable, while the latter calls into play as many variables as possible so that the result is multiple, open to change, rich in meanings that are accessible to everyone.'[93]

The first and still most impressive of De Carlo's experiments in composite structure is his dormitory for the Collegio del Colle (below), whose spatial form was strongly influenced by the Renaissance city of Urbino and, above all, the spontaneity of human choices along its footpaths.[94] The intent was not to reproduce the indigenous forms of a bygone era, but to learn from the way their multifarious routes accommodate timeless human actions and translate this energy into a contemporary idiom. While distinctly modern in shape and character, the Collegio del Colle is inscribed with many of the same projects and deeds as the pedestrian pathways of Urbino's steep hillsides.

Linking the splayed student rooms of the Collegio is a remarkable network of outdoor paths that step with the hillside (p. 152). There are many different routes a person can choose from while moving from one point to another, whether proceeding past or between clusters of rooms, descending to the parking below or climbing to the communal centre that forms a hub for the residential units fanning out on the slopes below. Each of the intersecting paths

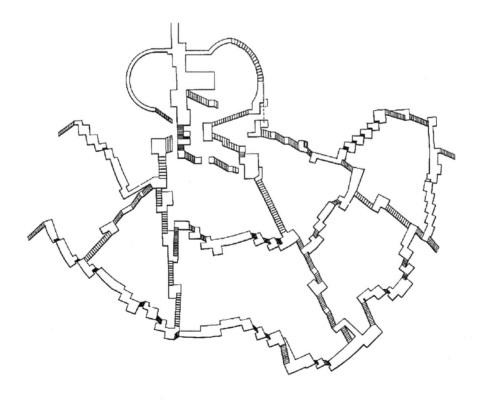

Giancarlo de Carlo, Collegio del Colle (1966), University of Urbino,
diagram of interlaced routes of stairs, terraces and bridges

is differentiated and made perceptible by concrete parapets with strong profiles. Some routes are direct and others discursive, with choices of mild or steep inclines, exposure to weather or shelter from rain, with each scenario slightly different in inward scenery and outward vistas to the countryside of Le Marche. Enhancing these deliberative powers are other contrasting qualities: routes that soar over bridges or burrow into earth; bends that widen into corners; and a persistent invitation to rest and sit upon benches in quiet alcoves (p. 116). The pathways are conceived not as narrow corridors, but as pedestrian streets where students are able to roam and manoeuvre on their own, or simply relax and congregate outside their rooms. The result is a network with hundreds of latent choreographies, each of which can be implemented freely, rather than predetermined as a forced or redundant move.

THE BINARY VALUES OF ALDO VAN EYCK

At the core of the ethos of architect Aldo van Eyck is a concept of doubleness based upon reciprocity. In reaction to the polarization of single values detached from and set against each other, epitomizing much of our current age and architecture, Van Eyck sought a binary fabric of 'multiple meanings', in which complementary qualities – large and small, light and shade, private and public – could be harmonized in a state of equipoise and 'intrinsic ambiguity'. The architectural means he developed to intermingle polar values was a configurative language he called the 'mild gears of reciprocity'. Rather than remaining isolated, contrasting qualities were integrated and made transparent to one another, so as to mutually enrich and cushion their experience.

Giancarlo de Carlo, Collegio del Colle (1966),
University of Urbino, alternate routes and choices for rest

The resulting structures are vaguely coherent but also diverse, and open to choice through equivocal readings in which some of each melds with the other. To characterize these compound properties, Van Eyck resorted to analogies from nature – the dual phenomena occurring, for instance, as water bathes the sand of a seashore (above left), as day and night shade into one another at twilight or a solar eclipse (above right), or as sunlight passes through a glass prism to fan into a spectrum of colours. Some of the surest embodiments of this idea are his tiniest works, such as the Sonsbeek Pavilion (p. 154), in Arnhem, Netherlands, and the entrance to the Schmela House and Gallery (p. 155) in Düsseldorf, where neighbouring worlds press into and interweave one another.

In his search for ambivalent meaning in architecture, Van Eyck found confirmation and a resource, as had fellow architects Frank Lloyd Wright, Maurice Smith, Herman Hertzberger and Giancarlo de Carlo, in folk cultures where dual-phenomena survive in humble, unpretentious forms. But he also drew on the simultaneity of twentieth-century art and its visualization of relativity, translating doubt into tangible form. Architecture inspired by these qualities was no longer absolute and fixed, but continually changing according to a person's own changing frame of reference. The boundaries between things are not sharp dividing lines, but interchanges in which each side and its properties mingle. Painters such as Cézanne, Mondrian, Georges Seurat and Robert Delaunay had long explored this view, as had artists from other fields including Constantin Brancusi, James Joyce and Arnold Schönberg, all of whom Van Eyck described as 'the entire Great Gang' (in which he also included architects Jan Duiker, Alvar Aalto and Le Corbusier). 'With breathtaking intelligence and artistry,' Van Eyck wrote, 'they too opened the field in which they worked and succeeded in tracing the outline of a world less strained – milder and more relative.'[95]

Lapping of sea and land along the Côte Sauvage, Brittany
(left) and in-between light of a solar eclipse (right)

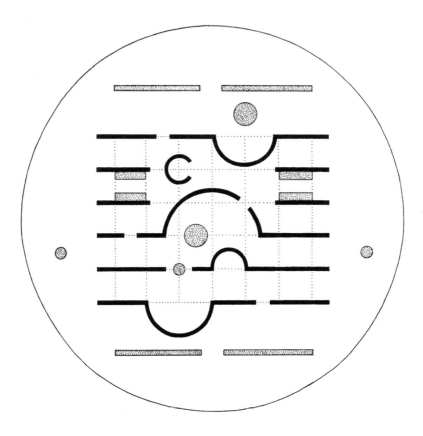

The significance of binary qualities for spatial action is that their qualities are inherently double and thus interpretive. Moreover, their complementary values mutually strengthen the appeal of each other. This interplay lies at the heart of Van Eyck's architecture, from the Hubertus House in Amsterdam (p. 156) to the ESTEC complex in Noordwijk, each conceived as a small city overflowing with opportunity. Rooms contain small nested zones of contrary but desirable character, and paths fork into alternate journeys with dissimilar but ever-hopeful futures. In a site as simple as the Hubertus entry, a person can move back and forth between being protected and exposed, and there are contrasting routes responsive to each direction of arrival, each with its own dual options to pause or rest, and each with its own foresight into the glassy walls of the building or, when departing, overlooks out to the city. These rich provisions of self-control culminate in the children's dwellings, where every boundary is interactive, pushing and pulling on neighbouring space to overlap associations and meanings, and diversify the ambience for gathering or eating, working or sleeping.

Aldo van Eyck, Sonsbeek Pavilion
(1966), Netherlands, plan

The reciprocal values that reverberate through Van Eyck's church in The Hague
(p. 157) are not dissimilar to the compound space of the City of God created by masons
in medieval Europe, but their character has been utterly transformed by emancipation
from axial control and repeating bays, and more generally from religious command and
rhetoric. Every spatial and material component is inscribed with alternate readings, whose
ambiguity is perplexing and provocative. Passage occurs through a tall transept with
multiple points to enter the sanctuary, while negotiating a floor that continually flows off
to the side to mingle with neighbouring space. The route is bordered with semi-cylindrical
chapels that straddle boundaries, being half in the transept and half in the sanctuary, their
curving volumes half open and half closed, each supplying a small domain to withdraw
from other worshippers and rest in private contemplation.

This leitmotif of double-vision reappears in almost every detail. The altar is set on
a piece of transept floor that penetrates into the sanctuary. Piers between transept and
sanctuary, moving and settling, fork into columns that rise separately to support roofs at

either side of contrasting height. Great cylindrical skylights extend half below and half above the roof plane, while dividing incident light into yellow sun and violet sky. Though echoing the myriad choices for movement and prayer in a Gothic cathedral, Van Eyck also attacks his model by eroding its spiritual authority: defining while breaking and scattering axes; establishing and then loosening control of the altar; eliminating any prescribed path to God. Gone is any burdening dogma, ordained propaganda or spatial directive, replacing gravitas with a playfulness that raises more questions than it answers.

Aldo van Eyck, Hubertus House (1981),
Amsterdam, entrance portico

Aldo van Eyck, Catholic Church (1969), The Hague, interplay
of transept, chapels and sanctuary (above) and semicylindrical
chapel straddling the border of transept and sanctuary (top)

Wachigaiya geisha house (1680), Kyoto, multiple
layers of open grillwork protect *shoji* on two storeys

4

depths of discovery

Among our inherent traits as human beings is an irrepressible curiosity about the world, expressed through an urge to investigate things around us that are intensely entrancing and promising, but also mysterious and largely unknown. When buildings are endowed with intriguing depths open to human discovery - residual spaces and enigmatic details, spaces fogged over by screens or membranes, provocative glimpses and inviting trails into the future - they grant a precious power to scrutinize and explore one's environment. Architecture such as this can never be completely exhausted of wonders or reduced to an object or commodity, for there is always a sense of something enchanting that is waiting for us to reveal its presence through the force of our searching, enabling us to delve into the world and find things out for ourselves.

Where hidden depths of architectural space allow us to probe and reveal their secrets, we become active seekers, rather than mere occupants or users of space (above and opposite). There is a sense of unknown country ahead, in which the adventurous spirit can work and from which it may continue forward. In the course of this inquiry, our acts bring to light unexpected reserves of our world that intrigue *us* and that *we* are able to freshly disclose, transforming the experience of architecture into a quest.

Unfortunately, this exploratory power has largely vanished from the architecture of the past century, to the point that we barely notice its absence apart from a vague awareness that buildings have grown increasingly shallow and explicit, devoid of the kind of promising questions that spark human scrutiny. A common but highly deceptive example is the largely transparent and overexposed volume of glass. While fully open to our gaze, there is nothing left unrevealed, no concealed depths or secluded corners to investigate. Equally demeaning is a space devoid of fascinating yet elusive features – details that recede from our grasp and resist being quickly resolved, or windows that blur and fog the space beyond – the absence of which leaves us with nothing of interest to study and disclose. Making us equally ineffective are spaces such as linear sidewalks or repetitive cells, so uniform that any course of investigation would lead to the same fixed, inevitable conclusion. In each instance we have been condemned to a predetermined experience, one divested of mystery and indifferent to our presence.

The inverse of total exposure guarantees fatalism in a different manner. When desirable spaces are sealed up and removed from view by solid façades or closed compartments, all incentives to examine the world are erased and architecture is closed to discovery. Spaces we might want to find could be present, but we are denied the power to detect them. When

Via Maestà delle Volte at sunrise, Perugia

opportunities of this kind exist but are totally hidden, obscuring any chance to recognize and disclose them, they are effectively buried opportunities. A more degrading means of thwarting human inquiry is to present opportunities that beckon from afar, and then deny access through barriers or a lack of trails to pursue. When this kind of attraction – such as a restaurant when we wish to dine or library when in search of a book – seduces us from a distance but can't be reached, it obstructs our pursuit of something we desire, even though we see it and wish to find it. These are thwarted opportunities, all too familiar to people with disabilities, which both tantalize and block human initiative. I am not suggesting that private space should be public, rather that private space should be less deceitful and public space more open to action.

It is important to mention one last form of human frustration – the detached architectural spectacle – for though it is less overtly insulting it is more insidious in deflating our powers, demonstrating again the crucial distinction between *energetic actions* and *passive reactions* to something externally caused and controlled. Consider the disturbing obsession of so many architects and critics with the sculptural display of façades and skyscrapers that we are meant to ogle but not enter, turning buildings into a form of public exhibitionism. We are frozen in place before these stylish objects, since there is no incentive or reward to our movement. Like theatregoers stuck in our seats and bombarded with stimuli, we may *passively react* but not *creatively respond* to the building before us. No matter how impressive

Discovery of the Piazza del Campo, Siena

and exciting these objects may be, if they fail to respond to our curiosity and encourage us to probe their mysteries, they are fundamentally dehumanizing.

Thankfully, there is a long history of architecture rich in exploratory freedom to point a way out of this culture of enervation. I am referring to buildings that, irrespective of their function or context, continue at every encounter to fascinate people about what is ahead and reward their curiosity by opening up breaches and depths to seek out, cultivating a spirit of inquiry. Our self-affirmation in this kind of structure derives from the investigative roles we are offered, and the powers we are given to track down and reveal things of importance through our own endeavours. We begin to divulge something important about ourselves: that we are curious about and involved in the world; that we are living forces venturing in space; and that we are agents able to carry out pursuits according to our own concerns.

SECRETS OF RESIDUAL SPACE

The simplest kinds of discovery occur in accessible but concealed space that is just beyond the limits of a room and marginal to its primary functions. These outskirts include the 'detached linings' and 'residual spaces' identified by Robert Venturi, such as the in-between depths of poché in thick walls, but they also include less-visited zones above or below the everyday realm of a building.[96] The climb up to an unfinished attic or descent into a dark cellar is never an entry to neutral space, but a venturing into uncertain depths where anything could happen. These domains are secluded from daily life and harbour their own memories and secrets, touching a nerve deep in the psyche that magnifies our sense of adventure.

Among the most common marginal zones are closets and cupboards, their voids concealed but also marked by the handles and outlines of doors. No matter how familiar they seem, these hollows retain a capacity of surprise, for in opening them we reveal them anew, along with the things stored inside. The contents might be different than remembered and the space has a startling freshness when brought to light. In *The Poetics of Space*, Bachelard considers the psychological depths found in these recesses to be 'very evident witnesses of the *need for secrecy*, of an intuitive sense of hiding places'. But these places, he continues, 'are objects *that may be opened*. When a casket is closed, it is returned to the general community of objects; it takes its place in exterior space. But it opens! For this reason, a philosopher-mathematician would say that it is the first differential of discovery.'[97]

These marginal spaces are normally so mundane they fail to stimulate our curiosity. But that is not the case in Shaker architecture, where a zeal for order and cleanliness led to intricate forms of built-in storage that suggest while extolling the promise within.[98] This allure is enhanced by woodwork, often stained yellow or orange, set off by the austerity of pure white rooms, as seen in the Church Family Dwelling (opposite) in Hancock, Massachusetts. The skylit attic, discovered not by dull ascent but by a momentous climb into falling light, often contains the most captivating storage units. In the attic of the Church Family Dwelling House in Canterbury, New Hampshire, there are over eighty drawers and seven walk-in closets: the yellow-stained pine wall is circumspect yet abundant with clues such as prominent joints around the compartments and handsomely turned wooden knobs.

Deepening the mystery of certain closets are cavities nested inside one another, with doors leading to more hidden rooms with their own concealed cabinets, like Chinese boxes set within boxes.

A related impulse in Japanese culture – to keep interiors simple and calm – inspired an art of residual space that permeates every part of its architecture, bringing an air of uncertainty as much to a teahouse or farmhouse as to an elaborate villa. The entire building constitutes, in a sense, a complex of secrets hidden behind a baffling array of sliding screens (p. 164). The layers resist extreme openness or closure, while supplying clues to the space beyond. The reticent mood is strengthened further by rooms that are free of association with a single function, in contrast to Western rooms that are assigned to, for instance, sleeping or eating. One can never be sure about what lies in a neighbouring room, in terms of occupants or activities, for it might be employed for meditation, congregation or work.

Church Family Dwelling (1831), Massachusetts, yellow-stained
cupboards and cabinets made from butternut and pine

The *fusuma* themselves are inscrutable, since those that serve as partitions between rooms are identical in appearance to those used for closet doors. A person might slide open a screen thinking it is a closet, only to find it opens to another room. Even a closet inspires doubt, for there is no indication of whether it contains books or bedlinen. When surrounded by screens to what may be a neighbouring room, storage closet or veranda, people are prompted to imagine what lies ahead, to hesitate before disclosing a space. Indeed, it is difficult to find a single wall in a Japanese house that does not contain some sort of space hidden within or behind it, creating a world that is highly receptive to revelation but also intrusion, by the gentlest stroke of a hand.

JAPANESE GRILLES AND BLINDS

A more pervious source of curiosity in the folk architecture of Japan is the wood lattice, whose porosity is carefully adjusted to haze over views while retaining the needed degree of privacy. Derived from a practical need to regulate the flow of light and air, these woven screens also appeal to a cultural preference for reserve and intimation, rather than outward display. Facing the external world, especially village streets, are grilles assembled from hundreds of narrow wooden slats, culminating in the *senbon-goshi*, or 'thousand-fingered' lattice (p. 158). Softer, more delicate screens face the innermost private garden, including gauzy *sudare* that gently atomize scenes beyond. As a result, the interior, especially in summer, is enveloped by meshes of varied filtration, each serving a different role in sifting light while admitting breezes, and protecting rooms from prying eyes through walls that mystify rather than expose or divide.

Juko-in Temple (1566), Daitoku-ji, Kyoto, *fusuma* with
screenpaintings by Kano Eitoku divide rooms and cover recesses

The intrigue of the Japanese lattice lies in the fact that it stimulates our visual questioning of the world; we can glimpse just enough of what lies beyond to excite our perceptual faculties (below). The contours and features of what we see have been half-erased and finely broken up by the intervening medium, making them more bewitching and giving added creative force to the eye by leaving something unseen to discover. In renouncing visual certitude and its predetermined facts, the wooden veil enlivens both the imagination, by affording it extra room to manoeuvre, and spatial action, for the filtration alters slightly with every step or turn of the head, keeping us involved and urging us on with the thrill of detection and the lure of something faintly forbidden. Though such deliberately imperfect views may frustrate the rational eye by deleting part of the literal world, it is precisely this loss that activates us as seekers and finders, giving us nothing but offering us everything.

These marvellous old veiling effects have been revived as a source of power by architect Kengo Kuma, who retains much of their timeless value while adapting them to modern technology. Especially convincing in drawing upon yet transcending the past is the densely woven and multilayered cedar lattice that partitions and covers his design for the Bato Hiroshige Museum. Changing views through the lattice, according to angle and motion, envelop the museum in what Kuma describes as a 'cloud of particles floating in the landscape', evoking a world fogged by rain or mist, as often depicted in the *ukiyo-e* woodblock prints of the artist Utagawa Hiroshige.[99]

Yoshijima House, Takayama, rear garden viewed
through *sudare* dappled with sun and cast shadows

Today, a more common source of secrecy is a membrane of finely perforated metal stretched across a sensitive boundary, as in the filmy envelopes of punched aluminium by Toyo Ito, Itsuko Hasegawa, Kazuyo Sejima and Jun Aoki. Interiors are secluded behind veils that are seductively luminous, their allure strengthened by evocative silhouettes or moiré effects from layering, persuading us to actively question their mysteries, which continue to change and emerge for the moving eye. Parallel sheets of glistening aluminium with cloud-like silhouettes and the interference patterns of overlapped sheets, for instance, covered Hasegawa's interior pavilion for the 1989 World Design Expo in Nagoya to suggest a floating mist full of vague impressions, an experience that resonates with the vaporous atmosphere of Japan. Though shimmering and industrial, and no longer dark and rustic, the burnished webs continue to express a preference for space wrapped in enigmas and capable of revelation.

An especially convincing inducement to exploration is the perforated skin of the Tepia Science Pavilion in Tokyo (above), whose architect Fumihiko Maki has stated: 'The illusion that there can be secret places must be maintained.' Large but very thin hangings of punched aluminium are inserted between inside and outside, turning the boundaries between city and building into beguiling curtains. Whether looking in or out, the space beyond is thrown out of

Fumihiko Maki, Tepia Science Pavilion (1989), Tokyo, perforated aluminium membrane with hazy view to staircase and street

focus and ground into fine particles of light, allowing the detection of indistinct shapes with fuzzy outlines and diluted colours that can only be resolved by taking action in space. Though we infer what lies ahead, we can never quite grasp it, and it sinks back into the veiled light as we try to fix or isolate it, attracting and leading us on.

FOREST-LIKE VENTURES

Though rarely as nuanced as their Japanese counterparts, Western screens have also played a dual role in providing seclusion while stimulating inquiry. Frank Lloyd Wright's inclination to overlay windows with complex webbings of leaded glass, epitomized at the Dana House in Springfield, Illinois (p. 168, top), creates an experience far exceeding surface delight, for it motivates the curious eye and adventurous soul. Geometric filigrees of slender, dark lines, obscured further by small panes of autumnal colour in complex patterns of chevrons and rectangles, are meant not only to *look at*, but also *see through*, gazing at the world as if through abstract prairie vegetation, echoing a primeval experience. 'By means of glass something of the freedom of our arboreal ancestors living in their trees becomes a likely precedent for freedom in twentieth-century life,' Wright wrote in his autobiography.[100] When peering through one of these 'light screens', as Wright called them, the space beyond is defocused and filled with both doubt and allure, retaining intimacy while inciting action.

These primeval associations would also seem to underlie the timber screens characterizing modern Finnish architecture, which derive in part from the availability of wood but also from a mode of perception that evolved in the northern forest. The infinitely fractured light and view when filtered through densely packed trunks and branches must have shaped the way the Finns see their world. The simultaneous ability to hide and seek, which largely determined human survival in the distant past, is maximized – especially in glaciated Finland – at the forest edges of clearings and lakes, where people can gaze out at the world from sites of filtered retreat and adjust this balance by simply moving back and forth, controlling the view of space beyond while minimizing their own detection.

Alvar Aalto, an early master of these atavistic powers, wrapped the most transitional zones of buildings – entrances, stairs, doors and windows – with baffles and poles. These vulnerable sites are thus given an intermingling of shelter and adventure, a forest theme that reaches its peak at the Villa Mairea (p. 168, bottom) in Noormarkku, Finland. The forest abstraction of layered slats that haze over space with splintered views continues to the present day as a central feature of many Finnish masterworks, from the Otaniemi Chapel by Kaija and Heikki Sirén to the more recent museums and schools of architectural firm Kaira-Lahdelma-Mahlamäki and the churches in Laajasalo by Järvinen & Nieminen and in Viikki by JKMM, all of which exude an air of mystery but also discovery.

As in Japan, the activated vision of veiled space is being reinvented in Finland with industrial meshes and thin steel framing, most persuasively in the skeletal fringes of Erkki Kairamo and shimmering grids of Heikkinen-Komonen, whose Rovaniemi Airport Terminal is largely defined by an ever-finer gradation of lattice along the journey from entry to flight. Inspired by the scrims of artist Robert Irwin and his aim to 'dissolve the object in the subject',

Alvar Aalto, Villa Mairea (1941), Finland, wooden poles and forest light of staircase (above); Frank Lloyd Wright, Dana House (1902), Illinois, leaded glass doors between corridor and reception space (top)

Heikkinen-Komonen used diaphanous screens to both puzzle and fuel vision.[101] A trail of exploration develops on the way to departure lounges by passing through spaces wrapped with increasingly denser lines and smaller holes, from airy screens to fine meshes, turning the short trek into a searching journey. The closer one gets to the moment of flight, the more one probes through vaporous images – building anticipation for the adventure to come.

THE MYSTERY OF SHADOWS

A human fascination with light has often diminished the appreciation of darkness, both its bewitching moods and way it can turn a fixed reality into one that is less distinct. Murky air obscures the limits of space, shrouding the definite contours of objects and pulling their shapes out of focus, lending the eye extra powers to actively search something unknown.

The capacity of shadows mixed with faint light to elicit feelings of *mysterium tremendum*, to use the phrase of Rudolf Otto, led to its playing a central role in the sacred architecture of most religions, and was fully exploited over the centuries by builders of churches, temples and shrines.[102] But beyond this mystical power, and provision of a symbolic death that made spiritual renewal possible, the cloaking of visible things in shade has the simpler and more immediate virtue of stirring the imagination, for as objects and space are half-obscured they lose their inevitability. This freedom from established fact can appear in both secular and spiritual spaces, and in landscapes and cities, as well as buildings, for anywhere shadows introduce doubt they also create a chance for fresh disclosure.

In his splendid book *In Praise of Shadows*, Jun'ichirō Tanizaki discusses the importance of shadows in every aspect of Japanese culture, from poetry and food to ceramics and architecture. The heavy darkness contained within an old farmhouse, primitive tearoom or lonely mountain temple creates a place of vaguely sensed things that seem caught in a dream-like or formative state (p. 170). Dark woodwork and paper screens gradually soak up the excess light, causing voluminous ceilings to dim, where only bits of beam and ceiling flicker in the blackness. The eye picks up hints of sensuous textures, sometimes a glint of bamboo or flash of gold, but struggles to make them out. Any conclusive or absolute reality is eroded, absorbed into dusky secrets that urge seeking while eluding measurement or logic.

The quiet simplicity and lack of adornment in a traditional Japanese room is misleading, Tanizaki insists, unless one considers what has emerged as a primary presence within the void: a play of infinitely graduated shadows. While physically vacant to an objective eye and mind, the bare room contains an elusive something the eye can't grasp or the mind comprehend. 'An empty space is marked off with plain wood and plain walls, so that the light drawn into it forms dim shadows within emptiness,' he writes. 'And yet, when we gaze into the darkness that gathers beyond the crossbeam, around the flower vase, beneath the shelves, though we know perfectly well it is mere shadow, we are overcome with the feeling that in this small corner of the atmosphere there reigns complete and utter silence … Where lies the key to this mystery? Ultimately it is the magic of shadows. Were the shadows to be banished from its corners, the alcove would in that instant revert to mere void.'[103]

Fushin-an teahouse, Omote-senke,
Kyoto, dimly lit interior

An equally palpable darkness developed in the medieval churches of the West, from the Norwegian stave church, whose black-tarred wood is barely lit by tiny high windows, to the cavernous shadows of a Romanesque church (above) or twilit Gothic cathedral, in each case offering something precious to human contemplation and scrutiny. Long after pupils adjust in these intensely dark sanctuaries, a person must still move about with caution by feeling a path through spaces resistant to outward sight, as if embarked upon a nocturnal journey in search of a world that can only be dimly and slowly gleaned by persistent searching over time.

While Renaissance churches onwards tend to be clearly bathed in light, a venturesome darkness reappeared in a few sacred works of the twentieth century. At Ronchamp, La Tourette and Firminy, Le Corbusier employed frail light not to eradicate shadows, but to stimulate wonder. The same is true of a few Scandinavian churches, whose eloquent darkness is fertile to our inquisitive powers. Among the high points in this line of descent are the dark brick churches of Peter Celsing, notably Härlanda Church in Gothenburg, Sweden; Viljo Revell's Vatiala Chapel in Kangasala and Aarno Ruusuvuori's Huutoniemi Church in Vaasa, both in Finland; and the Islev Church in Copenhagen and Nørre Uttrup Church in Aalborg, Denmark, by Inger and Johannes Exner.[104]

Vézelay Abbey (12th century), France,
dark narthex with triple portals

The most astonishing quests into darkness from the past century are two Nordic churches, from whose dense shadows eerie things emerge under the force of a searching eye: St Peter's in Klippan, Sweden, by Sigurd Lewerentz; and St Hallvard in Oslo by Lund & Slaatto. As we push visually into the heavy gloom at the former, we begin to make out the baptismal font of a huge white seashell (below), which draws the eye to a wave in the floor with a dark slot into which drips of water fall. Other strange features appear unexpectedly, most intriguingly a huge column of rusted steel at the centre of the nave, from which crossbeams spread to support the roof (opposite). Waiting to be discovered at St Hallvard is something equally startling: a convex ceiling that *presses down* into the darkness, as if the heavens themselves had pushed into the sanctuary. The most important elements of these churches are not expressed apart from our presence, nor are they noticed at first, but are revealed gradually without ever being visually exhausted. Though shadows do not fully destroy reality, they erode its control, converting rational objects into brooding subjects for the imagination.

While the suitability of darkness for religious architecture is more easily argued, could there also be secular settings where its mysteries are appropriate today? According to Alvar

Aalto the answer is yes, as he demonstrates so touchingly at the Säynätsalo Town Hall. The intensely dark council chamber is reached by a faintly toplit staircase, culminating a journey that began at the outermost steps in the landscape, and ends in a room that stimulates thoughts on the birth of democracy and its need for continued renewal. Light is cut down and warmed as it filters through pine-baffled windows, throwing a pleasing cloak of shade over the room, to slowly reveal for a patient eye the fan-shaped trusses overhead, supporting the roof like so many coordinated fingers.

A recent affirmation of secular darkness is Peter Zumthor's Therme Vals in Switzerland, its secret cavities calling to mind dark tunnels and magical caverns found in the earth (pp. 174-5). Hidden within the half-buried and dimly lit monolith are a number of mysterious stone chambers, each containing a secluded bath unique in qualities of light and sound, aroma and temperature. We are invited to search out these hidden places and then leisurely savour their sensory pleasures, in whatever sequence suits us – whether the Fire Bath or Cold Bath, Flower Bath or Sound Bath, Indoor Bath or Outdoor Bath.

We can at best guess the location of these hidden marvels concealed in shadow; to find them, we must set off through a trickle of falling light to explore folds in the tactile stonework, feeling our way through darkness by trial and error to disclose each newly enchanting room. The arrival becomes less important than the journey, for we get lost in the slow adventure. In commenting on these unhurried routes from pool to pool, described as 'the meander', Zumthor notes, 'it was incredibly important for us to induce a sense of freedom of movement,

Sigurd Lewerentz, St Peter's Church (1966), Sweden,
rusted steel structure obscured in darkness (above) and
baptismal font with mollusc shell (opposite)

Peter Zumthor, Therme Vals (1996), Switzerland,
descent into the underground caverns (above) and
beckoning space and light (opposite)

a milieu for strolling, a mood that has less to do with directing people than seducing them …
I'd be standing there, and might just stay awhile, but then something would be drawing me
round the corner – it was the way the light falls, over here, over there: and so I saunter on …
in a kind of voyage of discovery.'[105]

FOGGED IMAGES IN TRANSLUCENT WALLS

The seductive appeal of space melting into an uncertain glow, with soothing yet evocative
depths that incite inquiry, lies at the heart of Japan's indigenous architecture. Each backlit
boundary of white paper *shoji* behaves as a shadow-box, or rear-projection screen, on
which appear vague impressions of nature, conveying an amorphous yet fascinating world
open to human interpretation. Superimposed on the more nebulous images are slightly
firmer shadows cast by nearby vegetation or bamboo blinds, along with the crisper, denser
black lines of the thin wooden lattice on which paper is pasted. These overlays become
more compact on *shitajimado*, but further enriched by irregular shadows cast from reeds or
bamboo. In each of these membranes, fact is transformed into possibility, and concrete things
are replaced by elusive shadows, liberated from certainty. Space is compressed into two
dimensions, in the manner of a photogram, and no longer perspectival. We are amazed by
this evocative world, and spurred to look more closely, to ponder its mysteries by searching
with the moving eye and reaching back into the imagination.

If the amorphous images on paper screens could only be gazed upon as fixed
impressions, they would incite little power of action beyond quiet contemplation. Crucial
to their capacity for discovery is the way in which their contents and depths transform with
proximity. Randomly interwoven fibres appear in the paper as one draws near, as do slight
tonal variations of every scale, neither of which are evident from afar (opposite). Moreover,
with *shoji* the searching need not end at the membrane, for the screen can be opened to
suddenly expose a previously intimated world – disclosing the weather or angle of the sun,
the garden and landscape, encouraging one to step onto the veranda and assess newly
emergent possibilities. In other words, the screen's mystery offers a beginning rather
than end, a threshold rather than limit, transforming us from submissive audience to
active seekers.

The inexhaustible mysteries achieved in the past with paper screens are being
reconceived in glass by a number of Japanese architects. A particularly deft skill with this
medium has been demonstrated by Hiroshi Hara, who etches sheets of glass with suggestive
images of lines, dots, webs and circles, at times transparent figures on a translucid ground
and at other times the reverse. Complicating these impressions is the way in which he then
folds the glass wall into a many-pleated membrane. The optic effects of various layers are
superimposed, increasing their elusiveness and response to each person's vision and motion.
Rational space becomes diffused and broken up by the ricocheted light, including reflected
images from afar appearing on some angles of glass, an intermingling of reality and fiction
that culminates in Hara's Kenju Park 'Forest House' in Nakaniida and the Iida City Museum,
both in Japan.

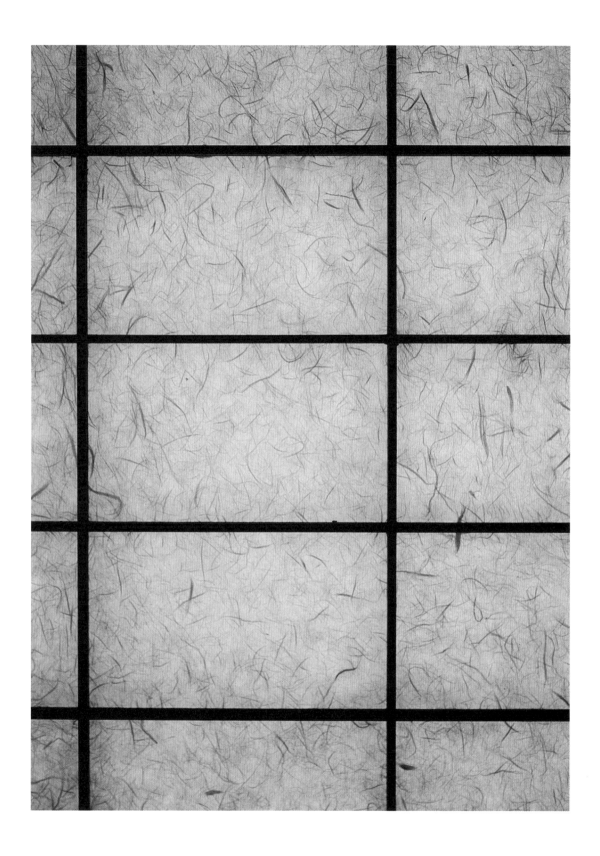

Hosen-in Temple, Ohara, detail of paper fibres in *shoji*

As elusive but more ethereal and understated are the curving glass walls of SANAA's Glass Pavilion at the Toledo Museum of Art (below), which exploit the capacity of glass to behave as both lens and mirror. As a visitor's eye roams about the interior, it peers through each undulant veil in search of exhibits or demonstrations. But superimposed on these views are the transported and slightly distorted impressions of neighbouring rooms with their own glass displays and human occupants, whose images have been warped and rearranged by the curvatures. A person might stumble on something attractive to pursue, only to have it fogged and invaded by enticements from unexpected locations, whose ghostly trail can be followed according to one's interests, route of perusal and speed in space.

One might imagine these optical intrigues are too subtle for Western architects, but this was disproved almost a century ago by the Maison de Verre, owing perhaps to the influence of architect Bernard Bijvoët, Chareau's collaborator, who had worked with Dutch architect Jan Duiker on his glass masterpiece, the Zonnestraal Sanatorium in Hilversum. Reality in the Maison de Verre is repeatedly fogged by assorted kinds of translucent glass under the influence of changing light, keeping their vague images fresh and able to sustain curiosity. The power of disclosure is most pronounced in the large walls of Nevada glass lenses (opposite), whose individual shapes are neither flat nor uniform, but indented and textured at three different scales. The translucid grid of dark steel and luminous squares seen from afar resolves at mid-range to a pattern of slightly concave circles; closer, a lemon-peel texture creates its own plastic impression. Finally, as the eye is brought up to the glass, it finds

SANAA, Glass Pavilion (2006), Toledo Museum of Art,
Ohio, superimposed, reflected and warped images

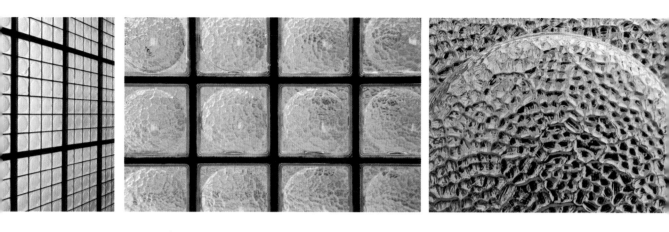

thousands of newly refracted glints in tiny gem-like facets – miniature highlights set against shadows, which on clear days are painted in a pointillist pattern of yellow sun and violet sky.

INTRICACY AND PATINA

The provisions for discovery in translucent windows, when possessing multiple scales responsive to changing viewpoints, raise the question as to whether similar powers could be inspired by opaque walls? Here, as well, the building art of Japan seems to point the way in its graduated range of details, possessing every scale. The searching eye in almost any part of a traditional building is able to find ever-new features in the same location, and when drawing near can detect and gaze into a microworld that resists any complete exposure and termination of action. Richly tectonic yet anonymous forms, freed from excessive control by their builders' persona, give the observing eye tremendous leeway in making its own startling disclosures, as if roaming through an uncharted landscape.

The intricate construction of an old Japanese teahouse, temple or shrine, or imperial villa such as Katsura or Shugaku-in, contains large features the eye can best detect from a distance, but offers new and ever-emerging attributes as it draws near, brought to light by each person's action. These powers are especially strong in buildings that embody the rustic simplicity refined and celebrated in the tea culture. Walls, floors and ceilings of natural materials have inherently scalar textures, often built up from overlaid elements that present a richly plaited structure with its own microperspective of receding layers. Additional scales of detail are found in highly visible joints and fastenings, and in the way the inherent grain of materials has been enhanced by human craft. The extraordinary depth of surface and assemblage in a bamboo ceiling or stone pavement continues to surprise at every new viewing angle or distance, disclosing something fresh for the eye. Weathering and use over time – the bleaching of the sun, splatter of rainfall, overgrowths of moss or lichen and erosion by human feet or weather – only magnify these depths further with patinas the Japanese conserve and treasure.

Pierre Chareau with Bernard Bijvoët, Maison de Verre (1931), Paris,
detail emerging with viewer proximity on Nevada glass lenses

Shimogamo Shrine, Kyoto, fence of bamboo branches; Imperial Pathway,
Katsura Imperial Villa, Kyoto, mosaic pavement of blue-black cobbles;
Sa-an teahouse, Gyokurin-in Temple, Daitoku-ji, Kyoto, earthen wall with
straw mixed into a blackened crust over reddish clay; Imperial Gate,
Katsura Imperial Villa, bamboo ceiling supported on a ridge beam
180   of unstripped oak (clockwise from top left)

Even something as monolithic as an earthen wall is transformed by Japanese hands into a realm of unlimited discovery. While the earthen mass may be simple, its surface opens up to human inquiry through a heterogeneous composition and a crust that is brittle, cracked and abraded. The granular texture and mingled colours of different clay and soil are complicated by small bits of straw, and in the walls of teahouses such as Taian at the Myokian Temple and Sa-an at the Gyokurin-in Temple (opposite, bottom right) in Kyoto, these small stalks protrude from an earthy substrate to imply unseen strata below. As the harmonious yet seemingly infinite depths – as involving as a landscape seen from the air or, conversely, through a magnifying glass – continue receding before an advancing eye, they embody the notion of life as a process, opening up a world in which people can probe beyond the outermost surface of reality.

The most iconic wall of this kind, the rammed-earth perimeter of the dry garden (*kare sansui*) at the Ryoan-ji Temple (above) in Kyoto, is also the most stimulating. Clays employed in the 'oil-earth wall', as it is called, were boiled in rapeseed oil to make them more durable. Over the years this oil has gradually leached out, along with the uneven iron content of the clay, to stain the surface with evocative patterns of subtle brown and orange tones mixed with cool greys. The abstract images are not static but change with viewing distance and angle, at every moment eluding logic while delighting human intuition.[106]

The investigative powers at Ryoan-ji are related to the more evocative crusts of twentieth-century art, from the haphazard scratches and earthen grounds of Jean Dubuffet and textured pigments of Antoni Tàpies to the peeling paint, eroded wood and abraded objects in the exquisitely detailed photographs of Edward Weston and Minor White. Materials conducive to impacts of time and weather have been seemingly infused with their own experiences and memories, turning the surface into a site for inspired vision and for active searching, inducing us to move closer and closer, to visually dig into and under the external skin. Beneath its rational operations, a liberated play of the mind is urged to probe the mysteries found before us, and to plumb one's own inner depths to disclose an unconscious pool of memories or make astonishing discoveries in the imagination. A mouldy wall might be simply a wall, or it might allow us to peer into its history, perhaps becoming a vast mountain range, its splash of brightness a molten planet or field of stars.

TINY IMMENSITY

Our ability to uncover new aspects of the world by the force of our own voluntary acts vanishes in a building whose features are either so scant or unchanging that there is no incentive to draw us near. The sterile volume declares at the outset it is not worth exploring, whereas eye-catching features that fail to mutate with differing viewpoints assure us more slowly, but no less completely, that we are mere spectators to a preordained display. Either scenario negates our existence and denies us the chance to take control of our immediate future, rather than having that future defined in advance by somebody else.

In sharp contrast to these deadening structures are buildings whose parts are related to the whole and display pattern inside pattern, allowing them to alter and reveal new depths. Close examination may be rewarded by something as small as a floorboard or stepping stone in a Japanese house or garden (opposite, left), or as large as the béton brut of La Tourette (opposite, right), whose monolithic walls were impressed with multiple scales of texture. The appearance of each begins to transform as we draw near, as if its smallest elements were lying in wait to further encourage our energetic inquiry. We are drawn into a playful game of hide and seek as we move about, advancing to examine it more closely and then stepping back, to see it in context, only to detect something new that was previously imperceptible. Such things are always incomplete in a perceptual sense, for as one pattern appears another disappears, and thus can only be grasped over time by a highly creative mind's eye.

Recursive architecture of this kind is open to discovery at many scales relative to each person's height, age and agility, not to mention curiosity and interest. It is incomprehensibly small and unimaginably large at once. It is both tiny and immense, containing what is large in something small, and something small in what is large. In a sense it lacks scale, for it contains important features at all sizes. As we draw closer, we may discern ever-smaller details of interest, but also find that beguiling new depths have come into view. Miniscule features and hollows appear and then expand as we near them, only to recede into unfamiliar realms of space, inviting us into their secret universe – 'to see the world in a grain of sand', as William Blake wrote. Microcosmic textures and joints, or infinitely minute details set inside other details, transport us into a kingdom that never fully releases its treasures, granting us the power to endlessly explore and rediscover them anew.

Obviously this scope of freedom requires something more than vacancy or bland repetition or, at the other extreme, sculptural bravado or lavish decoration, which remains unresponsive to our presence. The human potential of miniature things depends on what

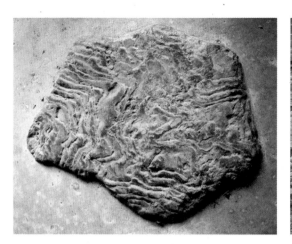

we can freely make of them, on the exploratory range and elasticity they offer us. But it also depends on a degree of anonymity to loosen details from the stylistic control of their maker, from our being reduced to the complacent audience of someone's creative excess and end product. When granted the power to enter something tiny that has been left open to our imagination, we experience what Bachelard considers an 'inversion of perspective', a 'source of freedom' especially abundant in nature, as when peering into the infinite depths of a tuft of grass or vein of a leaf, or in finding a compressed world in a glowing planet in the night sky.[107] This power in which the imagination serves as a human faculty, he argues, underlies in part the delight of small toys, taking us back to childhood.

While not physically small, the reiterated forms of a Gothic cathedral are so self-embedded as tiny hollows set into medium-size voids within monumental cavities that the entire structure appears in a state of fluctuation, now shrinking and now expanding. Every element displays recursion across many different scales (p. 184). Huge piers break down into clustered columns and thin colonnettes, and these into countless vertical lines. A single large bay sprouts into increasingly smaller repetitions of the same basic form, and by this gradation remains plastic with change and ever-responsive to human scrutiny.

The peak in a Gothic propagation of images, where what is small becomes large and vice versa, occurs in stained-glass windows (p. 185). Lancet windows echo the spatial forms around them, but also contain figures and landscapes with fresh details that continue emerging the closer the eye. What first appears a uniform colour is found to be pieced together from many different shades of the same basic hue, presenting a multitude of mosaic-like spots, whose internal facets can never be completely disclosed, even when inches away. Huge rose windows shatter into radiating sherds and fragments, each of which can absorb the eye in a squinting investigation of its mottled colours and gem-like complexity. As the observer moves back to grasp the whole window, or moves close to take in its detail, vision is ratcheting back and forth, widening to take in the breadth and then zeroing in to make out the source of a miraculous glitter that keeps receding out of reach.

Outer Arbour, Katsura Imperial Villa, Kyoto, geologic depths of a stepping stone, set into a floor of pounded earth (left); Le Corbusier, La Tourette (1960), Éveux, rain gutter and concrete imprinted with rough formwork in the east wall (right)

In *Heavenly Mansions and Other Essays on Architecture*, John Summerson proposes the cathedral is essentially an 'aedicular fantasy', whose attraction, stemming from multiple bays of 'little houses', is rooted in our 'primitive and universal love' for miniature shelters, such as a doll's house or the improvised houses we make for ourselves as children.[108] Each aedicula forms a small, empty and airy shrine harboured in ever-larger shrines, which are so profuse they give the cathedral an inexplicable tininess and grandeur at once.

'Gothic man seeks to lose himself', echoes Wilhelm Worringer in *Form in Gothic*, 'not only in the infinity of the great, but also in the infinity of the small. The infinity of movement that is macrocosmically expressed in the architectural structure as a whole expresses itself microcosmically in every smallest detail of the building. Every individual detail is, in itself, a world of bewildering activity and infinity, a world which repeats in miniature, but with

St-Ouen Abbey (begun 1318), Rouen, France, aediculae at every
scale (above); Amiens Cathedral (begun 1220), France, multiple
scales of form and detail in the west façade (top)

Chartres Cathedral (begun 1194), France, jewel-like
intricacy of south rose window (above); three scales
of discovery in lancet window of the apse (top)

the same means, the expression of the whole ... The crown of a pinnacle is a cathedral in miniature', Worringer concludes, 'and anyone who has sunk himself in the ingenious chaos of a tracery can here experience on a small scale the same thrill ... as he experiences in the building system as a whole.'[109]

Among the few architects who have tried to revive the plasticity of scale in a Gothic cathedral, albeit with touching modesty and ingenuity, is Fay Jones, whose skeletal chapels keep activating our relations to them. His unpretentious Thorncrown Chapel (above) in Eureka Springs, Arkansas, resonates with the surrounding forest in its abstraction of infinite trunks and branches, which themselves are echoed by the standardized lumber of Southern pine with which they mingle, helping the building share in the immensity of the receding trees. The framing is multiplied over and over to create an airy canopy of stick upon stick, but also form a primitive shelter that has the intimacy of an overturned bird's nest. Upon entering the chapel, its larger image equated with the forest reverberates through the timber cage, down into a repetition of small wooden lamps that line the nave. Each light is a miniaturization of the overall character of the chapel, its intricacy of line and space receding beyond the reach of the eye. The result is a building that breathes in and out, losing every fixed dimension as it expands and contracts.

The same supple language reappears more purely in Jones's later Pinecote Pavilion (opposite) in Picayune, Mississippi, where there is nothing left to distract the eye from the latticeworks at multiple scales, which carry the genetic code of the forest into the overall structure and down to its smallest components. Every part of the building keeps opening up to the searching eye with features that are at once huge and minute, galactic and nuclear.

Fay Jones, Thorncrown Chapel (1980), Arkansas, multiple scales of forest abstraction

SPATIAL ELASTICITY OF SIR JOHN SOANE

A more playful instance of miniaturized freedom – the capacity of tininess to liberate us from absolute facts and set dimensions – is Sir John Soane's Museum, in London. Designed both as a residence and a setting for Soane's collection of antiques and art, the house possesses every scale but no single scale, with compelling elements at all sizes. Rooms are surrounded by ever-smaller bays and zones, and smaller still are innumerable objects whose wonders are compressed into forms so tiny we must bring our eyes close to peer into their secrets. Hidden dimensions keep appearing for the inquisitive eye, as if squinting like Alice through her looking glass to find a magical realm that can only be partly entered, with unexpected dimensions and treasures, each 'curiouser and curiouser'.

It is crucial to remember we would never be drawn into this Soanean universe – large spaces harbouring ever-smaller subspaces, encrusted with plaster casts, etchings, paintings, bronzes and ancient urns – or would our eyes and imagination be inspired to conduct a leisurely exploration, unless the subjects of our scrutiny were inherently appealing and worthy of our attention, time and devotion. Among the peaks in this enchantment are diminutive architectural details, including lanterns over the Breakfast Parlour and Dressing Room with the scaled-down appeal of a doll's house (p. 188). These minute worlds are brightly illuminated and perceptually salient, attracting and then giving wide creative scope to the eye. In the case of the Dressing Room, the domical lantern is a model from Soane's architectural practice, now free of its previous function and scale.

A more optical source of spatial elasticity occurs in the small convex mirrors scattered about the house, but concentrated especially on the Breakfast Room ceiling. As we catch

Fay Jones, Pinecote Pavilion (1987), Mississippi,
self-similar structure and details

Sir John Soane's Museum (begun 1792), London, Dressing Room ceiling, with lantern incorporating Soane's model of the domical light in the Masonic Hall; Breakfast Parlour lantern, in Flemish stained glass with small convex mirrors below; view up into the dome (clockwise from top left)

their sparkle and then draw near to gaze into their curved reflections, perspective is inverted by shrinking the world in which we stand. The dwarfed and warped space is loosened from rational certitude, presenting something large in a tiny volume, a space we can enter only by reverie as we press the eye near to probe into its magical depths.

ENIGMATIC DETAILS OF CARLO SCARPA

No less playful but more perplexing is the way in which Carlo Scarpa liberates buildings from their prison of fixed dimensions. Spatial volumes in the Olivetti Showroom or the Fondazione Querini Stampalia (p. 190, top left and middle), both in Venice, are less interesting in themselves, shifting all attention to details that entice and provoke. Making these tiny details more surprising, and at times miraculous, is that they often belong to the most prosaic building elements, including, at the Olivetti Showroom, the logotype design in the entry, glass tesserae embedded into the floor and suspension hardware of black steel with brass joints near the ceiling. At the Fondazione Querini Stampalia is a puzzle-like compartment with gold-accented walls for twin radiators, bronze rails for hanging pictures and a cantilevered metal bracket for a glass wall in the entry hall, turning the most commonplace objects into subjects of rumination.

A more frequently repeated inversion develops for the untiring eye at the Brion Cemetery. Here, the smallest things have an involving power reminiscent of a medieval miniature placed in the margin of a liturgical text, where the eye is first caught by a shimmer of gold and deep blue pigments of lapis lazuli or azurite, but, when inches away, discovers that the smudge of colour contains within it an amazingly elaborate world, which recedes into nearly infinite detail – opening a window onto a microscopic realm of landscape, buildings, figures, sky and stars. As before a painted miniature, one must avoid being too hurried or rationally inclined to enter its tiniest wonders. Where a concrete wall terminates in a zig-zag edge, it is inlaid with Murano glass tiles, whose golden hue reveals, on closer examination, other tonalities within its filmy depths. Beneath the twin tombs are small drainage holes covered with perforated metal disks, their silhouettes shaped into tiny figures that one must get down on one's knees to make out. Similarly, the intricate door handle to the chapel, the marble font with its inscribed brass fittings, the bronze altar with its cloudy reflections and pattern of rivets and the strange, steel-edged skylight in the concrete roof of a subterranean service space (p. 190, bottom) serve in different ways to magnetize, collapse and expand space at once.

Most bewildering are the tiny metal objects embedded in the upper edgings of concrete wall (p. 190, top right). Their inexplicable shapes and odd locations fail to suggest any rational function, even while drawing us closer and closer in fascination. Like fossils found in ancient rocks, these things imply industrial detritus left and absorbed into the building. Perhaps they are accidents or vestiges from the time of construction, activating the imagination as an anachronistic presence and giving the smallest architectural elements the greatest degree of surreal mystery and suggestive power.

Carlo Scarpa, Brion Cemetery (1977), Italy, tiny skylight framed with steel
over underground service room (above); mysterious small details at the
Olivetti Showroom, Fondazione Querini Stampalia and Brion Cemetery (top)

THE PRIMORIAL JOURNEY

At first glance, the volumes of Le Corbusier's buildings from the 1950s onwards, but especially those of his few religious works, appear uncomfortably strange yet excitingly fresh. But something important underlies this mesmeric appeal, for their forms touch the innermost recesses of our psyche and resonate with the subliminal power of the past century's most primordial works of art, particularly the extraordinary vitality found in the work of Joan Miró, the metamorphic stone carvings of Isamu Noguchi or the congealed energy in the forged steel of Eduardo Chillida (below). We cannot help but look with amazement at the strange, voluptuous curvatures and openings at Ronchamp (p. 192), the startling tubes and archaic concrete at La Tourette or the volcanic cone and stellar flicker at Firminy (both p. 193), which tap into the kind of primary vision that Claude Lévi-Strauss calls the 'savage' mind, with its fascination for the 'mythical' and the 'magical'.

Unlike a painting or sculpture, Le Corbusier's animistic forms invite us to embark on an unforgettable journey, which allows us to continually reveal startling features that mediate between human conscious and unconscious thought. This seeking and finding transcends

Primordial shapes of forged steel by Eduardo Chillida

Le Corbusier, Notre Dame du Haut (1955), Ronchamp, south wall of embrasures
with hidden details in the chapel (above) and exterior of church (top)

Le Corbusier, St-Pierre (begun 1971), Firminy (above) and
La Tourette (1960), Éveux, church crypt with celestial orbs (top)

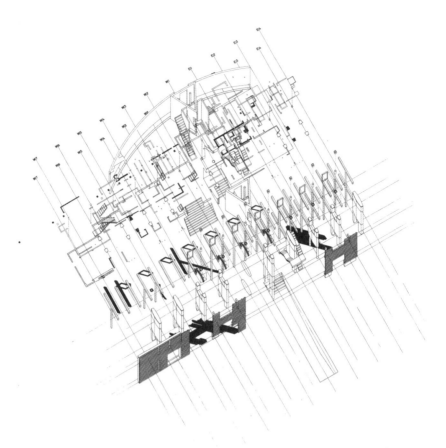

vision or logic, for it stirs something deep in the body and mind. It also exceeds any single moment of time, for the adventure keeps unfurling under the force of investigation as we feel our way into shapes and orifices that seem to both enchant and threaten, manifesting their architect's belief that 'to make architecture is to make a creature'.[110]

The transformation of architecture into a passionate search of discovery, where intensely cryptic things aim to enliven the journey, also resounds through the work of architect Thom Mayne and his firm Morphosis, although drawing on a more machined language of form. Their buildings are composed of strange yet vaguely familiar fragments, not unlike the alluring paradox of Picasso's broken figures or the fantastic images of the Surrealists, in both of which hallucinatory shapes with multiple viewpoints charm and disturb with physically vibrant sherds that flicker in the depths of the mind. The activating source in Morphosis's designs derives in part from a game of disrupting the world, and then setting it right again in an uneasy balance. The unity of absolute things is shattered and reshuffled, while strengthening the allure of some of those parts by making them highly enigmatic – charging the observer's imagination to enter into the perceptual tensions and pursue traces of things along various trails. The sympathetic beholder is given immense leeway in how these splintered forms are seen and, more crucially, the ways they can be explored in space by tracking and moving about them. Expanding the range of freedom are mysterious properties that are often alarming, even terrifying, but are sometimes favoured with a lyrical beauty.

Unpredictable worlds composed from what seem evocative scraps of industrial rubbish underlie the mesmeric appeal of Morphosis's buildings, from the Crawford House in Montecito, California (opposite and below), with its discursive entry and corridor sequence through a series of broken and evolving forms, to the Diamond Ranch High School in Pomona, whose outdoor pedestrian street weaves through mutating volumes embedded in earth on one side and cantilevered over a hillside on the other, and the San Francisco Federal Building (p. 196), with its stainless-steel scrim shading a public plaza before climbing and screening the neighbouring tower and rising into a fluttering tent over the roof. Each contains voids shaped by things that elude certainty, bending out of alignment or splitting into puzzling fissures, a fringe of enticements into the building and through its anatomy. We catch sight of one spatial pattern only to discover other patterns filtering through it, like a series of incomplete remains overlaid in an archaeological site, allowing a person to shuttle between several domains of space and time that permeate one another and provide many new points of departure. There is never an end but only edgings leading to trails of new beginnings.

Setting Morphosis apart from other exponents of ruptured form are fragments of reality whose fierce but irresistible things we faintly recognize. Magnetically drawing us on are strange totemic pylons that echo through space, emerging from the landscape as if caught at a moment of birth or death, implying there is buried space left to discover. Sheets of steel mesh waver in the air as veils shaped by invisible forces. Bizarre steel mechanisms exert

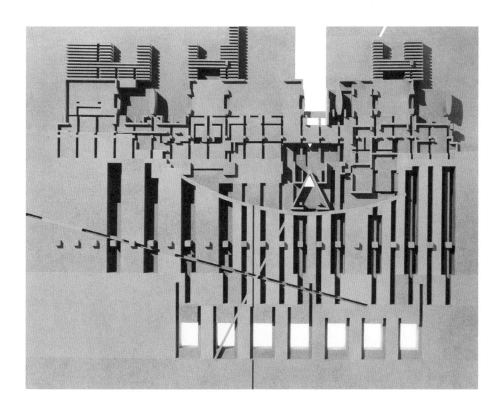

Morphosis, Crawford House (1990), California, conceptual relief model (above) and exploded axonometric (opposite)

an animistic presence, including vaguely anthropomorphic assemblies with the suggestion of bones or limbs. The vitalistic shapes turn vertical and hollow, even vascular, in the adventurous stairs of atriums at 41 Cooper Square in New York and the Perot Museum of Nature and Science in Dallas (opposite, middle and bottom). The magical intensity and pent-up energy radiated by these hollows, and the body heat found within them, are fascinating and disturbing. 'To be a human being in this world of ours,' Bruno Bettelheim reminds us, 'means having to accept difficult challenges, but also encountering wondrous adventures.'[111]

Some of the firm's greatest visions of undetermined space are large complexes, sadly unbuilt, which rise from a porous underworld. These include the superimposed slots and voids, flying bridges and platforms of the Artspark Performing Arts Pavilion for Los Angeles; the erosive edge along the Seine of the Paris Expo Architecture et Utopie competition; the half-buried egg and stratigraphy of a convention-centre competition in Nara and the Chiba Golf Club (opposite, top) in Kanto, both in Japan. The terrain of the golf club is scraped and gouged into a deep, partly subterranean relief, whose routes extend out and down into the land they inhabit. Perplexing built forms are extruded from this excavation as long, layered walls and reiterated frames, concluding with a pavilion lifted into the air, so as to vertically elaborate the routes of discovery while weaving them into and out of the contours.

We are reminded here of Wassily Kandinsky's account of the scattered and twisted reality found in Picasso's paintings, and the 'constructive dispersal of these fragments over the canvas'.[112] In a similar manner, the Chiba Golf Club and other Morphosis fragments trail

Morphosis, San Francisco Federal Building (2007),
overall view of public plaza and southeast façade

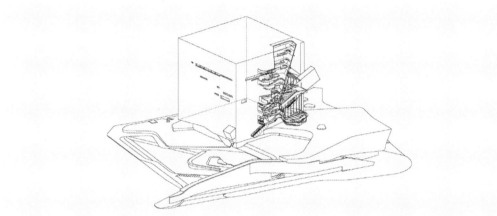

Morphosis, Perot Museum of Nature and Science (2012), Dallas,
vertical searches in the terraces, bridges and stairs (above) and
atrium diagram (middle); Chiba Golf Club (1991), Japan, model (top)

out over the landscape, with numerous baffling yet tempting things to investigate. Along any chosen route, and long before reaching an actual door, a person is able to discover and rediscover the work many times. The mysteries invite us not merely to reach our destination, but to actively engage with the multiplicity of places we find along the way. In the end, its promise is that the challenge of life should not be escaped in architecture, but lived with magnificent intensity.

THE COMPELLING GLIMPSE

One of the greatest motivating forces in architecture is the glimpse of enthralling space ahead, a stimulus to action subtly perfected in the gateways of ancient Japanese temples (above and opposite). Darkly weathered and grey timber portals heighten the allure framed ahead: intensely colourful moss; dynamic and energetic trees against a rectilinear frame; perhaps the start of an exquisite bamboo fence or series of stepping stones; bits of roof peeking over a wall or hedge. Each riveting hint grips our attention and inspires us forward, offering the promise of something to find around the next bend. The entire journey stimulates a vigorous search through a sequence of cues we are able to detect and uncover, multiplying the feats of discovery along a progressing state of holiness.

A similar art of hypnotic sightings to stimulate curiosity appears in the Arizona houses of Rick Joy, which withhold all but a few glimpses of carefully framed desert. The Tubac House (p. 200) is buried in an edge of terrain, largely hidden apart from rooflines breaking the horizon and beckoning us forward. Next to appear is an entry court that opens below, luring us down to water and shade. After reaching this secluded void, the way to the door is signalled by a neighbouring window framing a patch of distant landscape, its startling image of mountain and desert enhanced by contrast with the foreground – but puzzling, as

Honen-in Temple, Kyoto, thatched gate

Koto-in Temple, Daitoku-ji, Kyoto, gateway

well, for it implies the wall is nothing but a thin desert boundary. Upon stepping inside, that impression is dispelled by a new magnetic force: a panoramic desert vista, enhanced by the white interior. This kind of mesmerizing attraction mixed with surprise reoccurs in different forms throughout the house, and especially compelling at the end of corridors aimed on their own desert finds. Clearly demonstrated here is an appreciation of suggestion, restoring the chance for people to find things out for themselves, echoing Marcel Proust's observation that 'the real voyage of discovery consists not in seeking new landscapes, but in having new eyes'.

The art of concealing while hinting at beauty, in order that it can be freshly revealed, is apparent in Juhani Pallasmaa's Rovaniemi Art Museum (opposite), in Finland. The entry incorporates two sets of doors with narrow slits, bordered with glass and peripheral glances, ensuring that the world directly ahead can only be gleaned by peering through cracks to traces of future. Each slender glimpse at what lies beyond appeals to our innate desire to uncover secrets and resolve mysteries. Evidently there is something inside that is not left open to just anybody, nor will it be disclosed without our presence, awaiting us to slowly detect and search for meaning within its treasures. Like the African tribal masks that influenced the psychic improvisation of modern art, the building's doors prod the visitor to draw upon extra powers of vision – a fitting preparation for enigmatic works of modern Finnish art and their demand for insight and outlook.

Rick Joy, Tubac House (2000), Arizona, glimpse of the
Sonoran desert, framed by rusted steel at the entry

ENFILADES AND RECEDING THRESHOLDS

Where thresholds to desirable space are layered behind one another, leading from one revelation to the next along a succession of open portals, the power of discovery is multiplied into a chain of sequential acts. Each event anticipates the next, on and on, allowing us to foresee and avoid opportunities or hazards as we wish. These sequential disclosures in Western architecture tend to be organized along horizontal axes, as enfilades that form virtual tunnels through plural boundaries and rooms, providing a chance to deliberate over and set out in search of many different stages of future.

Underlying the intense human pleasure of walking through an enfilade are the multiple acts brought under our power to envision and prophesize. Numerous possibilities are grasped along a single line of sight, and are sufficiently visible around the edges to hint at what they withhold, expanding the spatial and temporal range over which we can exert our will. But these chances for disclosure only become real opportunities when they are worthy of our interest and are possibilities we care about. When sequential voids fail to do this, owing to being overly monotonous or vacant, they doom us to numbing repetition.

By contrast, consider the way repeating bays in a Gothic cathedral are so richly varied in their intensity and colour of light, and hidden attractions of stained glass, paintings and altarpieces, that any sighting along an axis picks up edges of many different destinies that

Juhani Pallasmaa, Rovaniemi Art Museum (1986), Finland,
sequential doors with sliver views at main entrance

are worth pursuing. A related anticipation occurs along Francesco Borromini's aisles at the basilica of San Giovanni in Laterano in Rome, where the repeating bays are turned into places worth seeking by contrasts of light intensity, the arresting chiaroscuro of cast shadows and lateral options to side chapels, each of which is uniquely shaped and magically toplit. And then there is the airy syncopation of colonnade and portico around The Lawn at Thomas Jefferson's University of Virginia, whose rhythms play off one another, rise or fall in terrain and arrive at fascinatingly lit and recessed entries to ten different pavilions. In each of these cases, the transformation of uniform bays into a sequence of desirable events is achieved by a richly flowing cadence of light, whose magnetic powers draw us on through a series of revelations.

Standing out among recent efforts to organize buildings around enfilades of discovery is Rafael Moneo's National Museum of Roman Art (above), in Spain, shaped to evoke the architecture it honours. Many thin layers of exhibition space are divided by tall brick walls pierced by various openings, the largest and most prominent being huge archways along the museum's centre line. When gazing about this plane-parallel structure, the moving eye is continually drawn to the edges of layers exposed along each recession, and their intimations of space and artefacts worth exploring. The extraordinarily deep probing extends throughout the entire building, as well as through openings carved out of the floors to signal further levels and art, including an underworld where remains are still embedded in the earth.

A different approach to turning procession into waves of discovery appears in the Shinto shrines of Japan, where approaching paths are galvanized by a series of ritual gateways, or *torii*, that mark the transition from the profane to the sacred. What is important about these gates in terms of human agency is the way in which they signal and lure while celebrating

Rafael Moneo, National Museum of Roman Art (1986), Spain

disclosure and, in the case of large shrines with multiple gates receding in the distance, present a chain of futures to deliberate and act upon, culminating in the thousands of mountain-climbing *torii* at the Fushimi Inari-taisha shrine in Kyoto (below). Even when the axes become discursive as repeatedly broken and angled segments, a progression used also in the approach to Zen temples, their staged discovery stimulates people to be curious and persistent, and to conduct a unified journey out of many small deeds of searching and finding.

While a discussion of the tremendous range of historical solutions to architectural narratives, many rooted in religious rituals and passage rites, goes beyond the scope of this book, it is important to mention the achievements of Tadao Ando in giving this episodic structure a contemporary form, and doing this in a way that embodies Hannah Arendt's precondition for agency, a 'startling unexpectedness' that appears in the 'guise of a miracle'. Ando's spatial sequences contain a wide margin of error, as well as opportunity. They cannot be followed carelessly, and at times threaten or confuse, but are always intriguing, even bewitching, ensuring that each disclosure becomes a genuine feat. Moreover, the journey contains hidden wonders, often simple things that are psychologically complex, giving travellers the power to find and reveal them by the force of their own actions.

The way to the chapel on Mt Rokko (p. 204) is masterful in its sequential disclosures, which recede ahead along an indirect route to the sanctuary. At the outset, a ramp soars off

Fushimi Inari-taisha Shrine, Kyoto

to one side before turning 180° to arrive at a circular pavement, whose floor is separated from a glass tube ahead by a crack between the meeting geometries, which one must alertly step over to enter a new stage of calming light, aimed towards a mesmerizing patch of landscape. Near the end of this peaceful segment is an intensely dark and seemingly unimportant recess to the right, allowing one to easily pass by and wonder if the trail has been lost. This provocative tactic at a critical moment in the journey wakens an ever-more conscious seeking, slowing the finding and making it into an authentic deed. The attentive walker will remember the chapel's rough location, and cautiously plunge into the darkness towards the sliver of light, a beacon succeeded by another right bend to returning light in the sanctuary. But here, as in many Nordic churches, the adventure does not end, for the room opens at the side through a huge glass wall to a secret garden whose slope indicates that the light-filled chapel is unexpectedly sunk in the earth.

The Water Temple (opposite) on Awaji Island is perhaps Ando's most baffling if euphoric quest, its every phase marked by puzzling obstacles and sudden revelations. After climbing a hill past the old temple, the visitor encounters a gate-like opening in a long concrete plane, succeeded by a curving wall that diverts motion around its edge while skirting a dazzling bed of white gravel, at the end of which the path bends 180° to reveal a lotus pond that seems to hover above the landscape. Following instinct rather than logic, one comes

Tadao Ando, Mt Rokko Chapel (1986), Japan, circuitous journey to the chapel upon an enigmatic slot in the water with a hidden stair that descends to what appears to be a dead end, below water level. Advancing again, aroused by curiosity, the visitor arrives at the base of these steps to find two facing entries, the one to the left more alluring but more bewildering and dangerous. Drawn in by the tempting promise of a reddish glow in the far darkness and a seat to rest upon, the visitor can't proceed directly to the light and is nudged instead into the only path available: a pitch-black corridor that curves out of sight. After feeling the way by hand, one finally reaches an opening into the temple itself, whose circular void and wooden lattice are saturated with sublime red light, turning the arrival into an ecstasy suggestive, in shape and colour, of rebirth. Clearly it is not merely space that is being discovered here, but also something about oneself and the human condition.

Tadao Ando, Water Temple (1991), Japan, arrival in the Buddha Hall **depths of discovery**

Louis I. Kahn, Salk Institute Laboratory Buildings (1965), California,
structure of holes in the bridges, porticos and scientists' studies

5

fields of action

Where architectural opportunities proliferate around us, we are given a seemingly unbounded scope of freedom. The surrounding structure is rich with invitations of agility and transformation, versatility and discovery, presenting an all-pervasive field of action. These circumambient possibilities are apparent in untamed landscapes and great cities, but also appear in buildings with exceptionally porous masses and ongoing cavities. In these spongy and eventful forms there is no end to the courses of action people can detect and decide for themselves. These buildings are essentially 'open works' and 'open forms', due both to their spatial continuum and to the wide range of prospects brought into view for consideration, which offer countless 'open futures' people are able to choose and govern themselves.

As the opportunities in buildings multiply – their invitations spread across and around the field of vision, above and below, right and left, ahead and behind, receding one after the other into the distance – a unique kind of structure is implied. Its possibilities may derive from the four basic kinds of spatial action discussed previously, but what is different is their scope and profusion, encouraging us to exercise agency to the fullest extent.

A building that offers such broad, deep and circumambient powers is inherently porous, transparent enough for the eye to scan over multiple options and penetrate into the futures they offer. But it is also opaque enough to define while withholding some tempting contents, conveying that certain locales are private, but also that hidden reserves exist that can be explored and disclosed. And lastly, if most urgently, it displays constellations of distinct and compelling places – alluring enough to spark our interest as choices worthy of consideration and the exercise of our powers. Instead of shrinking tightly around a single directive, or a few desperate choices we have to settle for, there is a tremendous abundance of choices we care about, providing us with chances to fulfill our desires.

A structure so open to human deeds will charm and entice us in almost any direction we look. We can identify diverse points of departure for routes into and through the permeable mass. Captivating elements stir expectation and compete to attract our attention and involvement. These incentives present an ample range of inviting acts for us to contemplate, and continue to lure us as we set off on one of many possible journeys. They arouse 'one of the deepest, one of the most general functions of living organisms', which is 'to look ahead, to produce future', notes French biologist François Jacob in *The Possible and the Actual*. 'There is not a single movement, a single posture that does not imply a later on, a passage to the next moment.' With each of our actions in a wide array of available futures, 'we are engaged in what will be'.[113]

The closed forms we are often condemned to encounter in buildings – impregnable façades, sealed voids, unrelieved tunnels and isolated cells – have been partially opened up to us. Impervious façades are breached with receding space, while solid masses are shot through with cavities that erode the volume from within, presenting the eye with indented silhouettes and hollowed forms. Permeability extends through the innards to break down cell walls of a normally shut anatomy of rooms and corridors, walls and ceilings, floors and stairs. Volumes leak into one another, just as the built envelope does not end abruptly at a closed and airtight border, but disassembles and feathers along its extremities. But it is important to reiterate that these possibilities will not spark our interest if they are amorphous or bland, irrespective of their number. Each must possess a strong and enchanting character to inspire our pursuit. At these times we no longer *look at* a neutral (even if useful or sumptuous) object, but *see into* an intersubjective complex that *includes us* in its forms, imploring us to assess its many opportunities and explore its innermost charms.

While there is no convenient or accepted name for such a structure, it essentially forms a 'field of space', whose various parts trickle, seep, spill or surge to some degree into their neighbours. Adjacent zones intermingle, rather than stay immune to each other. Ultimately, the most crucial property of this structure is not a matter of form or space, but *energy* –

the intensely charged *field of action* it offers to us, the wealth and propensity of its open futures, its chances to exercise our free will as we take off and infiltrate its space.

The underlying human potential of this field of action was first articulated by poets concerned with finding a way to overcome the predetermined stanzic structure and fixed stresses of traditional poetry, empowering the reader to become a more vital creative force. In a lecture at the University of Washington in 1948, William Carlos Williams described his poetry as an effort to construct a 'field of action', whose arrangement and spacing of words was shaped deliberately to activate the reader and encourage the avoidance of falling back into passivity or habit.[114] In breaking down the stiff and predictable flow of earlier poetry, and in the process abandoning the narrative continuity imposed on a reader, Williams, along with like-minded poets such as T.S. Eliot, Ezra Pound, Hilda Doolittle and Charles Olson, created units of words that were non-sequential and spatially charged. 'Poetry returns authority to man,' he writes, as the reader is now stimulated to move around the page and take control by seizing words from several different vantage points.

Equally central to the notion of a field is its universe of possibilities for many people to perform deeds that make a difference and where, conversely, as Wallace Stevens describes, 'hundreds of eyes, in one mind, see at once'.[115] But it was Williams who grew especially persuasive about this polyphony. 'We seek profusion', he notes in his essay 'Poetry as a Field of Action', 'heterogeneous – ill-assorted – quite breathless – grasping at all kinds of things – as if – like Audubon shooting some little bird, really only to look at it better ... It is as though for the moment we should be profuse ... we need to build up a mass, a conglomerate maybe, containing few gems but bits of them – Brazilian brilliants – that shine of themselves ... We must *see* our opportunity and increase the hoard others will find to use. We must find our *pride* in *that*. We must have the pride, the humility and the thrill in the making.'[116]

PAINTERLY IMAGES OF A PERVIOUS WORLD

To help envision a field of action, it may be useful to first consider its appearance in the fictitious space of painting, whose images entice us to penetrate their scenes. The great charm of the landscapes of Northern Renaissance art, for instance, is the way in which their porously complex terrain and buildings, abundant with beguiling features and mysteries we can peer into, draw us into a visual adventure where multiple layers of space never end but shade into others as they recede. Crucial to our participation in these panoramas of contrasting yet interlocked events is that they are not predestined to be followed in any given order, but can be visually probed according to whatever sequence we wish at that moment.

The endless surprise and overwhelming variety of space in the work of Hans Memling are made accessible to the eye by pervious volumes piled up in depth and leaking into one another. Buildings in paintings such as *Scenes from the Passion of Christ* (p. 210) have some façades peeled away or hollowed out by oversized windows and arcades, around which floors and vertiginous terraces, tilted to better expose their contents, descend in tiers to the foreground, with exaggeratedly low walls wrapping balconies and ramparts – hundreds of entrancing scenes animated by Biblical activity for the curious eye to pry open.

The aerated earth and fanciful volumes of Hieronymus Bosch's apocalyptic *Garden of Earthly Delights* (1503–15) similarly fill the canvas with a heaven and hell abundant with fascinating events, and features hypnotic in their allure and terror. The land becomes a terrestrial sponge, a hell into which figures sink and descend, while above ground is a realm of airy, transparent structures. The bewitching yet bewildering panorama, populated with nude figures, is full of secrets and marvels that never lose their power of attraction, offering a different scenario each time we gaze into the picture.

Less bizarre, if equally charged with undetermined spaces to probe, are the peasant scenes of Pieter Bruegel the Elder, where multiple vistas spread over a complex landscape. In *Netherlandish Proverbs* (1559), the earthly tableaux blend into a town whose masses are riddled with windows and doors, porches and arcades, columns and walls, balconies and terraces, jagged rooftops and towers. Packed into the picture are nearly infinite open cells that are clearly defined yet partly flow into one another, and are populated with scores of people involved in a flurry of activities occurring simultaneously (agriculture, hunts, dances, games, festivals), in plain view and around corners or beyond hills, in a world that conceals as well as reveals. In *Hunters in the Snow* (1565), Bruegel utilizes a high horizon and elevated point of view to expand our scope of involvement and allow us to project ourselves into the canvas to wander about without aim or purpose, disclosing one feature after another.

The captivating, almost cinematic overlays of these Northern Renaissance paintings, derive in part from 'condensation', as Robert Harbison notes in *Eccentric Spaces*, 'creating little worlds, even worlds within worlds', in the best of which 'the details swallow the whole to present an image of plenitude ... where you can lose yourself completely in a corner selected at random'.[117] But also amplifying the phantasmagoria of crowded forms and, for Bruegel, often droll subjects, is the variety and pattern of spatial recession – in foreground, middle

Hans Memling, *Scenes from the Passion of Christ*, 1470 (Galleria Sabauda, Turin)

ground and far distance, as well as above and below ground – so as to seize the eye while drawing it back to the front, to *us*, in a way that excites and empowers the imagination to move about freely as it detects and pursues its chosen trails of rewarding space.

UNDER CONSTRUCTION AND IN RUIN

A more tangible indication of the architectural field of action is found in buildings caught in transition, when their structures are either under construction or dissolving to ruins. At these moments the silhouette and envelope, as well as internal cell walls, are incomplete, permitting the observer to dissect visually a multitude of components and spaces that would normally be closed to one another, their possibilities removed from sight.

While the formative stages of architecture are fleeting, the unfinished torsos during this phase invite unusually intense scrutiny and fascinate us with their richness of virtual actions. The construction site with freestanding walls not yet covered by roofs, floors only partially sheathed, skeletal frames clad or infilled incompletely, presents a porous world whose implied opportunities and degrees of freedom shrink as the structure is gradually zipped up. This developmental stage is a central attraction of Bruegel's *Tower of Babel* (below), its ziggurat containing an encyclopedic diversity of spatial components and improvised footpaths up, into and through the incomplete vertical city. Even if we momentarily ignore the variety of construction portrayed, and the painting's larger message of the futility of man's efforts on earth, we find a protean image whose vast honeycomb is half-exposed. Immense arches, vaulting and unfinished cavities open up channels through and beyond the outer

Pieter Bruegel the Elder, *Tower of Babel*, 1563
(Kunsthistorisches Museum, Vienna)

façade, into receding cells, exposing layer upon layer of pervious space. Incipient volumes are stacked high and in depth, with sufficient closure in finished areas to make the uncompleted parts more suggestive as points of departure for the eye.

When architects portray, through drawings or models, their buildings in an incomplete state – deleting portions of the envelope or roof, internal walls or floors – it is usually for the practical purpose of explaining the anatomy of something closed, allowing themselves and their clients to probe a reality hidden in the finished work. At the same time they are depicting fictional and sometimes extraordinary fields of space, hinting at undreamed of structures. Cutaway perspectives and axonometric drawings are suggestive of a mode of building that is based on a field of broken forms. Beyond illustrating an architectural idea or composition, these depictions empower an imaginative eye to poke around in the fictive structure, to roam through its innermost reaches and undertake ventures that will be severely reduced, if not eliminated, in the final building.

Mesmerizing depictions of an architectural field are found in Joseph Gandy's watercolour interpretations of the building designs of Sir John Soane. Sectional elevations peel away boundaries, giving illusory access to different volumes and levels at once. We can deliberate over spaces and then enter and move about them, gazing up or down into neighbouring zones. Most astonishing of these fanciful worlds is Gandy's cutaway perspective of the Bank of England. Much of the roof has been stripped away, along with façades and cell walls, to reveal an interlocking maze of corridors and courtyards, carried so far that the building appears to be a ruin, conveyed by walls and columns split off at varying heights, often with seemingly timeworn edges, reduced in places to stumps in the ground or empty arches devoid of vaults. The viewer is urged to wander through an irregularly broken formation and peer into fissures and hidden corners – all in multiple random relationships that are not dissimilar to letting one's gaze wander across a Cubist or abstract painting.

The same desire is incited by pictures of ancient ruins, as in Piranesi's etchings of the remains of Ancient Rome (opposite) or the engravings of Egyptian temples produced by Napoleon's scientific expedition and published in the *Description de l'Égypt*. Piranesi's famous series of *vedute* depict a world of eroded forms spread over an equally porous ground, interlaced with infinite routes to explore. Huge tracts of ruins have missing parts, and some are still half-buried in the earth or veiled by vegetation that has taken root in their cracked textures. It is not only the incomplete carcass that is evocative for a searching eye, but also the sense of elements partially concealed beneath the ground, intensifying their presence by absence, dotting the picture with things people *could* unearth and bring to light.

The fractured beauty of actual ruins turns this inquisitive image into reality. There are probably no buildings on earth more fertile for simple human action and rewarding to deliberation than the great ruins: the temples of Karnak and Paestum (p. 214, top left), the Forum in Rome, Tintern and Rievaulx abbeys in Britain, and Jumièges (p. 214, top right) and Les Baux (p. 214, bottom) in France, Chaco Canyon in New Mexico, Machu Pichu in Peru, Angkor Wat in Cambodia. The once whole and relatively closed structure of each has been transformed, through age or violence, into one that is fragmentary and half-exposed.

Shattered things induce puzzlement and unease, but also fascination and wonder, for their unplanned forms and openings encourage interpretation and reveal an array of trails to seek out, exploring a multitude of hiding places and spatial secrets ripe with promise. Moreover, because its original order and function are weakened, a ruin frees people to initiate moves without regard to external directive or logical sequence, and to do this in any order, without any beginning or end.

The ruin is in many respects the touchstone for a field of action, its seemingly endless spontaneous opportunities devoid of both finished beauty and practical purpose. All absolutes have disappeared, leaving in their place a realm of pure exploits, where people can contemplate dozens, if not hundreds, of places to move through and around, ledges to sit on and gaps to slip through – an immunity from manipulation that is totally independent of the ruin's picturesque image, romantic appeal or archaeological value. As the eye probes broken cell walls, into an unimagined interleaving of planes and openings, it sees through a double-vision similar to viewing a collage. But the collage has become a three-dimensional lattice that one can now bodily enter and freely weave through, exploring its depths as each viewpoint shifts with a turn of the head, glance back or forward, advance or retreat.

Giovanni Battista Piranesi, *View of the Campo Vaccino*
(detail), 1772, from the series *Vedute di Roma*

Receding colonnades of Greek temples, Paestum, Italy; basilican fragments at Jumièges
Abbey, France; the porous underworld of Les Baux, France (clockwise from top left)

THE FIELD OF FORCES IN SCIENCE AND ART

The interactive field of action is diametrically opposed to the concept of architecture as a fixed object, whose volume remains constant and stable, closed and inaccessible, and thus unresponsive to what is around it – including us. Rather than being 'inert' (from the Latin *iners*, meaning 'inactive' and 'unskilled'), the field presents a cluster of reciprocal elements charged with energy and forces of attraction. Our experience of this structure no longer centres on independent physical things, but on the spaces between things, which are now the site of invisible yet real and activating powers.

The view of architecture as a field of forces parallels ideas about physical reality that began to emerge in the late 1800s, beginning with scientist Michael Faraday's conception of the world as an arena of electromagnetic happenings. In 1861 James Clerk Maxwell introduced the term 'field' to convey the existence of streaming lines of force active in space – various stresses and strains, attractions and repulsions, pressures and displacements, which fill space with neighbourhoods of energy. Maxwell's field theory challenged the static Newtonian view of reality as discrete particles behaving at a distance, showing instead that currents and lines of force extend through the intervening medium. Space could no longer be understood as empty and inert, for its domain is pulsing with unseen electric and magnetic intensities – forces that occur at every scale, from the microscopic to the cosmic, but are invisible to the naked eye and are fully evident only when recorded indirectly or through non-visual wavelengths of energy.

With the publication of his special theory of relativity in 1905, Albert Einstein further demolished the Newtonian belief in absolute measurable things, demonstrating that matter and space are themselves relative, and change with different observers and according to each observer's shifting perspective. Moreover, the established dimensions of length, mass and time transform with one's frame of reference. Physical reality alters with a person's speed and location, and is not independent of the observing eye – it is, essentially, not determinate. These relativistic ideas might have remained the province of science had they not also begun to appear in more concrete form within the arts, allowing them to be more easily grasped and directly experienced by a wider audience. By the late nineteenth century, Vincent van Gogh was already painting a reality whose physical presence is overshadowed by turbulent energy. In *Road with Cypress and Star* (p. 216), material things are less important than the vibrations around them. Waves and bits of coloured light swirl and resonate in patterns of motion and countermotion, within the air as well as the pores of solid matter, filling space with something tangible and penetrating solid masses with something active and fluid.

The growing abstraction of twentieth-century painting, along with other visual media, continued to explore the visceral and elemental appeal of this newly imagined magical field, with its multiperspectives and expanded vision. In describing this new world view, Paul Klee wrote: 'A sailor of antiquity in his boat, enjoying himself and appreciating the comfortable accommodations. Ancient art represents the subject accordingly. And now: the experiences of a modern man, walking across the deck of a steamer: 1. his own movement, 2. the movement of the ship which could be in the opposite direction, 3. the direction and the

speed of the current, 4. the rotation of the earth, 5. its orbit, and 6. the orbits of the stars and satellites around it. The result: an organization of movements within the cosmos centered on the man on the steamer.'[118]

Analogously, the observer of a picture by Klee is not given a literal or preconceived subject to admire with a passive gaze, but is challenged to enter into the painting itself, to linger over enigmatic brushstrokes and vague shapes that interact across the canvas and with the viewer's imagination, and to a great extent only take form in the mind's eye, rather than physical one. Its reality cannot be recognized or construed without the creative aid of an observer, giving that person a compelling degree of involvement and power that illusionistic art cannot equal. Developing out of the mosaic-like fields in paintings by Klee (opposite) and Cézanne, and the Cubist works of Braque and Picasso, as well as the diverse abstractions that followed, was a radical change in seeing the world. A wide number of simultaneous or incomplete views of an object are now juxtaposed and a dimension of unfolding time is introduced to the image on canvas. The faceting of things, and the interlocking of partially transparent planes to form rhythmical structures flowing through one another, produce

Vincent van Gogh, *Road with Cypress and Star,*
1890 (Kröller-Müller Museum, Otterlo)

a realm full of surprise and fascination, richly supplied with hints of things left to explore beyond the immediate reach of the eye. Painting becomes extra-retinal, something able to invite and charm, even disturb and trouble, but always including the audience as a creative participant in giving it momentary form. The inquisitive eye cannot coldly observe from a distance a painting by Delaunay or Pollack, Rothko or Tobey, De Kooning or Tàpies, for the eye is urged to peer into and explore a universe of endlessly puzzling things that pervades the entire canvas – a world that attracts but also, more importantly, incorporates us as visually inventive beings.

OPEN-FORM CITIES

Some of the largest but humblest architectural fields are vernacular settlements whose contents open to action within as well as without: the perched villages of Conques and Gordes in France; the white Andalusian towns of Casares (p. 218) and Olvera; the seaside hilltowns of Riomaggiore and Manarola in Italy; the Greek island villages of Santorini and Mykonos; the Saharan cities of Ghardaïa and Béni Isguen in Algeria; the Mesa Verde cliff dwellings of Colorado. The walls and roofs of these spongy cities keep supplying hints of latent space as they twist and turn, while receding in depth and spilling into the foreground to produce silhouettes teeming with possible things to explore. Cascading facets take infinitely varied angles that stimulate endless scrutiny, as if gazing into a broken rock formation (p. 219), its thousands of incidents catching the eye and tempting us to graze over and search

Paul Klee, *Ad Parnassum*, 1932
(Kunstmuseum Bern)

Cascading houses and paths in Casares, Spain

deeply into its facets – a structure also approximated in Cézanne's paintings of Mont Sainte-Victoire, whose steeply fractured landscape is modelled through various shades of the same basic hues. But appearing between the urban solids is something especially galvanizing: cracks and fissures of half-hidden space that imply trails to discover and pursue, intimating futures both promising and attainable.

Seen from afar, the hilltown silhouette bristles with faceted houses and strongly marked towers, ramparts and turrets, signalling like beacons that call to us. The almost hypnotic allure of these settlements is also due to the way in which the steep terrain keeps tilting their pattern of solids and voids into oblique angles of view, at times almost a bird's-eye view, expanding our ability to deliberate over the attractions. This enhanced perception is similar to the vantage points taken in paintings by Memling and Bruegel, which lower the middle ground and elevate the background to accentuate visual access to otherwise tightly knit worlds. While this scope of perception is greatly reduced and almost disappears when standing inside the slot-like streets of vernacular settlements, it returns and explodes when paths widen into plazas, or turn perpendicular to the contours to expose a section of cascading opportunities, prompting us to savour a series of receding futures (p. 220).

I don't mean to suggest a conscious intent by hilltown builders to construct open urban forms, since their primary concerns were defensive and climatic and, apart from their institutional landmarks, most of these settlements developed less by controlled design than from a tolerance for patterns built up over time by many different hands and circumstances. Nevertheless, the most entrancing and porous of these towns, as they exist today, present monumental fields of action whose latent deeds are almost as open to visitors as to the inhabitants.

Broken rock formation at Les Baux, France　　　　　　　　　　　　　　**fields of action**　219

Sudden cascade of opportunity in Urbino, Italy

Though rare in modern urban planning, the expanded field of a rich topography is a principle attraction of cities such as San Francisco and Lisbon, Prague and Rome, which have not ignored or levelled their terrestrial gifts. Slopes keep tilting possibilities into view and increase the detection of otherwise hidden architectural options, whose mere sight can elicit the simple and automatic pleasure of wanting to walk through their streets. Analogously the sinuous channels cutting through a great river city such as New York, London or Budapest, or equally the canals of Venice or Amsterdam, open up expansive fields and fresh paths of opportunity. These liberated zones expose forever the heart of a dense urban mass to a crossfire of courses of action.

Analogous to the dissection and revelation of space along a river is the manmade channel willfully carved through a tightly packed city, as in the dramatic axes of Paris and Rome. Long cuts through the urban fabric bring into view and stimulate our consideration of distant opportunities, inciting us to act on long-range prospects. Plazas and churches, paths and arcades emerge from afar and line up in succession to signal their presence, coaxing us to set off on adventures with plural destinations. These channels may also assert civic authority and control, but for a person strolling through an otherwise congested and disorientating city their revelations are liberating, for they offer chances to probe through miles of otherwise closed space and restore one's bearings and control of the future.

STONE FORESTS

Among the most entrancing fields constructed in the history of architecture are infinitely porous religious structures (p. 222). Putting aside their spiritual meaning and seeing them purely as deliberative space – a space just as valid for the non-believer as for the worshipper – their interiors supply a tremendous array of latent actions. Among the impressive points in this heritage are the colonnaded temples of Ancient Egypt, the spatial labyrinths of Buddhist and Hindu temples in India and the multitudinous cavities and columns of an Islamic mosque such as Córdoba. In every direction, one's gaze filters through many receding bays, catching hints of promising features and atmosphere. When setting off on any of the innumerable courses of action, the way remains half-concealed by a matrix of piers, stimulating decisions about how to meander through and among the spatial units. The interiors form, in a sense, huge abstract forests with seemingly endless opportunities that invite and bewilder, turning us into choosers empowered to think ahead and anticipate the world.

Another apex in the field of action was reached in the stone forest of a Romanesque basilica or, above all, a Gothic cathedral. For medieval Christians, the church was a vision of earthly paradise, formed to embody the spiritual mysteries of the Heavenly City, as envisioned in the Book of Revelation and later Dante's *Paradiso*. But it was also an arena for people in search of enlightenment, a prospect still intact today, even for those unencumbered by faith or simply in search of cultural insight and understanding.

Surrounding the towering nave of a great multi-aisled cathedral, such as Bourges (p. 223), Cologne or Milan, is a tangle of bays, multiplied and mystified by colonnades and further obscured by heavy shadows, producing an unsurpassed scope of opportunities that

are simultaneously entrancing and baffling. One can proceed ritually towards the altar or wander about aimlessly and easily get loss around the periphery. Important nodes of spiritual concentration – baptismal fonts, side chapels, the innermost core of the chancel – grip our attention with their rituals and hypnotic pools of light. But other attractions are scattered about, diverse in their lures of light and colour, statuary and glass. Enveloping us at any moment is a universe of beguiling details, all of which woo the eye and foster involvement, making us want to gravitate towards them. Dimness intensifies all these appeals, making the glimmers more magnetic and receding spaces more adventurous, summoning us in every direction, including descent when the floor opens up to the underworld of a crypt.

In certain regards it is but a small step from the forest-like structure of a cathedral to the fictitious prisons of Piranesi – the *Carceri d'invenzione* (p. 224) – as long as we confine ourselves to the phenomenal structure and ignore Piranesi's Kafka-esque mood of ominous cables and machinery. What is new in the Piranesian vision is an accessible range of upward freedom. A fantastic array of receding space along diagonal increments, up stair after stair, some angling, others spiralling, passing or intersecting bridges, and all continuing into the distance, fading from view through a lattice of stone archways and piers. The closest Gothic approximation of the *Carceri's* upward power is the large gallery of a cathedral such as Noyon (p. 225, top) and, though divorced from its interior, the open-air stonework atop Milan's Duomo (p. 225, bottom). While routes along the latter's roofs are highly controlled for safety, the terraced levels amid a tangle of arches and buttresses suggest a tremendous scope of

St-Hilaire-le-Grand Church (1049), Poitiers

Bourges Cathedral (begun 1195), France

freedom. Virtual and actual trails weave through and around thousands of slender marble spires, which foliate into screens and filigrees, catching and absorbing our vision, slowing us down but giving us choices on how we might scramble over the rooftops. As we negotiate our way through this multilevel lattice, one broken vista leads to another, with every step revealing spaces populated by visitors who are also walking or resting, climbing stairs or scaling slopes. Repeated to infinity are bay after bay, with columns against which to lean, banisters on which to rest arms, ledges of varying heights for sitting and tiers of balconies from which to gaze down onto the city below.

INTERLACED WEBS OF IRON AND GLASS

The field of space took a wiry turn during the Industrial Revolution, as engineers and architects took full advantage of the emerging technologies of plate-glass, cast-iron and later steel to turn buildings into huge webs of tensile lines. The repeating cage of Joseph Paxton's Crystal Palace for the Great Exhibition of 1851, the most spectacular if monotonous of these sinewy structures, contained two levels of structural bays, transparent to one another and housing a wide variety of exhibits. But it was less the bland, repetitive spaces that motivated human action than the thousands of intriguing displays and human activity coming to view at each turn. Since occupants and exhibits could be seen simultaneously from any vantage point, they invited deliberation over boundless possibilities of light and shade, trees and fountains, booths and events, all easily accessed by stairs and bridges.

Giovanni Battista Piranesi, *Carceri d'invenzione* (detail), begun 1745

Duomo (begun 1386), Milan, spire-laden roofscape (above);
Noyon Cathedral, France, interior (top left) and choir (top right)

More architecturally varied is the field conceived by Henri Labrouste for the Bibliothèque Nationale in Paris, using iron to construct intensely poetic and intricate skeletons. The Reading Room (above) contains nine different bays, each traced by cast-iron columns and crowned at the centre with a skylit vault. But it is behind an end wall that Labrouste's ferrous structure is fully exploited in a crowded, perplexing space – the *grand magasin* of the stacks, whose four different levels open to each other across the cleft of a light well. One can glimpse a hundred different zones lined with books and dozens of spiral stairs linking the levels and gridwork of bridges, and even peer through the floor itself and ceiling above, since their plates and stair treads consist of iron grates. 'These bridges, quite apart from their obvious utility, give a certain effect of power to the room,' writes Sigfried Giedion in *Space, Time and Architecture*. 'If there is a Pazzi Chapel to be found anywhere in contemporary architecture, it is here.'[119]

The huge steel cage of the Eiffel Tower (opposite) takes the skeletal field out of doors, transforming it into a gigantic lattice with many different vertical manoeuvres and points of command. In addition to the platforms and bridges, stairs and elevators, cafés and restaurants, often superimposed in each line of sight, there are other bays hidden in shade or obscured by the densely woven structure, whose presence disappears and reappears for a searching eye. Mixed into these aerial chances for action are Parisian attractions spread out below and reaching into the distance, giving a bird's-eye view to incalculable futures that cannot be seen or contemplated on the ground.

Henri Labrouste, Reading Room (1869), Bibliothèque Nationale, Paris

Extending the same kind of liberative powers to a different building type is the five-storey atrium of George Wyman's Bradbury Building in Los Angeles (p. 228), described by architect Charles Moore as a place where 'the thrill of discovery is there each time: it's always far more wonderful, more ineffable, more magic than memory allows.'[120] A visitor to the skylit void is presented with open corridors and stairs that lead to hundreds of glazed offices. Concealing and revealing these adventures is a web of wrought-iron grilles and railings, balustraded stairs, freestanding mail-chutes and a 'birdcage' elevator – an interwoven world that was compressed and stretched by Enoch Hill Turnock for his Brewster Apartments in Chicago (p. 229).

Playing on similar themes at smaller size, while intensely modest and warmly inviting, is the small universe built out of refuse and scrap metal by the Italian tile mason Simon Rodia for Watts Towers (p. 230) in Los Angeles, assembled by hand over a span of three decades. One enters to find a maze of half-enclosed rooms and walkways, their boundaries loosely traced by low walls and wiry enclosures, with a wide assortment of improvisational seats and ledges. Each zone is distinguished by playful colours and textures, derived from sparkling

Gustave Eiffel, Eiffel Tower (1889), Paris

228   George Wyman, Bradbury Building (1893), Los Angeles, atrium

Enoch Hill Turnock, Brewster Apartments (1893),
Chicago, lightwell and staircase

bits of broken glass and colourful ceramics, small mirrors and thousands of seashells, set
into hand-patted concrete walls. Rising above the porous ground are openwork canopies
and spires, culminating in three tall, lacy structures of steel rebars. One cannot help but be
captivated by this miniature city abundant with the kind of free will that is worth wanting,
for it secures for us great joy, as well as dignity.

INTERFOLDING SPACE FROM WRIGHT TO KAPPE

The vast multiplication of viewpoints and incentives to action achieved in the age of iron and
glass is not unrelated to the polymorphous vision of Cubism, a way of seeing that continues
to evolve in abstract art. The roots of this mode of perception in architecture, Sigfried Giedion
argued a half century ago, can be traced further back to late Baroque architecture, and the
synthesis of complicated and interpenetrative volumes by Francesco Borromini, Guarino
Guarini and Balthasar Neumann.

Whereas these historic precedents retain the authority of a dominant centre and a
fixed perspective from which to probe a fluid yet hierarchical space, Cubism sought multiple
centres and a discursive perspective, where vision is urged to roam free of external control

Simon Rodia, Watts Towers (begun 1921), Los Angeles

and take in unpredictable views of its subject. If the former remain tightly choreographed around horizontal, vertical and radial axes with a preordained control, the latter imply a free play of the moving eye as it deliberates and manoeuvres through a loosely governed space. Though fixed on canvas, the Cubist or abstract picture takes variable form since we can choose from among many starting points and virtual journeys into and around ambiguous features. The way we see has been utterly changed, since we are now granted a prominent role in circling, inspecting and assessing the subject, which is no longer an object as it now includes *us* in giving it form. This transformative power derives from the way Cubism 'views objects relatively ... from several different points of view', Giedion contends. 'And in so dissecting objects it sees them simultaneously from all sides – from above and below, from inside and outside. It goes around and into its objects.'[121] It is, at its core, suggestive of the freedom of action in a field of space.

It is perplexing that so many architects of the past century have failed to notice the liberating vision pioneered in neighbouring arts, and continue instead to shape buildings into over-determined objects, whose primary aim is evidently to impress, comfort or profit by an increasingly docile clientele. Fortunately, there have been architects working from a contrary set of values, who explore how buildings – throughout their anatomy and at every scale – could become wide-ranging catalysts for human responsibility and dignity. The most impressive of these efforts are found in some pinnacles of modern architecture, but also include a number of underappreciated achievements.

While Frank Lloyd Wright often retained dominant centres and orderly axes, he was continually multiplying their presence and working away at eroding their control, so as to build up a loose field of centrifugal actions around and within the cohesive forces. This balance can also be seen in his efforts to 'destroy the box' and its prison of space, which led not to excessive transparency, as it has in so much Modernist work, but to an interpenetrative structure in which rooms remain both half-closed and half-open to one another and nature. Boundaries of rooms are partially opened in each of many different directions, through breaks in walls, floors and ceilings, expanding the causal powers of people and transforming the building into a world of circumambient opportunities. These open futures became especially extensive in city-like interiors, including those of Unity Temple in Oak Park, Illinois; the Johnson Wax Administrative Building in Racine, Wisconsin (p. 233); and the Midway Gardens in Chicago.

Each person is emancipated, Wright observed, by letting his 'line of action be *horizontally* extended', releasing the confinement of every room through open corners and wraparound windows and shaping space into a 'figure of freedom'.[122] The inside was 'liberated to flow into outside space', as it pushes and probes, slides and weaves, rises and falls. Even a modest Usonian house was designed to provoke a complex of centrifugal actions in a relatively small volume, providing the 'fundamental realizations of freedom' in the simplest possible dwelling, where for each occupant 'power is now to become his own responsibility – power never dreamed of until he thus began to live as a free man. Power now is perpetually renewed from within himself, power appropriate to his new circumstances.'[123]

Many features for which Wright is renowned – long wings soaring away from massive, deeply rooted hearths; horizontal lines that echo the landscape; cantilevered roofs that seem almost in flight; jutting balconies and long terraces striving towards the horizon – are dramatic metaphors for a less conspicuous but more fundamental achievement of freedom in the field of space. Unlike his iconic expressions observed sympathetically from a distance, the porous interiors are endowed with powers we can bodily enact. A dynamic current of space sweeps through in every direction, angling up or down stairs and turning the entire structure into an arena of action. Inspiring this overflow of adventure was in part traditional Japanese architecture, but also Wright's notion of American democracy and the words of Walt Whitman, in the opening lines of 'Song of the Open Road':

> Afoot and light-hearted I take to the open road,
> Healthy, free, the world before me,
> The long brown path before me leading to wherever I choose[124]

In contrast to Wright's inclination for terrestrial liberty, Le Corbusier gave action a skyward inflection, cutting away volumes and magnifying deeds along stairs and ramps, by which 'one escapes from the street and climbs towards the light and fresh air'.[125] Opportunities are vertically tensed and dramatized to draw people upwards, culminating in elaborate roofscapes more liberating than the buildings below, displaying a French instinct for levity as inspired as the roofscape of the Château de Chambord. This gradation of porosity and its rising freedom helped to set free the boxy rigidity of Purist houses such as the Villa Garches and Villa Savoye in France and Villa Curutchet in La Plata, Argentina, disintegrating the top in an airy structure that playfully mingles many points of desirable space. Even the distressingly cellular blocks of the various Unités d'Habitation are joyously free on their multilevel roofs, teeming with differently shaped terrains and their uncertain futures.

Despite his reputation for elegant if petrified monoliths of steel and glass, a young Mies van der Rohe could also produce something as supple and adventurous as the German Pavilion for the 1929 Barcelona Expo (p. 234). While limited to horizontal manoeuvres along a plinth, the choices of action unfurl in every direction, supplying routes that jog and slide to shimmering pools of water. The field is activated by planes and voids that slip past, while infiltrating one another. And because practical use is eliminated from the playful opportunities, our spatial motives are distilled into pure desire. These are essentially choices of sensory pleasure: the thermal delights of sun and shade, the intensified contrasts of rough against smooth, the voluptuous materials that draw us near, from the sparkle of chromium-plated steel and quiet glow of grey, green and white-tinted glass to the mineral depths of golden onyx and green Tinian marble.

Springing from all these sources are the spatial structures of Paul Rudolph, who described his own buildings as free-flowing Miesian plans turned on edge as vertical sections. While Rudolph's boldly shaped masses often prioritized formal variety at the expense of genuine leeway for action, his cavities are marked by real opportunities. Consider

Frank Lloyd Wright, Johnson Wax Administrative Building (1936), Wisconsin

the multilevel balconies and alcoves of student lounges at Southeastern Massachusetts Technological Institute, the multilevel caverns and overlooks of the Yale Art and Architecture Building or the polygonal cavities of the lobby and annex of the Burroughs Wellcome Building in North Carolina, whose wide and rich degrees of freedom are instantly grasped in the remarkable sectional perspective drawings for which Rudolph was renowned (opposite). He is often faulted for being too pleased with the aesthetic effect of sculptural forms, but he was nevertheless a pioneer in expanding our vision of what is possible in a spatial field.

The most Piranesian of Rudolph's works were conceived for himself: his Manhattan office and, above all, his residential penthouse at 23 Beekman Place, in New York. By partially removing existing floors and then inserting new and slightly displaced levels, hollowing slots for stairs and light wells that vertically jog along their journeys, he transformed the given cellular structure into a multitude of half-open interflowing spaces. Each level forms a virtual room with its own slight enclosure and character, function and activity, while opening

234   Mies van der Rohe, German Pavilion (1929), Barcelona

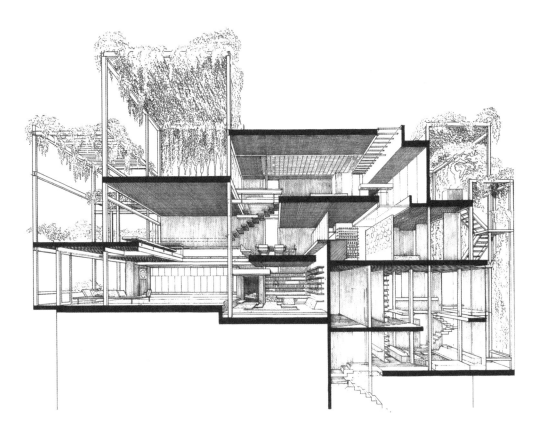

to other initiatives – a labyrinthian freedom that continues through glass walls and doors to a multistorey fringe of balconies and hanging gardens, making it impossible to grasp the building as a thing, and only as limitless vectors of experience.

Inspired by the open forms of Frank Lloyd Wright and interlocked planes of Theo van Doesburg (p. 236), Rudolph Schindler employed inexpensive lumber and plaster to construct richly indeterminate dwellings abundant with chances to act in space. Works in and around Los Angeles such as the Lovell Beach House and Elliot House (p. 237), along with the Bubeshko, Sachs and Falk Apartments, were built up out of fragmentary, interpenetrating and multifarious forms. Materials are treated as incidental, so that every resource could be applied to enriching the opportunities of raw space. Especially intriguing is the way solids and voids are loosened from one another and pulled apart, but also interlocked so that each possibility leads to another. Boundaries often dissolve at the ceiling, to mingle rooms without sacrificing privacy. Meetings of wall and floor fold into a habitable landscape of nooks and crannies and portions of plan rotate while interpenetrating others, opening rifts and trails to space beyond. From any room in a Schindler-designed dwelling, one is made aware of opportunities in any direction, stimulating what he called 'limitless power', horizontally, diagonally and vertically.[126]

Paul Rudolph, 23 Beekman Place (1977), New York,
sectional perspective of the penthouse

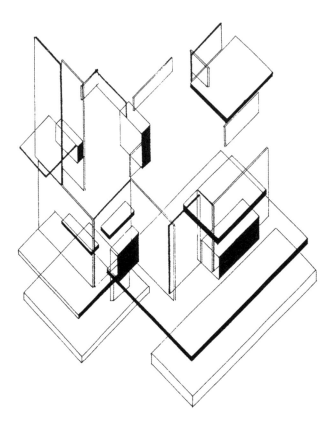

Among the Los Angeles architects expanding on the notion of buildings as unrepressed sources of human initiative is Ray Kappe. In the home designed for his family in Pacific Palisades, California (p. 238), rooms intermingle at multiple levels as they climb up the lush hillside. Supported on hollow concrete towers, devised to span natural springs, are seven different floor plates carried on laminated redwood beams and vertically shuffled to open rooms up to each other. From the entry deck we gaze down to a sitting area, look left into levels staggered above and below, including a studio, and right to a dining area and kitchen above, while other routes open to a wing of bedrooms and to bridges and terraces that climb the slope to a swimming pool.

Circumambient chances for action are composed differently in each of Kappe's later houses, with notable success in the Sultan/Price House in Santa Monica and the Keeler House in Pacific Palisades (p. 239). In the latter, a central staircase follows the site, its entire passage roofed with a skylight and glass floors to illuminate a slot through which to peer from level to level. The three main floors are stepped to form a cascade of mutually visible spaces, their opportunities strengthened by exhilarating overlooks and cozy alcoves and glass walls that carry the possibilities outdoors to decks cantilevered into the treetops.

Theo van Doesburg, *Architectural Analysis*, 1923

Rudolph Schindler, Elliot House (1930), Los Angeles

238   Ray Kappe, Kappe House (1968), California

Ray Kappe, Keeler House (1990), California

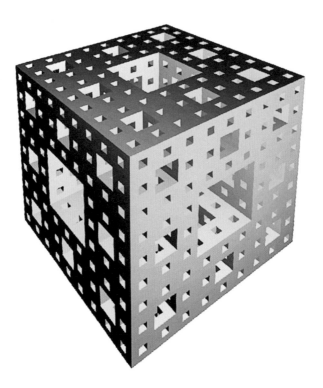

CONSTRUCTION OF HOLES

Evidently our actions in buildings depend as much on emptiness as solid masses. When these voids are recursive and self-embedded, creating a structure of smaller spaces inside larger ones, they form a porous matrix able to stimulate human inquiry at multiple scales and in multiple directions. The gradation of voids keeps drawing the eye into one space and then the next, revealing possibilities for action that lie ever deeper in the hollow elements of architecture. When this occurs, the boundaries of things are no longer sealed and Euclidean, and appear more as a fathomless surface of cracks, analogous to the geometric sponge conceived by Karl Menger in his search for the topological form of infinite holes (above).

A suggestive analogy to Menger's sponge is the outwardly massive yet cavitous architecture of Louis I. Kahn, whose elemental solids are carved and occupied with voids inside voids. These cavities include interior courts, their walls hollowed with huge geometric cutouts, ceilings that recede into concave vaults with openings to the sky and volumetric units loosely conjoined by the breathing space of prominent joints, all serving to deny closure and produce an onflow of human initiative. Despite their platonic geometry, the cavities are so inviting and nested inside one another that they supply a continuous spur to action, relaxing control of the otherwise static and over-determined masses and resulting in a rare counterbalance of vigour and inertia.

Representation of a Menger sponge

Kahn described his search for porosity as 'wrapping ruins around buildings', culminating in the highly ventilated structures suited to hot climates on the Indian subcontinent: the Indian Institute of Management, Ahmedabad, and the National Parliament House at Dhaka. Their monumental scale of nested layers, opened to each other by giant circular and triangular cutouts, tie them in spirit to the aerated stonework of such Mughal palaces as the Hawa Mahal ('palace of winds') in Jaipur.

An early masterpiece of Kahn's 'built ruins', for the semi-arid climate of the town of La Jolla in Southern California, is the Salk Institute Laboratory Buildings (below and pp. 242–3). While the laboratories themselves are by necessity sealed, placed between them is a freer structure of areas for study and open-air walkways bordering a central court. Without diluting its primary force as a huge channel onto the sea, the court leaks at either side into a network of spongy voids, a profusion of opportunities that recede through outdoor corridors and secondary axes, drawn along by mesmerizing patterns of light and shadow and concrete so sensuous that it glows like marble. These discursive manoeuvres are cut through at times by long, stroboscopic tunnels bored through the loggia and, perpendicular to these, from one side of the court to the other, simulating a crossfire of possible acts that beckon continually. Spatial initiatives are drawn to stairs that lead *up* to elevated pathways and bridges, airy porticos and teak-faced studies, and *down* to subterranean courts and gardens and, at the west end of the court, to a fountain with travertine seats – a welcoming belvedere onto the sea.

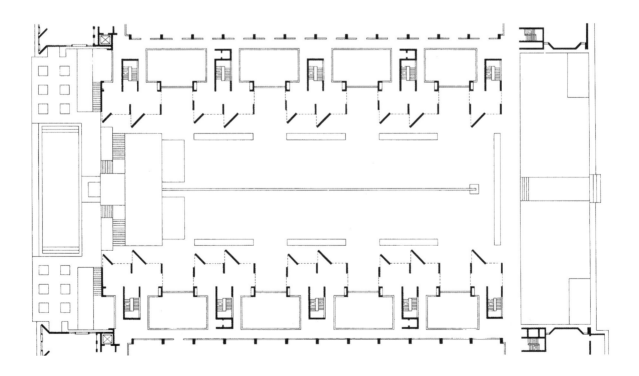

Louis I. Kahn, Salk Institute Laboratory Buildings (1965), California, ground-
floor plan of central court and loggia, lower terrace and fountain at left

Salk Institute Laboratory Buildings, enfilade of loggia with courtyard at right; view across bridge to portico of scientists' studies and courtyard beyond; structure of holes in the bridges, porticos and studies; and loggia with bridges to studies and sunken gardens and courtyards below (clockwise from top left); lower terrace with fountain and seating, and view to south wing of scientists' studies (opposite)

In many of Kahn's buildings, the ruins are inside, rather than outside, creating a hidden field of action. Such is the case at the Phillips Exeter Academy Library in New Hampshire (below), which forms a magical cavern inside a cubic brick mass that is surprising and startling every time it is entered. The tall central atrium, with walls containing circular cutouts, encourages arrivals to gaze about and peer into five different levels of book stacks. The wide scope of freedom was intended to incite 'a feeling for what a library should be – you come into the chamber and there are all the books.'[127] Each circle seizes the eye as a perceptual force, allowing one to 'feel the invitation of the books'.[128] Other opportunities emerge on levels above, as sightlines probe across the void and around the galleried perimeter that forms a promenade for strolling and surveying, perhaps stopping to rest and work in a carrel, each 'a kind of discovered place in the folds of construction'.[129]

It is instructive to compare Kahn's symmetric and orderly hollows with Joseph Esherick's rambling cavities at The Cannery in San Francisco (opposite). In order to transform the monolithic mass and systematic windows of the Del Monte Foods canning

Louis I. Kahn, Phillips Exeter Academy Library (1972), New Hampshire, atrium

factory into a new public market, Esherick carved and infilled the structure to eliminate its controlling geometry. While lacking the presence and scalar range of Kahn's voids, Esherick's understated design achieves a deeper, less predictable scope of action. Multiple layers of archways, some glazed, others left open, reveal options involving people and places, cafés and shops, shade and sun – receding up and down four different levels of space. The most varied freedom occurs along the pedestrian street excavated from the old structure. This winding channel open to the sky mingles into arcades at its edge, and swells periodically into small plazas, with each point in space linked to others by a maze of inviting stairs and escalators, bridges and porticos. The Cannery's total disinterest in formal aesthetics but rich provision of ongoing experience seem to echo the words of the poet Charles Olson: 'At root (or stump) what *is*, is no longer THINGS but what happens BETWEEN things, these are the terms of the reality contemporary to us – and the terms of what we are.'[130]

The idea that architecture might be conceived as a structure of holes reaches another pinnacle in Herman Hertzberger's Centraal Beheer office complex, in Apeldoorn, Netherlands (pp. 246–8). This headquarters for the country's largest insurance company, the kind of building usually reduced to an intolerant machine aimed at maximizing productivity and projecting a slick corporate image, is instead endowed at every point with human volition for its thousand workers. The building's monumental size is broken down by multiple scales of joints and cracks, beginning with its division into four multilevel quadrants, between which runs a continuous spine of multilevel pedestrian streets, all pulled apart from and opened

Joseph Esherick, The Cannery (1968), San Francisco, pedestrian street

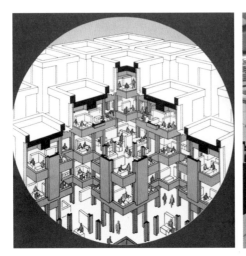

partially to their neighbours. It is loosened further by an assemblage of modular units, their square platforms detached from each other and linked by short bridges, establishing smaller corners within medium-sized platforms within larger domains, and leaving cruciform light wells between the units. The structure is inherently porous horizontally, diagonally and vertically, as well as both externally and internally, constituting a small city made pervious to action by a complex network of sightlines and pathways. Places for work and rest are semi-sheltered by parapets, columns and incomplete walls, keeping their opportunities partially accessible rather than isolated or invasive, and producing a world of mutual interaction that is extensive yet respectful.

Contributing to the finely tuned balance of refuge and outlook unique to each part of the building is a carefully modulated size, position and clarity of transparency. A revealing

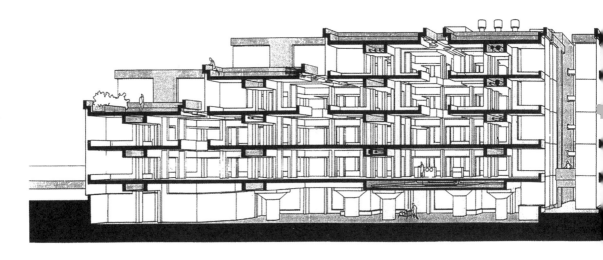

Herman Hertzberger, Centraal Beheer (1972), Netherlands, cutaway axonometric drawing of an office (top left); office and lightwell (top right); cutaway sectional perspective (above); fifth-floor plan showing the pedestrian street (light grey) and one office quadrant (dark grey) (opposite)

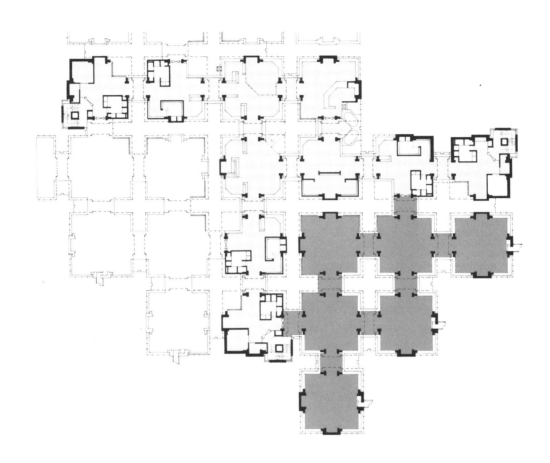

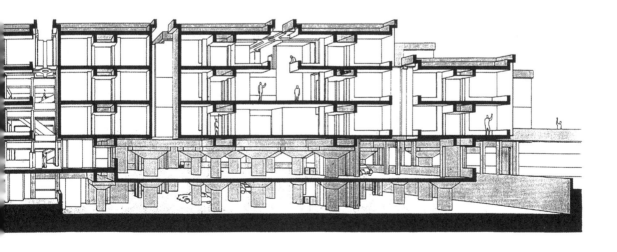

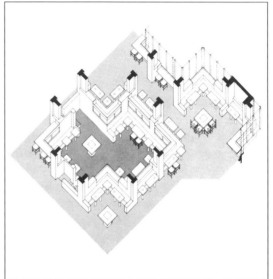

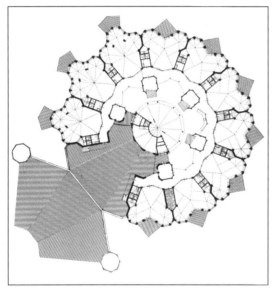

Herman Hertzberger, Centraal Beheer (1972), Netherlands, lightwell
between office and interior street (above right); interior street with office
corner (top left); cutaway axonometric of portion of cafeteria (top right);
Jan Verhoeven, Montessori School (1979), Netherlands, plan (above left)

instance of this equilibrium is found in the corner boundaries between office and street, where translucent lenses ensure a degree of discretion while vaguely connecting the worlds on each side. The diffusive veil is slightly opened by slivers of clear glass at the sides and a band of semi-transparent blocks at the height of the seated workers inside. The cafeteria, another small masterpiece of free will, contains a constellation of attractive places for people to dine, expanding on ideas broached in Hertzberger's student housing in Amsterdam, completed in 1966. Diners are faced with an abundance of options, some orientated back to the room and others gazing out through windows, perhaps sitting alone at a bar or joining a group at one of the differently sized tables. They can gravitate to each of several different floor levels or towards a cozy alcove sheltered within concrete piers or a panoramic bay in the folds of glass, and seek brightness under a rooflight or shade beneath a ceiling.

A more dynamic and public freedom is found in the building's pedestrian streets, their skylit channels overlooked by aerial walkways and mezzanines. At multiple levels is a diverse mixture of stairs, lifts, escalators and pathways, which are lined with seats and benches, cafés and restrooms. Inside this vast honeycomb of space, a person can detect hundreds of intriguing possibilities, each somewhat varied in ambience and furnishings. The 'profusion of invitations', to use William Carlos Williams's term, empowers people to survey and then freely select from a surplus of agreeable options, an interplay continuing through the entire structure and out to the routes of entry, and from offices out to roof terraces, also folded into alcoves and plazas lined with benches.

Sverre Fehn, Hedmark Museum (begun 1967), Norway   **fields of action**

Opportunity for many at once is the undisguised motive in Hertzberger's work, which in recent decades has struggled to conquer the amorphous character that can stem from repetitive and anonymous parts. Other Dutch Structuralists such as Piet Blom and Jan Verhoeven (p. 248, bottom left) have pursued similar humanist values, while searching for their own way out of the modular dilemma, the former through analogies to the Islamic kasbah and 'pole dwellings' and the latter more successfully through fractal-like, crystalline structures that echo in ways the richly clustered concentric space of Bramante's plan for St Peter's Basilica in Rome.

Scarcely less significant are the porous and self-embedded fields developed by other European architects: the multilevel temporal strata of Sverre Fehn's Hedmark Museum (p. 249); the skeletal edge of terraces threaded with stairs and escalators at the Centre Georges Pompidou (below) or Gae Aulenti's fabulous cascade of galleries, footpaths and seats at the heart of the Musée d'Orsay (opposite). The central human value of these buildings resides not in their outer appearance, but in their potential for self-affirmation. Each presents a 'continuity of possibility' deliberately stripped of 'inevitability', to apply the words of poet Robert Creeley.[131] The initial disorder and constant flux sensed in each building is of crucial importance, for it allows people to escape the prison of any fixed pattern of behaviour. The carefully worked-out frustration to order is a precondition for expanding the capacity of human beings to invent and actualize their own freedom.

Renzo Piano and Richard Rogers, Centre Georges Pompidou (1977), Paris

An especially promising vision of the spatial field taken to urban size is the ten-storey vertical campus of the University of Engineering and Technology (p. 252) in Lima, Peru, by Dublin-based Grafton Architects. Conceptual models indicate the way masses and cavities are repeatedly, and diversely, interlocked in plan and section, recalling the 'constructions' of the De Stijl sculptor Georges Vantongerloo and especially the houses of Rudolph Schindler, assembled from voids that are bent and spliced to clasp each other, ensuring that each spatial moment is inherently doubled and unfolds into new future. Courses of action may open wherever one looks, but their prospective trails are continually tucked around corners, zig-zagging into uncertainty, empowering people to launch spontaneous explorations, whose destinies are not preordained but under each person's control.

The generous room to manoeuvre derives in part from a huge concrete armature, or structural framework, used to support an additive complex of building units on the south side, away from the highway. The result is a hilltown-like cluster of loosely conjoined and differentiated volumes, whose patios step down to the ground. But unlike a hilltown, whose topological form rises from geographical features, the building is folded into the earth and airily interspersed in the sky, with its innermost core hollowed into a multilevel atrium. Set within this open-air cavern, extending the full height and length of the building, are the communal areas of the campus – classrooms and laboratories, cafés, terraces, library and dining hall – their opportunities linked by a rich complex of bridges and stairs, and pedestrian streets as full of adventure and human decision as Giancarlo de Carlo's for Urbino.

Gae Aulenti, Musée d'Orsay (1986), Paris

Grafton Architects, University of Engineering and Technology (2015), Lima, schematic
model; sectional study of space and mass; transverse section (clockwise from top left)

THREE-DIMENSIONAL HABITABLE FIELDS OF MAURICE SMITH

The Massachusetts houses of Maurice Smith carry implications far beyond their modest size. Each forms a city-like structure stimulating to human action, and so rich in projects and deeds that it defies description. At every location in space emerge new and multiple points of command, inciting us to endeavours in every direction, beginning at the outermost point of arrival and extending through the entire house, and then fingering back out to the landscape along porticos and retaining walls. With appealing lures spread out before us in all directions, any manoeuvre is going to entail instantaneous choices for and against, becoming a truly self-creative act.

The foundation for these branching opportunities at the Blackman House is a carving of the ground itself, and its vertical extension through interfolding walls of concrete block. Solid walls are never allowed to totally enclose any room, but instead commingle as incomplete pockets and corners, varied in size and complexity. These slight havens run over the hillside in jigsaw-like volumes (above), poking above or dropping below neighbouring walls. Rising from and interlocked with these broken shells is an equally manifold timber structure of framing and roofs, which form intricate webs over the masonry, in some locations left open as screens and others glazed for privacy or weathering. The result is an open cell structure abundant with chances for cozy retreat and energetic adventure, their possibilities gleaned by peering into spatial fragments that keep percolating into others beyond.

Maurice Smith, Blackman House (1963), Massachusetts, ground-floor plan   **fields of action**   253

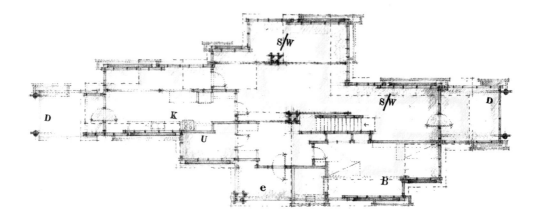

Another technique employed by Smith to ensure ongoing space is the passing connection: wall planes in section often terminate below the ceiling and rise or fall to varying heights, and in plan stop short of or slide past one another, as Mies van der Rohe had done at Barcelona and for his projected Brick Country House. Each wall thereby allows the detection of space beyond, whose presence and future are signalled by poking into view. Essentially the spatial boundaries are shuffled and interspersed, so that every point in space is linked to the edges of further possibilities, deepening and widening the scope to manoeuvre while intensifying its uncertainty. Rooms never seal up and become inert, but flow and interact with space beyond.

In a similar manner the external envelope of the Blackman House projects and recedes to tangle with nature, interleaving the two realms (pp. 256–7). The view out a window might reveal a wonder or threat in the landscape, and then continue back inside through another glass wall to disclose several nearby rooms and their occupants, and then through an interior window to find something of interest in a space beyond, before continuing back outside or along the perimeter, sandwiching together many spatial layers and their chances to *do something* that could *make a difference*. The result is a building, both as a whole and in its parts, which eludes being grasped as an object or image, volume or mass, and only appears as a superabundance of possibilities.

Serving as inspiration for Smith's intertwining of self and world is the poetry of Charles Olson, whose unexpected voids and shuffled words construct a field of space on the page that readers can negotiate in undetermined ways. Olson explained this process

Maurice Smith, Smith Summer House (begun 1989), Maine, plan

as an 'overflow of unrealized action', and identified its source in a structure that 'must, at all points, be a high energy-construct and, at all points, an energy-discharge'.[132] In his essay 'Projective Verse' (1950), he described his own method of arranging words in space as a 'COMPOSITION BY FIELD', a notion paralleling that of William Carlos Williams but greatly expanded upon, drawing a clear distinction between 'OPEN' form and closed form.[133] The former frees the reader to proceed along innumerable and unpredictable directions, while the latter remains fixed in traditional stanzas and prescribed patterns of reading. Olson thought these 'shapes of energies' could be 'boiled down to one statement': 'ONE PERCEPTION MUST IMMEDIATELY AND DIRECTLY LEAD TO A FURTHER PERCEPTION,' thus forming a 'PROJECTIVE VERSE'.[134] This projective power lies at the heart of Smith's architecture, for it implies a spatial continuum where incentives for action permeate and fertilize one another without termination, leading Smith to characterize his buildings as 'three-dimensional habitable fields'.

A similar point is made by Umberto Eco, who argued in both *The Open Work* and *The Role of the Reader* that the visual and acoustic arts, as well as literature, are raised to the status of exploratory media when they are able to be freely interpreted and cooperatively generated by the people who encounter them. The validity of Smith's architecture as an 'open work', using Eco's words, is 'precisely in proportion to the number of different perspectives from which it can be viewed and understood. These give it a wealth of different resonances and echoes without impairing its original essence form', which is 'quite literally "unfinished"'.[135] The spatial construct leaves parts to be 'welded' together by each person, in any order. It epitomizes an 'open work', owing to its 'susceptibility to countless different interpretations', causing each human initiative to be 'both an *interpretation* and a *performance* of it, because in every reception the work takes on a fresh perspective.'[136]

The poems of Olson and other 'poets of indeterminacy', as Marjorie Perloff calls them, deliberately serve as instruments for each reader's own self-affirmation and self-integration. This idea finds older roots in the poetry of Walt Whitman, who indicates in *Democratic Vistas* (1871) that writing should be based 'on the assumption that the process of reading is not a half sleep, but, in highest sense, an exercise, a gymnast's struggle; that the reader is to do something for himself, must be on the alert, must himself or herself construct indeed the poem ... the text furnishing the hints, the clue, the start or framework. Not the book needs so much to be the complete thing, but the reader of the book does.'[137] In his preface to a later edition of *Leaves of Grass* (originally published in 1855), Whitman notes further: 'I round and finish little, if anything, and could not, consistently with my scheme ... I seek less to state or display any theme or thought, and more to bring you, reader, into the atmosphere of the theme or thought – there to pursue your own flight.'

Smith's own writings take this freedom from narrative to an extreme.[138] Ideas are pieced together on the page in lines that are loosened from rigid control by the frame. Lines begin and end without a conventional stopping point or vertical alignment, so they may suddenly veer to the one below, leaving unexpected gaps and voids in the text, and coalesce into ragged paragraphs that slide, skew and zig-zag across the static page. These live paragraphs

Maurice Smith, Blackman House (1963), Massachusetts, view from stair landing looking east (above); view from upper corridor looking south to stair landing with living room below (top); view from stair landing looking west (opposite, top); view from stair landing looking north (opposite bottom)

Maurice Smith, Blackman Summer House (1993), Massachusetts,
interleaving of boundaries and space (top left); stair to sleeping lofts (top
right); spatial layers viewed through wood framing and screens (above left);
ground-level staircase opening to other levels and rooms (above right)

dart off at diverse angles, interacting with images and letters of contrasting size and character, some made by hand and others with rubber stamps, tilting to varied degrees on the page. Each word cluster is neither independent nor subservient to order, but jostles and interpenetrates others, producing a patchwork constructed of ink and words instead of solid material. Most challenging of all is Smith's recurring refusal to select a single word for certain phrasings, so that a sentence may flow briefly to a point where it sprouts into two or more alternate words, which can be substituted to form other shadings of thought. It is the reader who is urged to deliberate and choose which words to use in any rendition of the text.

Taking porosity to a skeletal extreme is Smith's own summer home in Addison, Maine (p. 254), and later the Blackman Summer House in Manchester-by-the-Sea, Massachusetts (opposite), each built of wooden frameworks with multiple layers of densely packed screens. At the latter, the field sifts through dozens of warm-coloured screens, filters from one room to another and encourages the detection of thousands of fragmentary clues to new opportunities. The lattice extends out to the sea and up to the sky, with each way ahead opening through a gentle Piranesian recession at multiple levels interlaced by stairs, bridges and mezzanines. But unlike the cavernous voids of Piranesi's *Carceri*, the Blackman Summer House has the gentle profusion of a forest, a world of infinite slender views. Forests, we are reminded by J.E. Marcault and Thérèse Brosse, 'with the mystery of their space prolonged indefinitely beyond the veil of tree-trunks and leaves, space that is veiled for our eyes, but transparent to action, are veritable psychological transcendents'.[139]

THE JAPANESE SPATIAL LATTICE

The traditional Japanese building constitutes in its entirety an intensely inviting spatial field, owing to its trabeated structure, filtered views and sensuous treatment of natural materials (pp. 260; 261, top). A multitude of latent acts are brought into view by a matrix of fixed and sliding walls, where even a closed boundary can hint at further possibilities. Chances to exercise power beckon in every direction, from discerning a neighbouring room or path to catching sight of a shady recess or sunlit veranda, with similar manoeuvres appearing outside at multiple levels. All these circumambient acts are further charged by slight distinctions in floor material, from the peripheral movement on smooth floorboards to the intimacy of soft, aromatic *tatami* mats, each dramatizing and giving profoundly different values to the choice of action along its surface.

The ability to pack such abundant human causation inside a small volume is an ancient and well-practised art, fully present in imperial villas, as well as in one of the country's oldest farmhouses, the Yoshimura House (p. 261, bottom). A maze of screens and incomplete walls ensures there are always opportunities beyond, filling each viewpoint with promise. The eye slips from one room to another, and can scrutinize a dozen or more half-hidden rooms that arouse curiosity and may be explored by moving only a short distance. At times the space between wall and ceiling is left open, intimating future even when out of sight. Receding layers of glimpsed space deny the termination of inquiry, as does the lack of any real centre or destination at which to arrive and conclude the journey.

The overlapping strata of Japanese screens have been often compared to the skins of an onion. The terms *ma* (a space between, charged with energy) and *oku* (an invisible centre) are used to convey this endless depth, where space is devoid of absolute boundaries. *Oku* also refers to a subjective zone, where multiple layers wrap around one another with vague, rather than clear, divisions, producing a fathomless space that defies measurement. Even a space as small as the guestroom at the west end of the Yoshimura house contains this perpetually layered structure. The room consists of two volumes, divided and linked by sliding screens and an open transom, and surrounded by alcoves, a built-in desk, a recess for making tea and shallow verandas at either side with contrasting exposure and scenery.

Among buildings that display the greatest profusion of human freedom are the Kusakabe and Yoshijima houses in the mountain village of Takayama (p. 262). From the moment of entry, visitors are greeted by appealing calls to become the locus and source

Shokin-tei teahouse, Katsura Imperial Villa (17th century), Kyoto,
veranda for tea preparation (above) and interior (opposite top)

Yoshimura House (1615), Japan, anteroom with alcove for
tea preparation and view to other half of guestroom (above)

Yoshijima House, Japan, view through timber frame and screens to interior
veranda (above left); view from one open hearth to another (above right);
earthen floor (*doma*) and interior veranda (*hiroshiki*) (top right); Kusakabe

House, Japan, view of elevated rooms from entrance (top left)

of action: to sit on a wooden ledge; to head to rooms clustered around open-pit fires; or to set off to other invitations gleaned through the filtered space. Emerging at each step are new meandering routes to explore. Crowning the more public zones near the entry is a huge structural cage of wood, allowing the inference of attractions or threats that are out of sight but sensed indirectly. Each room communicates with countless others, illustrating the Japanese penchant for continuity amid a state of mystery and surprise. Despite their elegant woodcraft and enchanting character, the Yoshimura, Kusakabe and Yoshijima houses are free of any formal or individual expression that would weaken spontaneity. They share both a submersion of ego and the ethos of never presenting an achieved experience that does not require our own presence. While this heritage has had limited influence on modern architecture, it does persist in the more porous works of Tadao Ando, Fumihiko Maki and SANAA, and the fantasy worlds of Hiroshi Hara and Itsuko Hasegawa.

Tadao Ando has been especially resourceful in giving new form to these causal powers, from his perforated box in Okinawa to the hilltown-like Rokko Housing in Kobe, and large, multifarious structures such as the Awaji Yumebutai complex in Hyogo and the diminutive Garden of Fine Arts in Kyoto (above). Descending below ground in the garden is an intertwined network of stairways, balconies and bridges, branching off in varied directions, drawn to hidden waterfalls and pools at three different levels, and the periodic appearance of large reproductions of Western and Japanese art. Stripped of any overt function, the spatial maze empowers visitors to pursue any one of many different routes. Ando commented: 'Here, I seek the experience of a contemporary, volumetric version of the stroll garden', a place composed of 'overlapping lines of motion and intricate vectors of vision', where people can revive themselves in action, free of any purpose or use.[140]

Tadao Ando, Garden of Fine Arts (1994), Kyoto

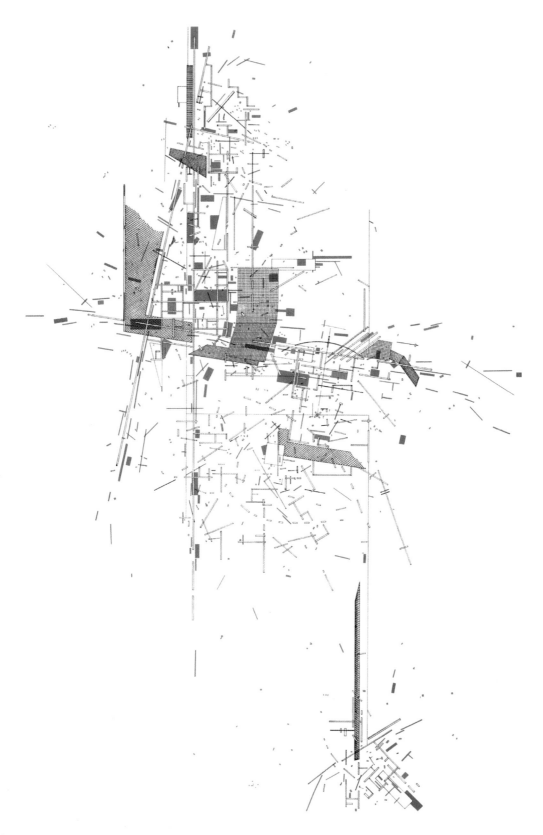

Ryoji Suzuki, conceptual drawing

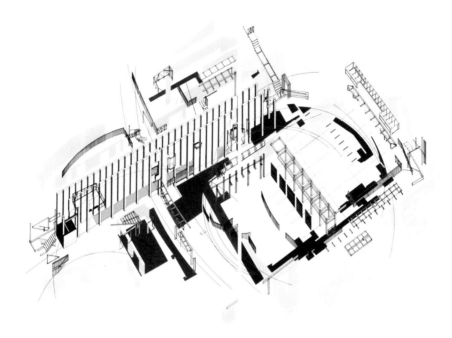

Reconceiving the causal fabric of architecture means, argues Ryoji Suzuki, 'an understanding of architecture not as a kind of solid entity capable of guiding disparate elements towards a synthesis, but of grasping it as a kind of centre of power, where various energies are free to pull in different directions'. Suzuki's aim in eluding determinism is to construct an 'open world' filled with doubt rather than answers, crowded with 'unexpectedness and strangeness' yet bursting with 'spontaneity'.[141] His buildings are composed from a dispersive mixture of masses and voids, which can only be apprehended as loose fragments with intermittent perspectives (opposite).

Each boundary of the Kohun-ji Temple in Tokyo (above and p. 266) is carved with slits of varying size and pattern. Cutting repeatedly through an unknowable whole are perplexing slots and fissures that pry open hundreds of spatial incentives, constructing a pervious world whose predominant quality is energy. These slivers of opportunity are layered to interact with others in weaving a complex network of cracks, causing people to repeatedly probe through boundaries at unexpected angles and depths, squinting to make out the slender futures. Hints of the space beyond appear in the crevices and joints between walls, gaps dividing modular elements, narrow skylights and window bands, interstices in colonnades, openings in frames of wood or steel, finely porous grilles and railings and incisions cut out of sheet metal or cast into concrete planes.

Another major figure in the Japanese attempt to recapture and redefine the field of action is Riken Yamamoto, whose roots extend to Herman Hertzberger and Le Corbusier

Ryoji Suzuki, Kohun-ji Temple (1991), Tokyo, conceptual axonometric

as much as his own cultural traditions. Apparently knowing that 'style is death', as poet Robert Kelly put it, Yamamoto loosely assembles a tremendous diversity of spatial events out of utterly plain industrial materials and makes them accessible through porous walls and generous gaps between solid things, as well as by a fringe of intermediate zones that playfully open and veil at once.

Yamamoto's cultivation of free will appeared first in a series of urban rooftop dwellings, including the Gazebo and Rotunda (opposite) in Yokohama, and Hamlet in Tokyo. Each consists of a loose assembly of small volumes, linked by openwork stairs and bridges and sharing a multilevel outdoor space sheltered beneath and unified by overarching canopies. Of Hamlet, Yamamoto commented: 'Differently sized social units overlap', so that 'at times the extended family acts as one; at other times the four households act separately; at still other times, each individual acts independently. No one unit is paramount. This is an apartment building that permits a high degree of freedom; that is, each occupant is free to choose how he or she will live.'[142]

This airy language takes on greater, more collective form in several later housing projects. Conceived as an antidote to what Yamamoto calls the 'self-sufficient' and 'closed' character of mass housing, with its 'dwellings arranged in rows and piled up in layers', Hotakubo Housing in Kumamoto (p. 268) was designed to form a more open world

Ryoji Suzuki, Kohun-ji Temple (1991), Tokyo, entrance to the main hall

Riken Yamamoto, Rotunda with dwelling on upper floors (1987), Yokohama

where territories intermingle and many people at once have a chance to act freely and responsibly.[143] The units, overlooking a grassy plaza from three sides, are pulled apart, shifted in depth and recessed from their concrete frame to accentuate the accessibility and presence of each home, as well as introduce a generous in-between zone. Within this pervious edge are found balconies, terraces, stairs and railings, bringing into view many indefinite but attractive opportunities that can change any moment with the ebb and flow of residents and weather.

Admittedly the interiors of Yamamoto's larger projects lack the warmth and porosity of old Japan, or of his earlier, more elaborate dwellings, but in compensation the internal spatial fields of the past have been turned inside out, concentrating human dignity in a semi-public realm instead of one that is hidden and private. This inversion is especially pronounced at Inter-Junction City, where an unprecedented scope of freedom is achieved along pedestrian streets threading between apartments and shops to a train station. Crisscrossing through the communal zone at many levels is an aerial network of footpaths, mezzanines, stairways and bridges, which gently melds into the porches of apartments. Constructed of modest materials, the volumes are hollowed at every scale, from the huge chasms of open courts and public walkways to the breathing space between units and unfilled gaps in the concrete frames, offering limitless subjects of scrutiny and action.

Especially evocative of the past is the Xystus complex (opposite and pp. 270–1) at the eastern end of Inter-Junction City, in which subtle veils of translucent polycarbonate have been used to give a reassuring modesty and shelter to residential thresholds, while infusing the entire street with mystery and surprise. From every point one can survey clues about hundreds of appealing destinations and encounters, along trails that lead off in varied directions and reappear across the street in facing apartments with their own

Riken Yamamoto, Hotakubo Housing (1991), Japan, external balconies
and staircases (left) and internal façade facing plaza (right)

inviting places and routes. But these incidents are sufficiently blurred so that the future remains somewhat clouded, invested with doubt and adventure. The nebulous maze does not present a fixed drama at which to gaze passively, but a drama in which we are meant to participate. As we assess and manoeuvre among these prospects, it is we, rather than the building, that become the centre of dramatic attention.

What is of utmost human importance in Yamamoto's architecture, including his designs for Saitama Prefectural University and Future University Hakodate, stems less from physical things than from forces awaiting each person to set them in motion. Attention has shifted to action rather than finished form, and its experience is almost the accidental concatenation of its parts. Occupants and visitors alike are drawn into a state of becoming, defining and creating themselves in action, where the end is always unknown. This kind of ever-present future is expressed more eloquently by William Carlos Williams: 'The virtue of it all is in an opening of the doors, though some rooms of course will be empty, a break with banality, the continual hardening which habit enforces. There is nothing left in me but the virtue of curiosity ... The poet should be forever at the ship's prow.'[144]

Riken Yamamoto, Xystus, Inter-Junction City (1992), Yokohama, street façade   **fields of action**   269

Suggested in Yamamoto's work, as well as in that of Frank Lloyd Wright, Rudolph Schindler, Louis I. Kahn, Herman Hertzberger, Grafton Architects and Maurice Smith, is a more generous form that our buildings and cities could take if we wished them to become places of inexhaustible opportunity. This freedom is not exercised through aimless or happy-go-lucky behaviour, but with inner direction, alert at every moment to alternatives and contrary desires, as new options are brought into view along the way. In doing so, people are repeatedly brought back to life as powers in space, living forces given the chance to initiate a wealth of acts placed firmly under their own control, with outcomes and deeds they care about, confirming over and again their basic existence as human beings.

Inter-Junction City, upper level with bridges and stairs to
dwellings (above) and internal pedestrian street, overlooked
by open-air bridges, stairs, corridors and terraces (opposite)

NOTES

1   Gaston Bachelard, *The Poetics of Space*, trans. Maria Jolas (New York: Orion Press, 1964), p. 15.

2   R.D. Laing, *The Politics of Experience* (New York: Ballantine Books, 1967), p. 23.

3   Fyodor Dostoyevsky, *Notes from Underground*, trans. Serge Shishkoff (New York: Thomas Y. Crowell, 1969), p. 32.

4   Ibid., pp. 32-4.

5   Luther Halsey Gulick, *A Philosophy of Play* (New York: Association Press, 1920), pp. 276-7.

6   Michel Foucault, *Discipline and Punish: The Birth of the Prison*, trans. Alan Sheridan (Harmondsworth, Middlesex: Penguin Books, 1977), p. 138.

7   Ibid., p. 154.

8   Robert Creeley, ed., *Selected Writings of Charles Olson* (New York: New Directions, 1951), pp. 58-62.

9   John Dewey, *Freedom and Culture* (Amherst, New York: Prometheus Books, 1989), p. 44.

10 Daniel Dennett, *Consciousness Explained* (Boston: Little, Brown, 1991), p. 209.

11 Lewis Mumford, *The Myth of the Machine* (New York: Harcourt, Brace & World, 1967), p. 76.

12 René Dubos, *So Human an Animal* (New York: Charles Scribner's Sons, 1968), pp. 128, 130-1, 132.

13 Erich Fromm, *Escape from Freedom* (New York: Holt, Rinehart & Winston, 1941), pp. 48-9.

14 Ibid., pp. 284, 288-9.

15 Jean-Paul Sartre, *Being and Nothingness: An Essay on Phenomenological Ontology*, trans. Hazel E. Barnes (New York: Philosophical Library, 1956), p. 438.

16 Ibid., p. 439.

17 Hannah Arendt, *The Human Condition* (Chicago: University of Chicago Press, 1958), p. 177.

18 Ibid., p. 179.

19 Dante (Dante Alighieri), *De Monarchia*, book 1, chapter XIII (*c.* 1312-13). This fine translation comes from Arendt, p. 175.

20 Gabriel Marcel, *Homo Viator: Introduction to a Metaphysic of Hope*, trans. Emma Craufurd (New York: Harper & Row, 1962).

21 Foucault, p. 139.

22 Arendt, p. 180.

23 Creeley, p. 55.

24 Bernard Rudofsky, *Streets for People* (New York: Doubleday & Co., 1969), p. 176.

25 Bernard Rudofsky, *The Prodigious Builders* (New York: Harcourt, Brace Jovanovich, 1977), p. 242.

26 Diane Ackerman, *Deep Play* (New York: Random House, 1999), pp. 19-20.

27 Gaston Bachelard, *Air and Dreams: An Essay on the Imagination of Movement*, trans. Edith R. Farrell and C. Frederick Farrell (Dallas: Dallas Institute Publications, 1988), p. 33.

28 Erik Erikson, *Childhood and Society* (New York: W.W. Norton & Co., 1950), p. 213.

29 The narrow intent of our well-intended accessibility codes has had an unfortunate levelling effect on our buildings and cities. In order to make every point in space equally accessible, the ground is being stripped of all real challenges and delights. A more thoughtful and truly egalitarian approach would be to diversify accessibility to include provisions of creative movement for all, including a wide range of challenges suited to the varying ages and capacities of people.

30 From comments made to the author in 1986 by architect Joseph Esherick, nephew and occasional assistant of Wharton Esherick.

31 Wallace Stevens, *The Collected Poems* (New York: Alfred A. Knopf, 1954), p. 83.

32 Akira Naito, *Katsura: A Princely Retreat* (Tokyo: Kodansha International Ltd, 1977), p. 148.

33 Kiyoyuki Nishihara, *Japanese Houses: Patterns for Living*, trans. Richard L. Gage (Tokyo: Japan Publications, 1968), p. 126.

34 Maria W. Piers, ed., *Play and Development* (New York: W.W. Norton, 1972), p. 133.

35 Ibid., p. 152.

36 Bachelard, *Air and Dreams*, p. 42.

37 Ibid., p. 121.

38 Mircea Eliade, *The Sacred and the Profane: The Nature of Religion*, trans. Willard R. Trask (New York: Harcourt, Brace & World, 1959), pp. 118–19.

39 Bachelard, *Air and Dreams*, p. 14.

40 Bachelard, *The Poetics of Space*, pp. 194–5.

41 C. Ray Smith, 'Rudolph's Dare-devil Office Destroyed', in *Progressive Architecture* 50 (April 1969): 98–105.

42 Henry Plummer, *Cosmos of Light: The Sacred Architecture of Le Corbusier* (Bloomington, Indiana: Indiana University Press, 2013), p. 10.

43 Erikson, p. 221.

44 Karl Groos, *The Play of Man* (New York: D. Appleton & Co., 1901), p. 161.

45 Erich Fromm, *The Anatomy of Human Destructiveness* (New York: Holt, Rinehart and Winston, 1973), p. 235.

46 Sartre, p. 580.

47 Ibid., pp. 580–1.

48 Friedrich Schiller, *Aesthetical and Philosophical Essays* (London: G. Bell, 1884), p. 71.

49 Johan Huizinga, *Homo Ludens: A Study of the Play Element in Culture* (Boston: Beacon Press, 1955), p. 7.

50 D.W. Winnicott, *Playing and Reality* (Harmondsworth, Middlesex: Penguin Books, 1980), p. 63.

51 Ibid., p. 66.

52 Piers, p. 127.

53 Ibid., p. 158.

54 Winnicott, pp. 75, 63.

55 Dubos, pp. 111–12, 175.

56 Cedric Price, 'Cedric Price Talks at the AA', in *AA Files* 19 (Spring 1990): 34. Price himself acknowledged the dangers of a disembodied world where mobile elements become detached from the human hand. 'An example is the automatic, electronically controlled door, activated by a light, sound or heat source,' he noted. 'A whole generation of sensitively designed, user-friendly door handles and door pulls is ignored or lost, while contemporary door-users wave around like triffids, in front of visually uninformative doors, hoping to activate something that will open them. Hands have been rendered useless … A lot of noise has gone out of things, and a lot of digital dexterity too.'

57 Martin Heidegger, *The Question Concerning Technology*, trans. William Lovitt (New York: Harper & Row, 1977), p. 5.

58 Jun'ichirō Tanizaki, *In Praise of Shadows*, trans. Thomas J. Harper and Edward G. Seidensticker (New Haven, Connecticut: Leete's Island Books, 1977), pp. 21–2.

59 Shigeru Ban, *Shigeru Ban* (New York: Princeton Architectural Press, 2001), p. 51.

60 Steen Eiler Rasmussen, *Experiencing Architecture* (Cambridge, Massachusetts: MIT Press, 1959), pp. 199–202.

61 Edward Connery Lathem, ed., *The Poetry of Robert Frost* (New York: Holt, Rinehart and Winston, 1967), p. 277.

62 Frank Lloyd Wright, *An Autobiography* (New York: Duell, Sloan and Pearce, 1943), pp. 310–12.

63 Paul Rudolph, *The Architecture of Paul Rudolph* (New York: Praeger, 1970), p. 42.

64 Arendt, p. 178.

65 Kenneth Frampton, 'Maison de Verre', in *Perspecta 12: The Yale Architectural Journal* (1969): 80.

66 Christopher MacGowan, ed., *The Collected Poems of William Carlos Williams, Volume II: 1939–1962* (New York: New Directions, 1988), p. 310.

67 Calvin Tomkins, *The Bride and the Bachelors: The Heretical Courtship in Modern Art* (New York: Viking Press, 1965), p. 146.

68 Steven Holl, *Intertwining* (New York: Princeton Architectural Press, 1996), p. 110; Steven Holl, *Parallax* (New York: Princeton Architectural Press, 2000), p. 234.

69 Holl, *Parallax*, pp. 226, 233.

70 Daniel Dennett, *Elbow Room: The Varieties of Free Will Worth Wanting* (Cambridge, Massachusetts: MIT Press, 1984), p. 145.

71 Russell Ferguson, ed., *Robert Irwin* (Los Angeles: Museum of Contemporary Art, 1993), p. 178.

72 Peter Prangnell, 'The Friendly Object', in *Harvard Educational Review* 39:4 (1969): 39, 41.

73 György Kepes, *Language of Vision* (Chicago: Paul Theobald, 1951), p. 77.

74 Marjorie Perloff, *The Poetics of Indeterminacy: Rimbaud to Cage* (New York: Princeton University Press, 1981), p. 119.

75 Wallace Stevens, *Opus Posthumous* (New York: Alfred A. Knopf, 1957), pp. 166, 178.

76 Bruno Bettelheim, *A Home for the Heart* (New York: Alfred A. Knopf, 1974), pp. 174, 177.

77 Ibid., p. 162.

78 Dennett, *Elbow Room*, p. 51.

79 Ibid., pp. 63, 73.

80 On a visit to the Olivetti Showroom in 1983, I witnessed a meeting of four people upon this stair, which wonderfully demonstrated its capacity to accommodate wide-ranging actions. One person sat on the bench below, another sat on a step high above, while a third leaned against the cantilever and a fourth stood on the wide bottom tread. Various steps found further use as places to set coffee and notepads. I have often regretted I did not have the wits to photograph this event.

81 Fromm, *The Anatomy of Human Destructiveness*, pp. 239–40.

82 Rudofsky, *Streets for People*, p. 191.

83 According to Michelangelo, the routes originally had a less liberal intent, with the privileged centre steps for the ruler and those on the side for courtiers.

84 Erikson, p. 212; Piers, pp. 133, 140.

85 Edgar Kaufmann and Ben Raeburn, eds, *Frank Lloyd Wright: Writings and Buildings* (New York: World Publishing Co., 1960), p. 92.

86 Ibid., pp. 317, 314.

87 Ibid., p. 313.

88 Wright, p. 162.

89 Herman Hertzberger, *Lessons for Students in Architecture* (Rotterdam: Uitgeverij 010 Publishers, 1991), p. 170.

90 Erikson, p. 213.

91 Herman Hertzberger, 'Montessori Primary School in Delft, Holland', in *Harvard Educational Review* 39:4 (1969): 66.

92 John Donat, ed., *World Architecture 4* (New York: Viking Press, 1967), p. 25.

93 Benedict Zucchi, *Giancarlo de Carlo* (London: Butterworth Architecture, 1992), p. 168.

94 See Giancarlo de Carlo, *Urbino: The History of a City and Plans for its Development* (Cambridge, Massachusetts: MIT Press, 1970).

95 Hertzberger, Herman, Addie van Roijen-Wortmann and Francis Strauven, *Aldo van Eyck: Hubertus House* (Amsterdam: Stichting Wonen, 1982), p. 89.

96 Robert Venturi, *Complexity and Contradiction in Architecture* (New York: Museum of Modern Art, 1977), pp. 78–82.

97 Bachelard, *The Poetics of Space*, pp. 81, 85.

98 Henry Plummer, *Stillness and Light: The Silent Eloquence of Shaker Architecture* (Bloomington, Indiana: Indiana University Press, 2009).

99 Kengo Kuma, 'Museum of Hiroshige Ando', in *JA The Japan Architect* 38 (2000): 12.

100 Wright, p. 339.

101 Ferguson, p. 113.

102 Rudolf Otto, *The Idea of the Holy*, trans. John W. Harvey (London: Oxford University Press, 1923), pp. 12-30.

103 Tanizaki, p. 20.

104 Henry Plummer, *Nordic Light: Modern Scandinavian Architecture* (London: Thames & Hudson, 2012), pp. 226-49.

105 Peter Zumthor, *Atmospheres* (Basel: Birkhäuser, 2006), pp. 41-3.

106 Analogously the fifteen rocks of the garden, placed in a sea of raked gravel, were skilfully arranged so that one rock always remains hidden behind others when seen from any viewpoint on the veranda, offering yet another freedom from logic and certainty and an inexhaustible stimulus to contemplation in which each person is left to fill in missing parts of the world.

107 Bachelard, *The Poetics of Space*, pp. 149-50.

108 John Summerson, *Heavenly Mansions and Other Essays on Architecture* (New York: W.W. Norton & Co., 1963), pp. 1-8.

109 Wilhelm Worringer, *Form in Gothic*, trans. Herbert Read (London: G.P. Putnam's Sons, 1927), pp. 165-6.

110 Le Corbusier, *Le Poème de l'Angle Droit* (Paris: Éditions Connivance, 1989), p. 136.

111 Bruno Bettelheim, *The Uses of Enchantment: The Meaning and Importance of Fairy Tales* (New York: Alfred A. Knopf, 1976), p. 155.

112 Wassily Kandinsky, *The Spiritual in Art* (New York: George Wittenborn, 1947), p. 39.

113 François Jacob, *The Possible and the Actual* (Seattle: University of Washington Press, 1982), p. 66.

114 William Carlos Williams, *Selected Essays of William Carlos Williams* (New York: Random House, 1954), pp. 280-91.

115 Stevens, *The Collected Poems*, p. 488.

116 Williams, pp. 284-5.

117 Robert Harbison, *Eccentric Spaces* (Boston: David R. Godine, 1988), p. 133.

118 H.B. Chipp, *Theories of Modern Art* (Berkeley: University of California Press, 1968), p. 186.

119 Sigfried Giedion, *Space, Time and Architecture* (Cambridge, Massachusetts: Harvard University Press, 1941), pp. 226-7.

120 Charles Moore, Peter Becker and Regula Campbell, *The City Observed: Los Angeles* (New York: Vintage Books, 1984), p. 24.

121 Giedion, p. 436.

122 Wright, p. 325; Kaufmann and Raeburn, pp. 284-9.

123 Kaufmann and Raeburn, pp. 264, 266.

124 Justin Kaplan, ed., *Walt Whitman: Complete Poetry and Prose* (New York: Library of America, 1982), p. 297.

125 W. Boesiger and H. Girsberger, eds, *Le Corbusier 1910-65* (Zurich: Artemis, 1967), p. 34.

126 David Gebhard, *Schindler* (New York: Viking Press, 1971), p. 192.

127 David B. Brownlee and David G. DeLong, *Louis I. Kahn: In the Realm of Architecture* (New York: Rizzoli, 1991), pp. 390-1.

128 'The Mind of Louis Kahn', in *The Architectural Forum* 137:1 (July–August 1972): 77.

129 Ibid.

130 Donald Allen, ed., *Human Universe and Other Essays by Charles Olson* (New York: Grove Press, 1967), p. 123.

131 Lewis MacAdams and Linda Wagner-Martin, 'Robert Creeley, The Art of Poetry No. 10', *Paris Review* 44 (Fall 1968): 180.

132 Creeley, p. 16.

133 Ibid.

134 Ibid., p. 17.

135 Umberto Eco, *The Open Work,* trans. Anna Cancogni (Cambridge, Massachusetts: Harvard University Press, 1989), pp. 3–4.

136 Umberto Eco, *The Role of the Reader: Explorations in the Semiotics of Texts* (Bloomington, Indiana: Indiana University Press, 1979), p. 4.

137 Kaplan, pp. 992–3.

138 See Maurice Smith, 'Not Writing on Built Form', in *Harvard Educational Review* 39:4 (1969): 69–84.

139 J.E. Marcault and Thérèse Brosse, *L'Éducation de demain* (Paris: F. Alcan, 1939), p. 255.

140 Tadao Ando, *Tadao Ando 1983-2000* (Madrid: El Croquis, 2000), p. 344; Tadao Ando, *GA Architect 16: Tadao Ando 1994-2000* (Tokyo: A.D.A. Edita, 2000), p. 48.

141 Ryoji Suzuki, 'Experience in Material', in *Japan Architect* 61 (November 1986): 93.

142 Wilhelm Klauser, *Riken Yamamoto* (Basel: Birkhäuser, 1999), p. 41.

143 Ibid., p. 48.

144 Williams, p. 26.

BIBLIOGRAPHY

Ackerman, Diane, *Deep Play* (New York: Random House, 1999).

Allen, Donald, ed., *Human Universe and Other Essays by Charles Olson* (New York: Grove Press, 1967).

Ando, Tadao, *GA Architect 16: Tadao Ando 1994–2000* (Tokyo: A.D.A. Edita, 2000).

——, *Tadao Ando 1983–2000* (Madrid: El Croquis, 2000).

Arendt, Hannah, *The Human Condition* (Chicago: University of Chicago Press, 1958).

Bachelard, Gaston, *Air and Dreams: An Essay on the Imagination of Movement*, trans. Edith R. Farrell and C. Frederick Farrell (Dallas: Dallas Institute Publications, 1988).

——, *The Poetics of Space*, trans. Maria Jolas (New York: Orion Press, 1964).

Ban, Shigeru, *Shigeru Ban* (New York: Princeton Architectural Press, 2001).

Bettelheim, Bruno, *A Home for the Heart* (New York: Alfred A. Knopf, 1974).

——, *The Uses of Enchantment: The Meaning and Importance of Fairy Tales* (New York: Alfred A. Knopf, 1976).

Boesiger, W., and H. Girsberger, eds, *Le Corbusier 1910–65* (Zurich: Artemis, 1967).

Brownlee, David B., and David G. DeLong, *Louis I. Kahn: In the Realm of Architecture* (New York: Rizzoli, 1991).

Chipp, H.B., *Theories of Modern Art* (Berkeley: University of California Press, 1968).

Creeley, Robert, ed., *Selected Writings of Charles Olson* (New York: New Directions, 1951).

Dante (Dante Alighieri), *De Monarchia*, book 1, chapter XIII, 1559.

De Carlo, Giancarlo, *Urbino: The History of a City and Plans for its Development* (Cambridge, Massachusetts: MIT Press, 1970).

Dennett, Daniel, *Consciousness Explained* (Boston: Little, Brown, 1991).

——, *Elbow Room: The Varieties of Free Will Worth Wanting* (Cambridge, Massachusetts: MIT Press, 1984).

Dewey, John, *Freedom and Culture* (Amherst, New York: Prometheus Books, 1989).

Donat, John, ed., *World Architecture 4* (New York: Viking Press, 1967).

Dostoyevsky, Fyodor, *Notes from Underground*, trans. Serge Shishkoff (New York: Thomas Y. Crowell, 1969).

Dubos, René, *So Human an Animal* (New York: Charles Scribner's Sons, 1968).

Eco, Umberto, *The Open Work,* trans. Anna Cancogni (Cambridge, Massachusetts: Harvard University Press, 1989).

——, *The Role of the Reader: Explorations in the Semiotics of Texts* (Bloomington, Indiana: Indiana University Press, 1979).

Eliade, Mircea, *The Sacred and the Profane: The Nature of Religion*, trans. Willard R. Trask (New York: Harcourt, Brace & World, 1959).

Erikson, Erik, *Childhood and Society* (New York: W.W. Norton & Co., 1950).

Ferguson, Russell, ed., *Robert Irwin* (Los Angeles: Museum of Contemporary Art, 1993).

Foucault, Michel, *Discipline and Punish: The Birth of the Prison*, trans. Alan Sheridan
(Harmondsworth, Middlesex: Penguin, 1977).

Frampton, Kenneth, 'Maison de Verre,' in *Perspecta 12: The Yale Architectural Journal* (1969).

Fromm, Erich, *The Anatomy of Human Destructiveness* (New York: Holt, Rinehart and Winston, 1973).

——, *Escape from Freedom* (New York: Holt, Rinehart & Winston, 1941) .

Gebhard, David, *Schindler* (New York: Viking Press, 1971).

Giedion, Sigfried, *Space, Time and Architecture* (Cambridge, Massachusetts: Harvard University Press, 1941).

Groos, Karl, *The Play of Man* (New York: D. Appleton & Co., 1901).

Gulick, Luther Halsey, *A Philosophy of Play* (New York: Association Press, 1920).

Harbison, Robert, *Eccentric Spaces* (Boston: David R. Godine, 1988).

Heidegger, Martin, *The Question Concerning Technology*, trans. William Lovitt (New York: Harper & Row, 1977).

Hertzberger, Herman, *Lessons for Students in Architecture* (Rotterdam: Uitgeverij 010 Publishers, 1991).

——, 'Montessori Primary School in Delft, Holland', in *Harvard Educational Review* 39:4 (1969): 58-67.

Hertzberger, Herman, Addie van Roijen-Wortmann and Francis Strauven, *Aldo van Eyck: Hubertus House* (Amsterdam: Stichting Wonen, 1982).

Holl, Steven, *Intertwining* (New York: Princeton Architectural Press, 1996).

——, *Parallax* (New York: Princeton Architectural Press, 2000).

Huizinga, Johan, *Homo Ludens: A Study of the Play Element in Culture* (Boston: Beacon Press, 1955).

Jacob, François, *The Possible and the Actual* (Seattle: University of Washington Press, 1982).

Kandinsky, Wassily, *The Spiritual in Art* (New York: George Wittenborn, 1947).

Kaplan, Justin, ed., *Walt Whitman: Complete Poetry and Prose* (New York: Library of America, 1982).

Kaufmann, Edgar, and Ben Raeburn, eds, *Frank Lloyd Wright: Writings and Buildings* (New York: World Publishing Co., 1960).

Kepes, György, *Language of Vision* (Chicago: Paul Theobald, 1951).

Klauser, Wilhelm, *Riken Yamamoto* (Basel: Birkhäuser, 1999).

Kuma, Kengo, 'Museum of Hiroshige Ando', in *JA The Japan Architect* 38 (2000).

Laing, R.D., *The Politics of Experience* (New York: Ballantine Books, 1967).

Lathem, Edward Connery, ed., *The Poetry of Robert Frost* (New York: Holt, Rinehart and Winston, 1967).

Le Corbusier, *Le Poème de l'Angle Droit* (Paris: Éditions Connivance, 1989).

MacAdams, Lewis, and Linda Wagner-Martin, 'Robert Creeley, The Art of Poetry No. 10', in *Paris Review* 44 (Fall 1968): 180.

MacGowan, Christopher, ed., *The Collected Poems of William Carlos Williams, Volume II: 1939–1962* (New York: New Directions, 1988).

Marcault, J.E., and Thérèse Brosse, *L'Éducation de demain* (Paris: F. Alcan, 1939).

Marcel, Gabriel, *Homo Viator: Introduction to a Metaphysic of Hope*, trans. Emma Craufurd (New York: Harper & Row, 1962).

'Mind of Louis Kahn, The', in *The Architectural Forum* 137:1 (July–August 1972): 77.

Moore, Charles, Peter Becker and Regula Campbell, *The City Observed: Los Angeles* (New York: Vintage Books, 1984).

Mumford, Lewis, *The Myth of the Machine* (New York: Harcourt, Brace & World, 1967).

Naito, Akira, *Katsura: A Princely Retreat* (Tokyo: Kodansha International Ltd, 1977).

Nishihara, Kiyoyuki, *Japanese Houses: Patterns for Living*, trans. Richard L. Gage (Tokyo: Japan Publications, 1968).

Otto, Rudolf, *The Idea of the Holy*, trans. John W. Harvey (London: Oxford University Press, 1923).

Perloff, Marjorie, *The Poetics of Indeterminacy: Rimbaud to Cage* (New York: Princeton University Press, 1981).

Piers, Maria W., ed., *Play and Development* (New York: W.W. Norton, 1972).

Plummer, Henry, *Cosmos of Light: The Sacred Architecture of Le Corbusier* (Bloomington, Indiana: Indiana University Press, 2013).

——, *Nordic Light: Modern Scandinavian Architecture* (London: Thames & Hudson, 2012).

——, *Stillness and Light: The Silent Eloquence of Shaker Architecture* (Bloomington, Indiana: Indiana University Press, 2009).

Prangnell, Peter, 'The Friendly Object', in *Harvard Educational Review* 39:4 (1969): 36–41.

Rasmussen, Steen Eiler, *Experiencing Architecture* (Cambridge, Massachusetts: MIT Press, 1959).

Rudofsky, Bernard, *The Prodigious Builders* (New York: Harcourt, Brace Jovanovich, 1977).

——, *Streets for People* (New York: Doubleday & Co., 1969).

Rudolph, Paul, *The Architecture of Paul Rudolph* (New York: Praeger, 1970).

Sartre, Jean-Paul, *Being and Nothingness: An Essay on Phenomenological Ontology*, trans. Hazel E. Barnes (New York: Philosophical Library, 1956).

Schiller, Friedrich, *Aesthetical and Philosophical Essays* (London: G. Bell, 1884).

Smith, C. Ray, 'Rudolph's Dare-devil Office Destroyed', in *Progressive Architecture* 50 (April 1969): 98–105.

Smith, Maurice, 'Not Writing on Built Form', in *Harvard Educational Review* 39:4 (1969): 69–84.

Stevens, Wallace, *The Collected Poems* (New York: Alfred A. Knopf, 1954).

——, *Opus Posthumous* (New York: Alfred A. Knopf, 1957).

Summerson, John, *Heavenly Mansions and Other Essays on Architecture* (New York: W.W. Norton & Co., 1963).

Suzuki, Ryoji, 'Experience in Material', in *Japan Architect* 61 (November 1986).

Tanizaki, Jun'ichirō, *In Praise of Shadows*, trans. Thomas J. Harper and Edward G. Seidensticker (New Haven, Connecticut: Leete's Island Books, 1977).

Tomkins, Calvin, *The Bride and The Bachelors: The Heretical Courtship in Modern Art* (New York: Viking Press, 1965).

Venturi, Robert, *Complexity and Contradiction in Architecture* (New York: Museum of Modern Art, 1977).

Williams, William Carlos, *Selected Essays of William Carlos Williams* (New York: Random House, 1954).

Winnicott, D.W., *Playing and Reality* (Harmondsworth, Middlesex: Penguin Books, 1980).

Worringer, Wilhelm, *Form in Gothic*, trans. Herbert Read (London: G.P. Putnam's Sons, 1927).

Wright, Frank Lloyd, *An Autobiography* (New York: Duell, Sloan and Pearce, 1943).

Zucchi, Benedict, *Giancarlo de Carlo* (London: Butterworth Architecture, 1992).

Zumthor, Peter, *Atmospheres* (Basel: Birkhäuser, 2006).

PHOTO CREDITS

INDEX

ACKNOWLEDGMENTS

The underlying ideas of this book owe many debts. They were stirred initially long ago as a graduate student at MIT, and benefited from the experimental atmosphere and human ethos of the school at the time, including the leadership of Donlyn Lyndon as department head, and the influence of teachers including György Kepes, Imre Halasz, Kevin Lynch and Minor White, but above all Maurice Smith, whose exploratory studio helped spark and challenge many of the thoughts explored here.

The possibility that architecture could be a source of human power and action in space was developed and tested further in my own studio and seminar teaching, as well as thesis supervision, primarily at the University of Illinois in Urbana-Champaign where it benefited from lively exchanges with students. At the same time the subject was pursued in a number of articles and photo essays in professional journals, and for this I would like to give special thanks to Toshio Nakamura, former editor of *a+u*, who encouraged and published what was to be a series of essays under the title 'Vessels of Power', only two of which were completed.

As the architectural visits and photography for this book extend far back in time, a debt is owed to many institutions supportive of the research and travel. Though most grants and fellowships were awarded for studies on the art of light in architecture, they afforded me chances to also observe and photograph other architectural qualities that came to form the foundational material for this book. For this I am grateful for three fellowships from the Graham Foundation, as well as fellowships from the Gladys Krieble Delmas Foundation and American-Scandinavian Foundation, the Lawrence Anderson Award from MIT, and a large number of research and travel grants from the University of Illinois.

On a personal level I am thankful for the generosity and patience extended by so many architects, owners, occupants, directors, and staff of the buildings examined here, who are far too numerous to list but whom I nevertheless want to acknowledge. And I am equally grateful to the many colleagues who have helped me obtain photographic permissions or written letters of support for grants: Wayne Andersen, Stanford Anderson, Jack Baker, Botond Bognar, Mohamed Boubekri, David Chasco, Walter Creese, Joseph Esherick, Alan Forrester, Kenneth Frampton, Jonathan Green, Fay Jones, György Kepes, Alejandro Lapunzina, Kevin Lynch, Donlyn Lyndon, Henry Millon, Toshio Nakamura, Bea Nettles, Juhani Pallasmaa, Richard Peters, Robert Riley, Maurice Smith, Minor White and A. Richard Williams.

A more immediate gratitude goes to Lucas Dietrich, architecture editor at Thames & Hudson, who has embraced this project from the outset and shown confidence at its shakiest moments.

None of the work underlying this book would have been remotely possible without the unwavering support and buoyant spirit of my wife Patty, from cushioning the demands of solitary writing to the wear and tear of overseas trips, but especially for providing the best of company on a long series of architectural quests. My heartfelt thanks.

*For Maurice Smith, who opened my eyes
to what is of central importance in architecture,
and for Patty, who continues to help me keep
an eye on what is of value in life itself*

300 illustrations

On the cover: *front* Rundetårn (17th century), Copenhagen; *back* Rick Joy,
Tubac House (2000), Arizona

The Experience of Architecture © 2016 Henry Plummer

First published in 2016 in hardcover in the United States of America by
Thames & Hudson, Inc., 500 Fifth Avenue, New York, New York 10110

thamesandhudsonusa.com

Library of Congress Catalog Card Number 2016931262

ISBN 978-0-500-34321-0

Printed and bound in China by C&C Offset Printing Co. Ltd.